Lonergan and the Theology of the Future

Lonergan and the Theology of the Future

An Invitation

David M. Hammond

PICKWICK *Publications* · Eugene, Oregon

LONERGAN AND THE THEOLOGY OF THE FUTURE
An Invitation

Pickwick Publications
An Imprint of Wipf and Stock Publishers
199 W. 8th Ave., Suite 3
Eugene, OR 97401

www.wipfandstock.com

PAPERBACK ISBN: 978-1-4982-0515-3
HARDCOVER ISBN: 978-1-4982-0517-7
EBOOK ISBN: 978-1-4982-0516-0

Cataloguing-in-Publication data:

Names: Hammond, David M.

Title: Lonergan and the theology of the future : an invitation / David M. Hammond.

Description: Eugene, OR : Pickwick Publications, 2017 | Includes bibliographical references.

Identifiers: ISBN 978-1-4982-0515-3 (paperback) | ISBN 978-1-4982-0517-7 (hardcover) | ISBN 978-1-4982-0516-0 (ebook)

Subjects: LCSH: Lonergan, Bernard J. F.

Classification: B995.L654 H22 2017 (print) | B995.L654 H22 (ebook)

Manufactured in the U.S.A.   01/24/18

For Pamela

Contents

Acknowledgments

I HAVE ACCUMULATED MANY intellectual debts over the years. Some of them can be discerned from the footnotes and bibliography. The limitations and mistakes in this book are mine alone, but what I got right I likely owe to Fr. Lonergan's writings and the many Lonergan scholars from whom I have benefitted. There is a great deal of help to be found for anyone who wants to explore Lonergan's work beyond this book's introductory level by consulting the marvelous web site *lonerganresource.com*, constructed by Robert Doran, S.J.

Special thanks to Bill Loewe, who taught me many of these things, and whose scholarship continues to inform and inspire. Thanks also to Dennis Doyle and Bill Portier for inviting me to discuss an earlier version of chapter seven, "God with us," with their grad students at the University of Dayton. Some years ago, Dennis Doyle and I hashed out some of the issues in chapter four, "God and Creation," and I am grateful for his constructive comments. Finally, I am very grateful for the editorial patience and good cheer of Matt Wimer and others at Wipf and Stock, as I assembled this book.

Introduction

Why Lonergan?

I HAVE WRITTEN THIS book to introduce the value of Fr Bernard Lonergan's work on theological method; my hope is that it will encourage students of theology to explore Lonergan's writings for the sake of the future of theology.[1] The intent is not to valorize an individual, but to point to a liberating instrument for doing theology. Lonergan did not romanticize the individual genius; he understood that those who make great intellectual leaps are those who have come up to the level of their own times, bringing a "new orientation or a sweeping reorganization," but the times have been prepared by "the competent and conscientious workers that slowly and unconsciously have been developing positions and heading towards the reversal of counter-positions."[2] By the middle of the twentieth century, updating in Catholic theology was long overdue, and Lonergan was one of several figures who worked to bring it up to the level of the times.

Through decades of dedicated and sustained effort, he produced what Frederick Crowe has called a *Novum Organum*, a new instrument for the future. The instrument, however, is not primarily a set of techniques or ideas, but a liberating discovery that places the operations of the human subject in clear focus and at the service of theology. This "generalized empirical method" is generalized because it is universal; it is always operating when the human mind is conscious and at work. It is empirical because the operations

---

1. "All culture does involve this *haute vulgarization*." An appropriate defense of the faith within the appropriate context is necessary, but such defense was for centuries in Catholic theology "out of reach for people without advanced degrees" (Lonergan, *Early Works 1*, 272).

2. Lonergan, *Insight*, 419. See also p. 704 on the work of genius and the need for collaboration.

of human intellect are experienced and can be known.[3] It is a method not in the sense of technique—the way to perform a particular task using a specific rule or formula—but in the sense that one proceeds methodologically by an acknowledgment that these universal operations of consciousness provide a control for any inquiry. Lonergan's turn to the subject is built upon earlier achievements, but he presents them in a much more empirically precise, and therefore practical, form. The turn is an invitation to self-knowledge that can become the *Novum Orgamum* for a theology of the future.

An Introduction

This book is an effort to introduce the importance of Lonergan's work by illustrating some of his key insights, primarily by reflecting on the meanings of central Christian doctrines. In one sense, Lonergan's work is difficult to read; the exercises in the first five chapters of *Insight* taken from mathematics and natural sciences, to name but one example, are often not accessible to readers of theology. However, because his basic focus is human experience itself, the key example to be understood and appropriated is the reader's own operations. Theologians familiar with Lonergan's achievement need to communicate it in ways that are intelligible to beginning students of theology. I have tried to write this book in simple and straightforward language, appealing to technical terms only when necessary, and offering ordinary examples. There are many specialized studies of Lonergan's development and the ways his thought can provide insight in several different fields beyond theology. It will be clear to those who know these studies how much I have relied on them. My purpose here is not to contribute a specialized analysis of any one aspect of Lonergan's achievement. I simply intend to introduce his thought to those unfamiliar with it by illustrating some of the ways it has helped me to understand what was "going forward" in Christian theology as it has come to us from the past and as it develops into the future. In the chapters that follow I hope to provide an accessible entrée to Lonergan's achievement. We begin at the center of it all: the human subject.

---

3. "Generalized empirical method operates on a combination of both the data of sense and the data of consciousness: it does not treat of objects without taking into account the corresponding subject; it does not treat of the subject's operations without taking into account the corresponding object" (Lonergan, "Religious Knowledge," 141).

The Subject and Theology

Self-knowledge is a difficult and sometimes painful achievement. We human beings are complex creatures; moreover, most of us need to spend a great deal of time and energy working to achieve the basic requirements of life in the body. "Who am I?" might seem an impractical question at best, and a waste of time at worst. The novelist Walker Percy begins his humorous essay *Lost in the Cosmos: The Last Self-Help Book* with a series of alternative subtitles, the fourth of which reads: "Why is it possible to learn more in ten minutes about Crab Nebula in Taurus, which is 6,000 light-years away, than you presently know about yourself, even though you've been stuck with yourself all your life?" It's a good question.

Doubts about the value of pursuing self-knowledge find an echo today. Not only is the world faced with an explosion of information in all the disciplines, but there is increased pressure to invest money and time in a way that will contribute to future economic and financial security. From a different point of view, however, it is precisely *because* of, not in spite of, this ever-burgeoning fund of information and the rapid development of our ways of knowing that self-knowledge takes on an even greater importance today. Questions about what the various ways of knowing have in common, and how or whether diverse truths can be reconciled and integrated, cannot be answered without attending to the locus of that potential integration: the human person. What could be more practical than knowing yourself, considering the fact that, no matter what you think or decide or do or become, it is always *you* at the center of it all. From this angle, Socrates's precept "Know thyself!" can still be recommended as one of the central aims of human development.

In a more obvious way than other forms of inquiry, theology demands a certain degree of self-knowledge. Faith, after all, is a very personal commitment to a personal God, and theology also requires a thinking human being, as well as the religious elements—the doctrinal, ritual and structural expressions of the religion—that the theologian attempts to illuminate. Whenever any element of religion becomes the object of attention, there is always someone attending to it. There is always, in other words, a person's "subjectivity" intending that object. That attending "subject" of theology is a core concern running through this introduction to Lonergan's thought.

Many Christians, even students of theology, ask what the academic study of theology has to do with their personal response of faith. They properly look for guidance in how to respond to the new insights and sometimes-disconcerting theological claims they encounter. The study of Christianity can deliver a fund of information about the people, ideas, movements and implications of Christianity. Such information, however, is never so "objective" as to be without the need of a subject who receives it and asks questions about it. Lonergan offers an aid to the process whereby one begins to sort through the plethora of concepts, images, theories and opinions touching on the Christian faith that one inevitably encounters not only in theology and religious studies courses, but throughout the intellectual life of Christian experience.

Saint Paul exhorted the Corinthians, "Examine yourselves to see whether you are living in faith" (2 Cor 13:5). There are different kinds of questions for self-examination "in faith." Most important are religious questions that seek to discern whether one is an authentic Christian (which was Paul's concern in this text). The sort of explicit self-knowledge with which this book is largely concerned is not a requirement for everyone trying to be an authentic person of faith. Still, increasing numbers of people in the developed and developing world cannot claim simplicity and intellectual innocence. Educated religious people are under an obligation to do theology in the manner appropriate to their various situations in life. The level of sophistication in one's religious understanding is relevant for one's ability to respond in faith to the complex challenges of life today.

Theology Today

In 1976 Lonergan noted that "today the word, theology, denotes not some well-defined form of thought but rather an aggregate of quite different and often quite nebulous forms."[4] His observation continues to ring true. A variety of theological options and approaches offer fresh and enriching insights, but much of contemporary religious thought can be disorienting and disconcerting for the student of theology. On the one hand, responsible theological work does not imply an excessive caution that stultifies free and creative scholarship. Bold exploration is necessary in every disciplined inquiry, and occasionally one cannot know whether a particular path is a theological dead-end until someone travels on it a while and then reports back. Such exploration, even when it results in ideas that the faith community must eventually reject, can be of value. Certain dead ends in the development of theology can best be understood, in Lonergan's phrase, as the church's "self-correcting process of learning."[5] We must tolerate for a time what seems to us to be error, the nineteenth century convert John Henry Newman once argued, if we are eventually to arrive at the truth.

4. Lonergan, "Ongoing Genesis," 146.
5. See Lonergan, *Insight*, 197–98.

Sometimes truth only reveals itself when error becomes explicit and then calls forth its own correction.[6]

Academic freedom in any area of inquiry, on the other hand, requires not merely freedom but academic rigor. There is a bewildering array of methods and standards among theologies today. If the theologian is under no constraints to follow the canons of competent work, as other scholars and scientists must, then why should anyone care about, let alone trust the outcome of theological inquiry? In such a situation, theology becomes idiosyncratic and unverified opinion, musings that need not be taken seriously. There are rules for any game, even when part of the game is to discover how the rules of the game need to be brought up to date in changed circumstances.

More than most methods of inquiry, theology depends upon the theologian as much as it does on its sources. In my judgment, the work of Lonergan provides the best contemporary help in the pursuit of the kind of self-knowledge needed to liberate the spirit of inquiry. Lonergan was convinced that to understand what precisely happens when we attend to an experience, understand it, judge that understanding to be true or false, determine the good to be done, and finally decide upon a course of action based on that knowledge, is to possess a generalized method for investigating anything that can be known. A method of inquiry that recognizes this permanent and universal pattern of operations enhances the investigator's control of the process and therefore of one's confidence as a questioner; the goal is to promote a set of insights *in* the person *about* the person.

Attending to one's own believing, imagining, thinking and questioning does not imply selfish conceit. On the contrary, self-knowledge is an ally of humility, which requires the self-knowledge to know what you do not know. Nor is self-knowledge the same as "subjectivism," the notion that reality is merely what we think it is or want it to be. Awareness of the difference between having an idea and judging that idea to name reality provides a basis in self-knowledge for eliminating the mistaken notion that "thinking makes it so." The turn to subjectivity is not subjectivism.

6. "If he has one cardinal maxim in his philosophy, it is, that truth cannot contradict truth; if he has a second, it is, that truth often *seems* contrary to truth; and, if a third, it is the practical conclusion, that we must be patient with such appearances, and not be hasty to pronounce them to be really of a more formidable character" (Newman, *Idea*, 372).

Theology: Practice and Skill

Sensitive to the rapidly changing cultural currents of the nineteenth century, John Henry Newman cautioned that "[t]o unsettle the minds of a generation, when you give them no landmarks and no causeway across the morass, is to undertake a great responsibility."[7] Such responsibility today cannot be laid at the doorstep of any particular group, such as scientists or theologians or philosophers; the multi-faceted cultural changes of modernity allow for no simple reductionism. Nonetheless, change today is rapid, widespread and still potentially unsettling, and so the situation in theology calls for a reliable "causeway." Lonergan's work can provide an excellent one, provided one approach his contribution not as a set of ideas proposed by a famously intelligent thinker, but as an invitation to discover what makes us human. By comparing theological method to an elevated road above a swamp, Newman did not mean that the road is ready-made. The causeway must first be built, for it is nothing other than one's own self-knowledge. Lonergan's foundational work is not a theory to be learned much less a set of concepts to be applied but a program for personal transformation.

Books and teachers can encourage this change but learning is never automatic. Thomas Aquinas observed that the teacher's job is to assist the learner's efforts to understand "from outside," much like the physician assists the inner healing processes of the body "from outside" through therapies that liberate the learner from misleading myths about knowing and believing.[8] Teaching only happens when there is learning, and learning occurs *within* the learner and not outside. Understanding is not mechanically induced through the machinations of the teacher or the sheer delivery of information. Just as a physician tries to find out what is impeding health and prescribes therapies in the hope that a remedy will occur, so does the good teacher have an ear for possible obstacles to understanding. The teacher assigns activities—reading, writing, discussion—that may eliminate obstacles and open the way to learning. Strictly speaking, physicians prescribe therapies, not "remedies." If the therapies work and the patient is restored to health, there is a remedy. No matter how routine the illness, the body must heal for there to be a remedy. Health is an inner reality; only the therapy, which may or may not be successful, comes from the outside. So also with learning: teachers, books, maps, languages, videos and web pages can be of significant help to anyone who wants to learn (and of course they can also set up obstacles to learning). But learning,

7. Newman, *Letters*, 465. Newman was responding to the historical and literary methods of biblical interpretation that had recently arrived on the theological scene.

8. Lonergan, *Topics*, 115.

like a successful therapeutic remedy, is a change within the person, and no amount of good teaching or intelligent writing can cause learning to occur without the cooperation of the student.[9]

Theology requires the skills that self-understanding provides, and the only way to acquire those skills is by practice. Imagine planning a construction project before you have had much experience with a saw and hammer. Let's say you want to make a dog house for Rex. First, you get a book from the public library on how to build simple projects. The chapter on doghouses is clear; the wood in the pictures is straight and the cuts that the author has made are square. All the pieces fit together and the author has driven the nails into the wood without bending them or splitting the wood. The completed doghouse looks so good—out there in the book—that the dog in the final picture seems to be smiling.

Now it is time for you to stop reading about how to make a doghouse and actually make one. Soon, however, you discover that the project is not going quite as smoothly as it appeared to go in the book. The saw you are using is dull and you have trouble holding it; as a result, your cuts are slightly short. Now what? And why do the nails bend half way into the board as you drive them with your hammer? This is harder than it looks. The problem, it seems, has to do with your box of tools and your lack of skill in using them. The book showed a doghouse made by a skilled carpenter with excellent tools; you, on the other hand, have had little practice measuring, cutting, nailing. In the midst of the project, you realize that you do not possess the quality tools or the carpenter's agility with hammer and saw, and this lack is making for a doubtful outcome.

Although the weekend carpenter's first backyard construction project turned out to be more formidable than anticipated, the second and third projects will probably be a bit easier because of the tacit knowledge and skill that come only with experience. Theology also requires a familiarity with tools: just as carpenters must know their tools and how to use them, so theologians must know their own intellectual operations, since these are the most important "tools" of the theological project. Familiarity with one's own intellectual and spiritual reality is the first step in developing

---

9. On the notion of self-appropriation as therapy, see Gregson, *Lonergan*, 10–15. David Burrell also uses this analogy: see Burrell, *Aquinas*, 133. Lonergan himself refers to the clinical psychologist Carl Rogers's client-centered approach as analogous to self-appropriation. See Lonergan, "Religious Experience," 117, as well as the interview *Caring About Meaning*, 107. See also his response to the question whether his approach is Kantian: "I wrote the book [*Insight*] to give people the opportunity to experience their own understanding, their own ability to get the point, and so to be able to stand on their own feet" (*Philosophical 1965*, 69).

theological skill. "Your method," Lonergan once said in a lecture, "is you operating as a theologian."[10]

Theology and the church

We can think about the relationship between the individual and the communal tradition of Christianity by noting that the Christian faith, as it is embodied in history and society, has three essential elements: worship, order, and theology. These elements are necessarily related to one another but are also distinct. Christianity is first of all worship and devotion: Christians relate to God through prayer, the sacraments and various devotional practices. They also form a community which organizes itself according to standards of belief and practice; Christianity is a way of life committed to God's revealed truth, whose meaning must be articulated, intellectually defended, and transposed so that the gospel may grow in ever new soil; this is the task of theology.

The church cannot exist without each of the three elements. In the actual life of the church, however, the three make up a delicate balancing act. Newman succinctly identified the principles, means and weaknesses of each element:

> Truth is the guiding principle of theology and theological inquiries; devotion and edification, of worship; and of government, expedience. The instrument of theology is reasoning; of worship, our emotional nature; of rule, command and coercion. Further, in man as he is, reasoning tends to rationalism; devotion, to superstition and enthusiasm; and power to ambition and tyranny.[11]

Given the limitations of the human condition, there will be inevitable tension and sometimes even conflict among the three elements. It would be virtually impossible for bishops, for example, never to irritate theologians by the way they use their power, just as it would be almost impossible for the discoveries of theologians never to shock the pious believer, who in turn sometimes appears to the theologian as having a superstitious or naive faith. Hence the conflict we observe within the church, as illustrated by many turbulent events throughout history and in our own day. Newman's point is that a certain amount of such tension must obtain if the deficits are to be

10. Lonergan, *Early Works 1*, 268.
11. Newman, *Via Media*, xxxviii–xliii.

supplied and the weaknesses corrected while maintaining the values and insights of all three essential elements.

The church has witnessed much theological tension in recent years and theology has often become suspect in the local churches. Theology's purpose is not to shock the devout, even if that is sometimes its effect. New thinking, if one is not prepared to receive and integrate it, can be disorienting. Nonetheless, to the degree that they are capable of it, believers have the duty to ask questions and thus reflect on the meaning of Christianity. In the process of aiding such reflection, teachers and books of theology will necessarily call into question certain common sense assumptions that impede a better understanding of faith. As we shall see, Lonergan's notion of the differentiation of consciousness can help to sort out conflicts that arise when tensions among the three orders of church life produce conflict. The Christian's common sense is not competent to deal with all questions, and the discovery of that fact can serve as a useful introduction to the kind of thinking that theology requires.[12] Because common sense is only common among those of a particular group, teachers of theology must know the common sense of their audiences, and in their efforts to clarify and interpret the gospel of Christ, theologians will sometimes need to call into question some of the assumptions that particular believers hold dear. They should always perform this work with sufficient respect for all and with humility proper to the situation at hand. It is my hope that this book will help to reduce the level of unnecessary or destructive tension within local churches by encouraging the kind of self-reflection that leads to greater mutual understanding among Christians.

Finally, there is an ecumenical spirit animating the approach of Lonergan's work and I want this introduction to encourage creative ways of overcoming some of the obstacles in the way of ecumenical understanding and so, in the long run, promote Christian unity.

Summary of Each Chapter

Chapter 1, "Knowing, Knowing Yourself, and Doing Theology," discusses the event of understanding, how the imagination functions in thinking, the role of evidence in making judgments, and the nature of objectivity. The chapter's basic point is that, although images are a vital help in coming to understand things, understanding goes beyond the image. With the help of Lonergan's pioneering work in cognitional analysis we will explore

---

12. Lonergan the teacher argued that "questioning of the omnicompetence of common sense seems to me a very good propaedeutic to philosophy" (*Understanding*, 322).

an understanding of our own conscious acts of understanding and thereby challenge the common but erroneous idea that getting the point is like having a visual picture. Within a clarified understanding of the human thinker as the "subject" of theology we will explore the communal and historical dimension of faith. God's grace is the reality that makes faith possible. Christian faith holds that God has first loved us, and our response in faith is a result of that prior divine gift. Faith implies the transformation of a life, not merely the acceptance of propositions. As the response to divine love and transforming grace, faith supports hope and fosters love. Faith, which is our awareness of and response to God's love, engages the whole person. Our response of love that answers God's invitation is a matter of reason, feeling, commitment and action. Faith is not a deduction from pure reason, but neither is it blind or irrational. Self-transcendence has as its terminus the knowledge of God.

Believing is thus an essential ingredient in all facets of human living, not just to religion. Intellectual responsibility, far from forcing us to choose between knowing and believing, requires that we believe many things. However, believing can impede understanding when it represses questions that head toward fuller understanding. The principle of growth in human history, including the history of Christianity, is the dynamism of human questioning. "Historical consciousness" is the most striking modern example of the way in which new questions encourage authentic Christians to re-examine what beliefs they hold or how they are to hold them.

Chapter 2, "The Drama of Religion and the Theory of Theology," examines the distinction between two different patterns of human experience: dramatic and intellectual. There is a need for the theologian to develop what Lonergan calls the differentiation of consciousness. The poet John Ciardi has noted that the "movement *from the specific to the general* is one of the basic formulas of poetry."[13] The specificity of images and symbols are essential carriers of Christian meaning and value such as we find in the bible, liturgy, devotions and the history of Christian art. A naive interpretation of the symbolic communication found in religion, however, creates conflict between religion and elements of modern culture such as scientific theory. The concrete images and symbols of religion which we encounter in the dramatic (or common sense) pattern of experience often raise questions that cannot be answered simply by referring to other symbols. When two symbols seem to refer to contradictory meanings, the question of meaning arises but cannot be answered within the symbolic realm. A shift to the intellectual pattern of experience, in which theory can

13. Ciardi, *Poem*, 671.

be distinguished from common sense symbolism, allows for such questions to be answered. The differentiation of consciousness reveals the stages of meaning in human development.

The viewpoint of Chapter 3, "God and Creation," stands within the distinction between symbol and theory presented in the previous chapter to explore the use as well as the limitations of imagination when thinking about God. The value of symbol as carrier of meaning is here balanced by reflection on the incomprehensibility of God, the source of all being, who is finally beyond material images. As the font of all being, God is intimately involved in the world and in human history. For those who take the bible as God's word, this is not in dispute. But *how* does God operate in the world? How can we talk about God in the world?

Chapter 4, "Grace and Human Freedom," discusses ways of understanding God's action in human life. With the help of Lonergan's historical analysis of the theology of grace the chapter seeks to understand God's saving presence and activity in a world that does not put God's redeeming and creative providence in competition with any created power, even the power of human freedom.

Chapter 5, "Redemption," addresses the process of salvation. Most religions seem to share a basic two-fold structure: there is something wrong with the world but there is also a way of correcting the wrong, healing the ill, solving the problem. What, according to Christian faith, do we need to be saved from? Lonergan considered evil to be a problem and not a mystery. If that is true, what is the basic problem that calls for correction, and what is the solution to the problem? In addition to the goodness of creation there are also natural disasters that cause enormous suffering. In addition to human benevolence there is also human sin. Faith in God's salvation is not a private affair with implications only for the individual. Faith is a social and historical value, foundational because it allows God's plan of redemption to be carried out through collaboration in history and society. Belief is one of the conditions for the possibility that the kingdom will be built "on earth as it is in heaven." The chapter thus presents some of Lonergan's insights regarding the corporate nature of salvation. Christ died for the world, not just for the select few, and all things are to be brought within his providential care. Conversion is the engine, on the personal level, that makes possible the transformation of structures of collaboration necessary for the healing and creativity that constitute salvation.

Chapter 6, "Incarnation," explores the central reality of the Christian faith, the Christ event, the coming of God in the flesh as the man Jesus. This chapter summarizes Lonergan's interpretation of the development of that doctrine from the earliest experience of the risen Jesus through the early debates concerning the identity of Jesus. We then address some of the stumbling blocks to faith in the Incarnation in the modern and post-modern mentalities.

Chapter 7, "Trinity," complements the previous chapters by tracing some of the salient points in the development of the Trinitarian mystery. From very early in its existence the church has confessed and baptized in the name of the Father, Son and Holy Spirit. The chapter explores some of the implications of Lonergan's Trinitarian thought, especially his interpretation of the psychological analogy, for the church's redemptive action in the world.

Chapter 8, "The Church and its Doctrines," continues the discussion of the corporate nature of redemption. Through the actions of Jesus' disciples, the church mediates and effects God's salvation. The gospel thereby becomes a force for progress in history to counter the opposing forces of decline. If redemption is to occur in history, therefore, God's redeeming message must be preserved and lived by the community of his disciples. In a historically conscious church the gospel message will be expressed and objectified in a variety of ways in its preaching, sacraments, Christian action, and education. Doctrines are judgments made by the church concerning the truth of the gospel but religious education opens onto forms of diverse communication according to the needs of the hearers and doers of the word. We conclude with a brief discussion of what sense it makes to pray.

1

Knowing, Knowing Yourself, and Doing Theology

IN THIS CHAPTER WE will summarize and illustrate Bernard Lonergan's groundbreaking thought on the basic structure of human thinking. The purpose here is not to learn what Lonergan said about thinking, but to use Lonergan's work as he intended, as an invitation to discover our own cognitional operations; his most important contribution to the theological enterprise is not a teaching, or doctrine, or even a model that one might choose. Rather, it is a summons, a call, an invitation to grasp the operations within ourselves that, when assembled, produce knowledge. As important as Lonergan's theological opinions are, what Lonergan himself thought matters much less than what we can discover about our own operations. Lonergan's writing helps us to begin that journey of self-discovery so that our "self-appropriation" can serve as a sure foundation for our own theological work.

Knowing Is Not Like Looking

Our initial experience of the world is purely through our senses. An infant's universe is the world of touch and taste, smells, noises, and blurred images. It wants merely to eat, sleep and cuddle. Soon, however, there develops the rudiments of language through which the child is introduced to a world of meaning that goes far beyond what can be received by the five senses. Eventually the child begins to ask questions: what is that? Why does that happen? Where does it go? How does it work? The world is now a wonderful and sometimes overwhelming surplus of meanings, seemingly made to order for the little engine of inquiry that not that long ago appeared simply as a wet, whining bundle of bodily needs.

Because the needs of the five senses come first in human development and continue as needs throughout life, it is a natural inclination to revert to what is given in the senses when we think about our own thinking. What's that? Well, take a look—see what it is. But questions for meaning (what? why? how?) are not resolved by a return to sense perceptions. One can look but not understand what one sees, listen but not understand what one hears. Only gradually does language open us to a world that is mediated to us not merely by sight and touch and sound, but by meaning. Knowledge starts with perception but it is not the same as perception. Lonergan's oft-repeated reminder is that knowing is not like looking. Vernon Gregson lists a few helpful examples of Lonergan's point:

> One does not really *see* a nation, or a city, or a university. One does not *see* a wife, or a president, or a criminal. Surely one sees land and buildings, but one only understands and judges that a particular expanse of land is under the jurisdiction of a particular group of people. Does a disputed plot of land *really* show you which nation it belongs to? The same group of buildings which you call a college or university can become a low-security prison with a change of ownership (a change of understanding and meaning) and look exactly the same. Surely one sees a woman but recognition of whether she is wife or president or criminal is a matter of understanding and judgment and not merely vision. No, knowing is not merely looking, it is experiencing and understanding *and* judging.[1]

We can add innumerable examples to verify this claim that knowing is not like looking. Language is an obvious example of the fact that getting the meaning is not reducible to the ocular gaze. If you study Spanish but have never learned any German, merely looking at a German sentence will not result in understanding its meaning. Looking gives sensory data to be understood; in this case, you can see mostly familiar letters, but not much more, because you cannot decode the meaning of the printed letters you are looking at. Looking at a page cannot substitute for understanding what the marks on the page mean. Or consider a climate: it is not sunshine or a storm or rain or temperature or any combination of these. A climate is a statistical construct; it cannot be looked at. And yet, who would want to claim that there is no such thing as a climate?

A good detective with bad eyesight is better at solving crime than someone with 20–20 vision but no police training. Many a good detective story hinges on a detail at the crime scene or elsewhere that, to untrained observers, can be seen yet means nothing, but the police officer "detects" something

---

1. Gregson, *Desires*, 27.

more than what meets the eye.[2] All the lab data in the world does not substitute for an insightful police inspector.[3] Good detection is in part the result of police training and not good eyesight. An aviator at that crime scene will not do much better police work than an electrician or a school teacher. That same aviator, however, might be helpful to the investigators at an airplane crash site. Similarly, the historian looking through a microscope in a science lab will be at a distinct disadvantage compared to the scientist.[4]

If you have ever visited an art museum with someone who knows how to interpret paintings, you know that you can both gaze at a portrait or an ancient sculpted torso, a still life or a reconstructed altar piece. Both of you will get the same visual data, the same stimuli on your retinas. Nothing is different for the two of you, except the two of you! A trained art historian will "see" more than an amateur; notice, however, that I have put the word "see" in quotation marks because there is the same visual data equally available to both of you. The difference is not in the painting's impact on the other person's eyeball; the difference is in the other person's understanding.

There are many examples in the natural sciences that knowing is not like looking. The physicist John Polkinghorne notes that "[q]uantum entities do not have the properties of simultaneously possessing exact position and momentum, of being visualizable."[5] He puts the same principle in more ordinary language by noting the "counter-intuitive character of a world governed by Heisenberg's uncertainty principle (which says that if we know where an electron is we don't know what it is doing)."[6] This "superposition principle" is a change from Newtonian theory, which required that a particle be either here or there; in quantum theory, a particle can be both here and there at once: "the particle will sometimes be found 'here' and sometimes be found 'there.' Thus, the superposition principle underlies the unpicturability and statistical character of the quantum world."[7]

Our first contact with the world is through the immediacy of the senses; understanding modern physics, however, is not a matter of keen perception. Quantum physics seems odd when one first hears about it because our

2. Lonergan begins the "Preface" to *Insight* with a reference to what a good detective story entails: all the clues are present but their meaning is not known. The denouement coincides with the "unique explanatory arrangement" of the clues.

3. For examples see Tekippe, *What*, 21–26.

4. For the example of the historian looking through the microscope ("to describe what one sees—that's easy; to see what ought to be described—that's difficult") see Febvre, *Combats*, 8, 22–23, and 431; as cited by Komonchak, "Vatican II," 17n.

5. Polkinghorne, "Quantum," 335.

6. Ibid., 334.

7. Ibid., 335. The term "superposition principle" was coined by Paul Dirac.

inclination is to fall back on our senses as the foundation for our knowledge. Physicists have found that light is a wave when measured one way and a particle when measured another. We can't just look to see which one it really is; light turns out to be not picturable. The theory of light will make sense only if one does not insist that it be picturable.

Many of these examples deal with experts having particular kinds of insights. That's because the more we know, the more informed and practiced we are before attempting any interpretation, the more likely we will understand the data we are considering. A New Yorker cartoon makes this point with humor.[8] It pictures the interior of a renaissance school room; through its window one sees gondolas, a bridge, and a palace. A student standing at his desk says to the teacher, "The Doge ate my homework." If you think this is funny (or, if you think it's distinctly not funny but you still get the joke), it's because you brought and successfully employed previously acquired knowledge of history, geography and popular culture. Getting the joke, in other words, is not the result of merely looking carefully at what the cartoonist has drawn. What knowledge do you need to bring to this cartoon to understand it? You need to know that gondolas are emblematic of Venice, that Venice during the renaissance was ruled by a "Doge" or leader, that the style of the dress in the picture is consonant with the halcyon days of Venice under the Doge and, finally, one must be familiar with the clichéd student excuse for not being prepared: "the *dog* ate my homework." That's quite a bit of knowledge that must be brought to bear in interpreting a little cartoon. Yet, if one considers what goes into any event of understanding, one realizes that, in most successful interpretations there is required a great deal of background knowledge.[9] One should be careful, then, not to reach too quickly for another well-worn expression of scholastic exasperation: "This doesn't make any sense!" The truth might be that *the person trying to figure it out doesn't understand it.* As Lonergan reminds us, "only the man that understands everything already is in a position to demand that all meaning be simple and obvious to him."[10]

Experiencing the Desire to Understand

You have perhaps noticed on occasion that you have a desire to understand by *feeling the frustrating absence* of understanding. Imagine a high school student being given an assignment to report, in one's own words, on the

8. Sam Gross, Cartoonist. *The New Yorker*, March 18, 1996.

9. Tekippe, 27–33, has accumulated examples of understanding through jokes.

10. Lonergan, *Insight*, 581.

ideas of a famous scientist. Now imagine reading about the scientist and his or her discovery but not having any understanding of that discovery. The celebrated idea is for the student simply words. How frustrating it would be to put into one's own words an idea that is not understood. Getting the point is more than the mere manipulation of words; it is an intellectual event. The frustration that emerges when we can't understand is, however, proof of our implicit grasp of the fact that we really do not understand. When we feel the difference between reading words and catching on to the meaning of those words we can notice that we want to understand, and that awareness is a significant indication of the natural desire to know.

The experience of wanting to understand is quite common. The human mind is always on the move, never static. We don't merely gape, repeat or memorize; we puzzle and wonder and ask. We feel the dynamic "pull" of a desire to "get it," and when we don't, we feel tension and frustration. Of course, there are many things that any particular individual at any given time is simply not prepared to understand. Children ask about much more than they are capable of understanding. Their engine of inquiry, however, is open: it points toward greater understanding when it asks about any particular object of knowledge.

The importance of intelligence is nicely illustrated in the first chapter of Genesis in which the Creator transforms an undifferentiated chaos into an ordered cosmos. Creation is portrayed as a separation of the abysmal waters and a separation or differentiation of the earth and its inhabitants from the waters. In the cosmos coming into being, light is not darkness, earth is not water. This is not that. All of it is good. Later in the narrative (Gen 2: 19), Adam, made in God's image and likeness, takes up the divine work of intelligence by naming and thus distinguishing the animals. Adam understood that a horse is not a tiger, a bird is not a fish, and none of them is a worthy spouse. It was important for him to get this right.

We have named that which is intended by our questions for understanding an "object" but our discussion of knowing as not reducible to a simple matter of looking should make us wary of any attempt to imagine the object of knowledge as merely a physical body. The object of our intending is the meaning of whatever it is we are trying to understand. That object is normally given in sense data but it could also be given in the operations of one's own subjectivity—what Lonergan calls the data of consciousness—that manifest one's intentionality.

Judgment and Truth

We have drawn attention to the human desire for understanding and have noted that children ask lots of questions: how? who? why? where? how many? These are questions for meaning that express the desire to understand; they can be asked and answered in a virtually infinite number of ways. Eventually, the child will also begin to ask another sort of question—the kind that intends not simply meaning but also truth. These are "Yes-or-no" questions. A child comes home from school, for example, and asks, "Billy said that there's a ghost living in the restroom. Is that true?" Notice that this is a different type of question from the ones that seek meaning. A "yes-or-no" question, unlike questions for meaning, can be answered only one of three ways: "Yes," "No," or "I don't know." The answer is a judgment about the truth of some idea or understanding that is being proposed as true. Either the idea has been verified (it is true) or it has not (it is false or perhaps one doesn't know whether it is true or false). This second type of question seeks to know not merely what people happen to think about things or situations or states of affairs; it seeks to verify whether what they think is in fact the case.[11] These questions for judgment are essential if we are to know what is really going on and not merely what people imagine.

The difference between thinking and knowing is the judgment that my thinking is or is not true. Self-knowledge requires that each person answer questions such as "Do I seek meaning?" "Do I judge the veracity of my ideas?" If I recognize this act of judgment entailed in my assessment of my cognitional operations, then I should appropriate that fact, take it seriously, and notice the very significant consequence, also expressed in a judgment: I am a knower. One can verify for oneself that judgment is inescapable: judge what you are reading to be either correct *or incorrect* and you will prove that you are a knower.

The ancient Greeks had a standard philosophical move that they employed to deal with people who claimed that there is no truth: they would ask the speaker to notice that the claim disqualifies itself. If there is no truth, one cannot know such a claim—that there is no truth—to be true. The move doesn't get us very far beyond exposing the silliness of such relativism but it does point to the fact that the operations of the human subject should be kept in mind when making claims about reality. For whenever you inquire into some reality in the world, you—an attentive and questioning human

---

11. The best one can achieve in many situations is the judgment that something is probably the case—but this is a judgment that "p" (standing for a proposition) is probably the case and so, one is making a truth claim, but about a probability. See Lonergan, *Insight*, 324–29.

subject—are already engaged. To claim that you cannot know is to forget—or perhaps intentionally to ignore—who you are and what you do. Knowledge is never simply about the object to be known; it is also necessarily about the subject as well. There are standards or "imperatives" (Lonergan's term) built into your very self. If you are to be authentic and not phony, it is "imperative" that you be (1) attentive to experience, (2) intelligent about interpreting that experience, (3) reasonable in judging the veracity of that understanding, and (4) responsible in your actions.

The operations and patterns of consciousness that correspond to these imperatives provide a starting point for serious philosophical reflection. Philosophy, after all, is not about learning the opinions of famously smart people. Philosophy is preeminently the achievement of self-knowledge. Socrates demonstrated at the dawn of Western philosophy that, if you know yourself, you can know what you know and what you don't know. As Lonergan once remarked, philosophy isn't in books—it's in minds.[12]

Of course, a relativist is confusedly aware of something very important, namely the frequent difficulty we experience in arriving at true judgments. Life is complex; catching on to the meaning of certain states of affairs is often quite difficult. Those whose primary concern is certitude, those who experience little doubt about things that require specialized knowledge, are probably further from finding things out than the cautious searcher. Attitude and personality are important factors in the acquisition of knowledge. Some are too quick to judge; perhaps they lack the persistence required to pursue the matter until all the relevant questions have been asked. Perhaps they fear the answer that they vaguely expect to find and so refuse to give full reign to the drive for understanding. They are reluctant to admit that they simply don't know what is going on. At the other end of the spectrum of attitudes, however, there are those who are reluctant to make judgments. Perhaps they want to be fair to the other side of the issue, or they fear being wrong, or perhaps they do not want to appear arrogant. There are, perhaps, as many reasons for these two psychological extremes as there are people. For our purposes, however, we simply want to acknowledge (1) that knowing isn't necessarily easy and (2) there is a myriad of reasons why any particular individual might have difficulty either making a judgment or making a good one.

What we correctly judge to be the case is not simply what we happen to think. This does not, obviously, imply infallibility. In fact, our recognition of error illustrates the fact that judgment is inescapable. If I say, "I was wrong; I thought *p* was the case, but it turns out not to be," I am making a judgment.

12. See Liddy, *Transforming*, 106; see also Lonergan, *Insight*, 421.

That I had been wrong in my judgment about some state of affairs is itself a fact arrived at through judgment. If I could not judge I would not know that in some particular matter I happened to be wrong. Words like "objective" are properly used in relation to a judgment about whether some state of affairs is the case. In the example we are using here, my error is objective—it's not that I merely think I was wrong; rather, my error is a fact and I know it. The correction of my mistake makes sense only within the context of a factual judgment that I have erred.[13]

Some might claim that any form of realism—the position that one can arrive at true judgments, which makes it the opposite of relativism—is a form of arrogance. They imagine that making judgments is the same as being "judgmental" or imposing a controlling narrative on experience and thus excluding alternative perspectives. If that were true, it would be virtuous—a morally good thing—to be a relativist. In fact, however, realism requires deep humility because the truth is often such that I do not *want* to know it. My ego would prefer not to face what, in many cases, will require me to change my comfortable habits and to abandon self-serving illusions about myself, my patterns of behavior or the groups with which I identify. Openness to alternative understandings is vital if we are to develop as individuals and make progress as a society; a fearful need for certitude can close off insights. Judgments are limited commitments and raise further questions for understanding. The dynamic drive toward higher viewpoints is not discouraged by judgment because there are further questions to be answered. But relativism discourages self-understanding and thus trivializes the quest for knowledge and the personal transformation it requires. It lets us off the hook—there is no urgency to broaden our horizons if there is no way of knowing what is or ought to be the case. Unreflective skeptics would not be responsible for their judgments if there is no such thing as truth.

If we cannot attain true knowledge (and if we can't, we will never *know* that we can't) then intellect takes a back seat to will. We might as well allow the corporations, governments, or their militaries to pursue their goals with no questions asked. But notice how easily such radical skepticism can turn matters of truth into matters of power. Before he had him crucified, Pilate interrogated Jesus concerning the charge that Jesus had declared himself to be the king of the Jews. Jesus responded that he had come into the world to testify to the truth. Pilate's famously dismissive retort was, "What is truth?" Pilate's question, to which he expected no answer, was the end of their conversation, and he walked out. There was nothing left to do but initiate the

---

13. On correcting mistaken beliefs see Lonergan, *Insight*, 736–39.

wheels of Roman force against an innocent man who dared to speak about truth (John 18: 28-40).

Judgments of fact are determinations that this is the case and its opposite is not the case. But there are also judgments of value: determinations that this is good and its opposite is not good. Take the following example of a judgment of fact: "There are, in fact, thousands of starving people in that country because government officials have impounded the food aid before it can get to its hungry citizens." Now contrast that factual judgment with the following judgment of value: "It is wrong for government officials to impound the food aid before it can get to its starving citizens." Knowing what is factually true in this case prompts further questions: is it good that the government is doing this? If not, what is at stake and what ought to be done about it? The common revulsion at the government's policy can be traced back to a judgment of value, a judgment not about what is but about what ought to be or not be.

Are There Any More Questions?

A key point in Lonergan's account of cognition is that we attain a secure judgment when no further relevant questions arise. When consulting the data to determine whether a judgment is correct, we are seeking to understand whether there are any more relevant questions to ask. If not, the judgment is secure. But how do we know that there are no more relevant questions? Is it not equally possible that, for whatever reason, we have not permitted the relevant questions to arise? This question, however, is another question for reflection; to ask it is to repeat the operation that is in doubt. Operations of consciousness, in other words, are matters of concrete and particular fact; when we ask about them we are exhibiting them. The issue is an existential one that each person must handle individually. The self-affirmation of the knower is not an arrogant claim that one is free of error or the capacity for error; it is rather a recognition of the fact that to correct error, one must be able to know it for what it is.[14] To the relativist Lonergan retorts, "You warn me that I have made mistakes in the past. But your warning is meaningless, if I am making a further mistake in recognizing a past mistake as a mistake."[15] The conclusion is inescapable: "Errors are just as much facts as are correct judgments."[16] "A reviser cannot appeal to data to

14. Ibid., 344.
15. Ibid., 368.
16. Ibid., 371.

deny data, to his new insights to deny insights, to his new formulation to deny formulation, to his reflective grasp to deny reflective grasp."[17]

The hermeneutics of suspicion points up the difficulty of honest judgments. Difficulty and hopelessness are, however, two different things. Lonergan points out that Marx and Freud were intending to act intelligently and reasonably in their critiques of reason, but this reply does not go to the heart of the matter. A fuller response lies in Lonergan's discussion in *Insight* of genuineness, or what he later came to call authenticity. Genuineness "has to be won back through a self-scrutiny that expels illusion and pretense: and as this enterprise is difficult and its issue doubtful, we do not think of its successful outcome when we cast about for an obvious illustration of genuineness."[18] Lonergan is not a superficial optimist; correct judgments depend upon a genuine human development that is difficult and far from guaranteed. And yet, the eros of the mind means that the human person is capable of the leap to a higher synthesis. There is, in the end, freedom to foster or inhibit the leap, and so the self-appropriation of the knower is more than an intellectual ideal; it is a concrete, personal achievement that entails an ongoing and cumulative process of self-correction.[19]

The foundational and heuristic value of Lonergan's understanding of understanding cannot be overestimated. Neither idealist nor naïve empiricist, Lonergan's notion of judgment allows him to distinguish between thinking and knowing. Knowledge is not perfect understanding but rather the correct affirmation of a particular understanding; judgment is "a limited commitment." What we get when we know is the real or "being." But there is always the further question for understanding that heads toward a fuller grasp of the reality one intends to affirm in a judgment.

To summarize, the self-appropriation of the knower, the recognition of what one does when one knows, establishes an invariant base (the invariant and thus normative operations of subjectivity) from which to evaluate diverse insights, philosophies and programs. Lonergan begins with the concrete human subject who neither logically deduces not naively looks at the world of things but rather affirms it through intelligence and judgment. His position takes into account the impediments that block understanding and so the self-affirmation of the knower entails fully human growth toward genuineness. Lonergan's work can initiate a process of liberation from the illusion that knowing is illusory; it can restore a proper sense of sovereignty

17. Ibid., 360.

18. Ibid., 500–504.

19. Ibid., 311.

to the individual in the post-modern world who, in Walker Percy's phrase, too often feels bad and does not know why.[20]

Insight Precedes Concept and Logic

We have noted that thinking means paying attention, trying to figure out what is going on and determining whether we've got it right. In many cases we will need to go further and ask what is good so that we might decide what to do. It should be clear by now that thinking is not a simple matter of logical deductions. "Logic" is a word with multiple meanings but in general it refers to the reasonable arrangement of claims so that one might arrive at a true conclusion. The truth of a logical deduction, however, depends in part on the truth of the "premises"—claims that one presumes to be true at the start of the reasoning process. To take a silly example, if I presume that all dogs can talk and that Rex is a dog, the conclusion—that Rex can talk—will be valid. I will have arrived at the conclusion using strict logical deduction; I didn't make any mistakes in the process. But the truth of the conclusion will depend, obviously, on whether all dogs can talk. Since most of them can't, then no matter how careful my deduction, I'm probably not going to arrive at a true conclusion.

The process of thinking does, of course, employ logic all the time—we would be merely silly, for example, if we were constantly violating the oldest and most basic element of logic: the principle of non-contradiction. But if we start a deduction with an idea that turns out to be false, we can be perfectly "logical" in our thinking without being correct in our conclusion. And the fact is, we are always starting with something that we presuppose to be true; we never start from a blank slate. The principles of logic are not meaningful unless they are employed in a larger context in which understanding and judgments of truth and value play their part even before we start the process.

Theology and Intellect

If theology mediates religion to a particular culture, as Lonergan's empirical approach insists, the principal task of theology will be one of interpreting the religious tradition and the culture, then transposing that tradition. Theology employs logic, to be sure, but the enterprise is much more than deducing conclusions from already established truths or first principles. As

20. See Percy, "Loss," 46–63.

Saint Ambrose once put the matter, it did not please God to save His people by logic.[21] Theology seeks to interpret these expressions of God's revelation and thereby to develop a keener understanding of the divine mystery itself. But meaning is always within a context, and so in its task of seeking understanding, theology must mediate religious living within particular cultures. The "conclusions theology" of an earlier era in Catholic thought has given way to a manifold of approaches. Theology has many specialized tasks to perform but all of them require thinking by human minds. For that reason, the self-understanding that we have been exploring in this chapter is most relevant to the doing of theology, for just as error in other realms of inquiry can sometimes be traced to mistaken notions of human cognition, so too can theological error. The physicist who insists on "seeing" the location of electrons in the atom will never understand what is going on there. In like manner (as we shall see in chapter five), the theologian who insists on imagining the way in which God's grace cooperates with human freedom will never understand that cooperation.

Lonergan speaks of an intellectual *eros*—an appetite constitutive of being human—a desire to go beyond one's present state of human development. To be ourselves, it seems, we must always go beyond ourselves. The end or goal of this desire is God who as Creator has instilled in the creature a desire to return to its Source. I do not choose my ultimate end or goal—that has been set for humanity by God, and that goal *is* God— and that end comes first in the sense that it is the origin of my desire, my seeking, the reason for my journey. This desire is not automatic or mechanical; it can be dampened or distorted. After all, most good things can be distorted by failure, stupidity or malice. Still, this human longing for more than what one presently understands cannot but be a fundamental element of the theological enterprise.

Anselm of Canterbury (d. 1109) famously defined theology as faith seeking understanding, by which he meant a reflection driven by questions about the meaning and truth of the revelation of God in Christ. For several centuries prior to the time of Anselm, theology was largely a monastic enterprise that proceeded according to the logic of prayer, reflection on authoritative sources (especially the Bible) and commentary on these sources. Anselm, like his monastic predecessors, placed his reflections within the context of prayer. But the rigorous questioning of his method and the concern for the systematic coherence of precisely defined

---

21. "*Non in dialectica complacuit Deo salvum facere populum suum.*" Newman placed this sentence as the epigraph to his justly famous book on religious knowledge, *An Essay in Aid of a Grammar of Assent.*

and interlocking terms marked a shift in the way theology was being done in medieval Europe.[22]

Much has changed in theology since the twelfth century; Anselm's abstract definition is true enough but today the methods to be used for understanding require specificity. His questions are not identical to our questions. In the medieval period to seek understanding meant primarily to be in dialogue with Platonic and Aristotelian philosophy. Theology is still an enterprise whereby a person of faith asks questions about the meaning and truth of that faith, but theology has of late come to acknowledge the need to engage in team work with other disciplines besides the traditional one of philosophy. If the twelfth century spoke of reason as primarily philosophical, today reason is understood within various socially and historically mediated situations and so calls for the human social sciences. For this reason, Lonergan has redefined theology as the mediation of a religion in a culture.[23] The thinking that the theologian does today must take into account not merely philosophical reason; he or she must also consider the insights of psychology, anthropology and sociology, economics, the natural sciences, and other ways of knowing. In other words, for Christians to contribute to the progressive redemption of the world, theologians must be willing to employ the insights of the sciences that study and make actual the healing and creative meanings and values that orient, ground and promote progress.

Some will object, however, that the various sciences are disparate and lack integration; perhaps integration isn't even possible. There are many diverse ways of knowing and any effort by a single science to integrate them will inevitably result in the hegemony of one form of knowing over another. Post-modern thinkers, for example, have objected to the "logocentrism" of western science, which attempts to dominate all knowledge and thus obscures alternative ways of knowing. Our "scientific culture" is simply a moment in history, relative to the contemporary western mode of thinking and not the sole guarantor of authentic knowledge.

In light of these observations, the question arises, is there any common ground on which all sciences and modes of inquiry might stand? Is there anything universal in human reason that can acknowledge the many of ways of knowing that contemporary pluralism makes possible and unavoidable? For example, does the method of the physicist have anything in common with what theologians do? By now we know that Lonergan's answer is yes: the thinker is that common ground. Thinking, no matter the subject matter, is a

---

22. For background and context, see Chenu, *Nature*, 270–309. For the turn to theory in Anselm, see Loewe, *Lex Crucis*, 71–101.

23. Lonergan, *Method*, xi.

recurring human activity that exhibits a certain structure or pattern of operations. The thinker's attentiveness to experience generates questions for understanding (e.g., what is that? Why is it that and not something else? What's going on? What does that mean?) as well as questions for verification (is this what I think it is? Do I have it right? Have I caught the correct meaning?). Lonergan asks his readers to do their own examination to see if it is possible to avoid either of these sorts of questions. The physicist might think about her subject matter very differently than the poet, and yet they are both asking about meaning and attempting to discern whether the meaning at which one has arrived is true, or at least true to some degree of probability. There is a common base of operations in all human thinking and this base, this rock on which all inquiry is built, can be discerned if one makes the full "turn to the subject" that has been evolving over the past two centuries.

When we come to know in ourselves these basic operations we have a powerful tool for controlling our cognition. When we know that our knowledge is constituted only when the assembly of these operations—as attentive questioning in search of truthful meaning—we will be less prone to mistake spontaneous images or clever explanations for truth. Truth results from a correct judgment regarding the way things happen to be. The key task is not to make assumptions about thinking but to discover the operations that constitute it.

Christian theology requires thinking about God's self-revelation as Creator and Savior. As *thinking*, it is also a recurring human activity that exhibits a stable structure or pattern of operations. For this reason, the theologian's grasp of what constitutes the activity of thinking will make a difference in the theological project itself.

The Turn to the Subject in Philosophy and Theology

In this section I briefly outline the philosophical tradition that preceded Lonergan's revolutionary insight. (For those readers who are not interested in Lonergan's place in the tradition of modern epistemology and metaphysics, they can skip to the next section without losing the thread of this chapter.) With the advent of the scientific revolution the ancient and medieval philosophical starting point—the philosophy of being, also called metaphysics or ontology—was replaced by the philosophy of knowledge or epistemology. The medieval approach to being, with its "stark and scandalous . . . array of disputed questions"[24] could not account for the scientific discoveries that were occurring during the Enlightenment and the

24. Lawrence, "Fragility," 57.

scientific revolution of the seventeenth and eighteenth centuries. Although Lonergan was educated at a time when Catholic philosophy and theology were stalled in a reaction against modern thinking, his early commitment was to the integration of the values of modernity into theology while exposing and criticizing its errors.

Whereas ancient philosophy concerned itself with the explication of being, modern philosophies focus on the *explicator* of being, the knower. The characteristically modern question is not "What do I know?" but rather, "What are the conditions of the possibility of knowledge?" Modern philosophy is critical of what seems to be the ancients' naive presumption that world and the mind are somehow fundamentally related. Some of our epistemological difficulties (confusions over what constitutes knowledge) can be traced back to the fourteenth century scholastic Duns Scotus and the tradition that followed (late medieval nominalism).[25] No matter what its antecedents, the philosophy of knowledge since the seventeenth century has been caught in a rather thorny thicket. On the one hand philosophy broke free from its naïve assumption that the unproblematic objectivity of knowledge can ignore the conditions for its acquisition in the knowing subject. On the other hand, the critique of knowledge has led philosophy to eschew the ancient and medieval assumption that the mind is constituted to know the world and the world is constituted to be known by the human mind.

The beginnings of the modern turn to the subject can be glimpsed in the work of Rene Descartes (1595–1650), whose dissatisfaction with the decadent scholasticism that he learned as a student at the Jesuit college of La Flèche in France motivated him to develop a method that he hoped would ground and unify all the sciences. To do that Descartes was convinced that his philosophical method must begin with radical doubt and then move toward a foundation of certitude. The movement was from the certain existence of the *res cogitans*—the thinking subject—to the *res extensa*—the world of sense experience. This approach involved Descartes in a detour through an ontological argument that the innate idea of God implies God's existence. From the existence of a God who does not deceive (a god who deceives is not God), he deduces the existence of the world of bodies. Throughout his philosophy Descartes relied on the widely held assumption that knowing is an immediate result of a mental view of what is present, namely the thinking thing itself.

Although most of his project has come under severe criticism, Descartes achieved something important. His famous conclusion, that because he thinks he must exist (if you are *thinking*, then *you* are thinking), manifests

---

25. On Scotus, see Burrell, "Aquinas and Scotus," 105–29.

the germ of Lonergan's insight that he called the self-affirmation of the knower.[26] Although the Cartesian way of affirming the existence of the knower is through the mistaken notion that we look inside ourselves, he did achieve through inquiry the clear and distinct affirmation of the subject's existence.[27] But the contents of consciousness are known not by looking inside but by asking and correctly answering questions. Descartes failed to make explicit what he was actually doing when he was affirming his own existence.[28] In like manner, considering knowledge of the rest of reality, Descartes's *res extensa* (bodies) is out there in the world, outside the mind, known by confronting what is there as if by a mental looking. Rather than imagining a world of bodies, as Descartes does, Lonergan affirms *being*, by which he means the goal of intelligent grasp and reasonable affirmation. Rather than taking a look, the knower brings to the data of experience a grasp of its intelligibility, and then affirms that understanding as true.

The key figure in the turn to the subject after Descartes is the great German philosopher Immanuel Kant (1724–1804). His "Copernican Revolution" was an enormous challenge to so much of the philosophy and common sense of Europe. Kant intended to establish a theory of knowledge that criticized and eliminated the unwarranted confidence of logical, deductive reasoning (a tradition since Descartes usually named continental rationalism) as well as the naïve focus on sensations (associated with British empiricism). Kant knew that without the operations of the mind, the sensations were just sensations, but he also knew that his inherited rationalism (thinking with little attention to the data of sense) could discover precious little. But how are sensation and reason related so that we can have authentic knowledge? Instead of thinking that the mind adjusts itself when it receives the world of objects via sensation, Kant proposed that we turn our thinking around and consider that the objects that we intend to know adjust to our thinking. Just as Copernicus placed the sun at the center of the planetary system where the earth was thought to be, so Kant placed the subject—the knower—at the center of thinking, displacing the objects of knowledge.

---

26. In his critique of Etienne Gilson's naïve realism, Lonergan points to the performance of questioning by the subject. "No doubt, that performance will be interpreted or overlooked in different manners when assumed within different horizons; but it is given to be interpreted or overlooked whether or not it is assumed. Nor can any doubt be entertained about the fact of the performance. To doubt questioning is to ask whether questions occur. The condition of the possibility of doubting is the occurrence of questioning" ("Metaphysics," 199–200).

27. Lonergan, *Insight*, 413–14.

28. Ibid., 339.

The revolution raised the question, what exactly does the knower do when knowing anything? Here is where Kant's revolution stumbled. Kant says that we can know the appearance of things only; the thing itself, out there in the world, is unknowable. Still, we humans all have a common mental structure that shapes our sensations in the same way, and so science is possible because we are all doing the same thing with the data that we receive. We can speak intelligently of causality, for example, because causality is a universal characteristic of human cognition which the mind applies to the sensations it receives.[29]

In spite of his radical proposal to bring our thinking and knowing to center stage, Kant's preoccupation with the *contents* of cognition left his understanding of the subject incomplete and misleading. Thanks to Kant, philosophy began to move away from the naïve objectivism and rationalism that dominated it in the eighteenth century. Yet there remained an ambivalence in his critical philosophy that required a further liberation: the often-unacknowledged tendency to imagine knowing as the task of bridging a gap between the knower and the known. Lonergan sometimes calls this common misunderstanding of knowing the "confrontation" theory; its assumption is that the real is "the already-out-there-now-real" and that to know it is a matter of a mental gazing. With Kant, we are stuck with this imagined gap: we can only know appearances, but appearances of what? The thing itself is unknowable so we can't know that what appears are the appearances of the thing itself. At the same time, Kant insisted that there is no knowledge without sensation; reason without the data of sense is empty. Lonergan traces this assumption that we know only the appearance of reality back to Galileo's distinction between primary and secondary qualities, where the primary are the really real and the secondary are what appear to common sense.[30]

Although Lonergan did not accept the full answers that Kant provided, the fundamental questions raised in his *Critique of Pure Reason* were key to Lonergan's intellectual development.[31] Kant overlooked the fact that

29. The eighteenth-century Scottish philosopher David Hume was convinced that the only thing we know is what comes through the senses, and so the causality we ascribe to what we sense is merely a customary way of interpreting those sensations. This makes science impossible, and Kant was determined to respond to Hume's challenge and establish a firm philosophical foundation for science. See Kant's "Preface to the Second Edition" of *Critique*, 22.

30. Lonergan, *Insight*, 363.

31. Mathews, "Anomalous," 85–98. In Lonergan's view, Kant's version of scientific or theoretical knowledge is constrained by the *a priori* conditions of what Kant called *Anschauung*, and usually translated as "intuition." For my discussion of the intuitionist principle in Kant, I rely on Sala, *Lonergan and Kant* for many of the details of the

when we understand, we grasp meaning in an image. The image itself is not the insight but it provides the opportunity to grasp the meaning of what is given in sense or in consciousness. Nor is insight a pre-determined concept. The intellect is not like a factory with fixed tools that only makes one set of fixed things. Rather it is more like a universal machine tool "that erects all kinds of factories, keeps adjusting and improving them, and eventually scraps them in favor of radically new designs."[32] Insight, in other words, precedes concept.

Finally, Kant has a weak notion of judgment. Recognizing Kant's original revolutionary insight, Lonergan also turned to the subject but found that conscious operations, when assembled, constitute knowledge. The real—being—is what is correctly affirmed in any judgment, which is a "limited commitment" about a particular insight. Judgments are made within concrete contexts; the vast majority of our judgments concern contingent facts and so are not about what is always and everywhere true. In both Kant and Hegel, it is precisely the role of judgment (as Lonergan uses the term) that is missing. Hegel is fascinated by the infinite intelligibility of phenomena and is never content with any explanation that does not account for all data. Lonergan shares with Hegel a commitment to the unrestricted desire to know; the eros of the mind is the central motivating force behind the incessant and profound analyses of Hegel's *Phenomenology of Spirit*. But because Hegel conceives of knowing as complete understanding, he is unable to affirm either the knower or the known as a unity-identity-whole. Lonergan, on the other hand, recognizes many examples of particular judgments, each of which attains a virtually unconditioned. Without judgment, cognition remains at the level of understanding, which is in itself infallible: one thinks what one thinks, and there's an end of it. To solve this problem, Hegel appeals to the final and complete understanding that he names Absolute Spirit. But a further question arises beyond any particular and limited insight. Is my idea about this, my understanding of this, my thinking on this, true? That further question is essential if thinking is to terminate in knowledge of the real. Knowledge is not the already-out-there-now-real, nor is it the conceptualization of what appears in intuition. Rather, knowledge results from a series of self-assembling operations that culminates in

comparison between Kant and Lonergan. Lonergan finds a Scotist assumption operating in Kant's critical philosophy: that there is a duality or gap between object and subject at the base of the intuitionist principle. Kant wrote as if the object is already given in the sense data. Experience (*Erfahrung*) "tells us, indeed, *what is*, but not that it must necessarily be so, and not otherwise" (Kant, *Critique*, A.1).

32. Lonergan, *Insight*, 430–31.

a judgment that is virtually unconditioned—a conditioned in which all the conditions happen to be fulfilled.

In the complex act of knowing we grasp intelligibility in the data of experience and affirm that understanding reasonably through judgment. Not until we ask the truth question, not until we judge, can we properly claim knowledge. Judgment is secure when no further relevant questions emerge. At that point the judgment is a virtually unconditioned, i.e. a conditioned in which all the conditions happen to be fulfilled. We come to know that this is indeed human cognitional structure when we affirm the process in our own behavior. The question, "What am I doing when I am knowing?" admits of an answer available in the intelligent grasp and reasonable affirmation of one's own conscious operations. For cases in which one cannot know whether there are or will be further relevant questions, the judgment will be probable; in other words, in a probable judgment, one is heading toward the ideal of answering all the relevant questions even if one has not yet achieved that ideal. Judgment, however, does not close off the openness that leads to ever new discoveries, and so most judgments will affirm a probability rather than an absolute.

The vital role of judgment eliminates the need to imagine that Galileo's "secondary qualities" are unreal, and thus no need for Kant's noumenal "thing in itself." Instead, the inquiring subject asks questions for both understanding and truth, and answers them. Accordingly, the fact of insight coupled with Lonergan's notion of judgment means that the world of things does not remain unknown but is instead infinitely knowable. For unless we can identify the thing as a unity-identity-whole, science would never reach beyond appearances.[33] The necessity of judgment as the completion of the cognitional process means that knowledge does not consist in a final and exhaustive explanation of the thing it affirms (Hegel's solution, which entails complete understanding), but rather in the affirmation of an intelligent grasp of this particular assemblage of data.

For Lonergan, in other words, the solution to the problem of knowledge is not to abandon the turn to the subject, content to imagine that knowing is like seeing what's out there already (a naïve empiricism). Nor is the solution an appeal to logic, as if we can make progress in our understanding of the world simply by deducing truths from first principles (an abstract rationalism).[34] Kant provided a strong impetus for a focus on the subject, but if we pay intelligent attention to our own thinking we can discover that we do not confront a gap between our minds and the reality

33. Ibid., 275.
34. See Lonergan, "Healing," 104.

outside of it. Rather, knowledge is a matter of assembling the elements that our cognitional operations provide as we attend to our experience, ask questions, think, imagine examples, think some more and finally judge whether what we *think* is going on really *is* going on. The completion of the turn to the subject does not stop at understanding, as it seems to do with German idealism. Beyond thinking there is the operation of judgment: asking whether one's thinking is true. The complete turn to the subject fully rejects the myth of knowing the "already out there now" by a kind of looking. Judgment is a matter of asking and correctly answering all the relevant questions that arise regarding the understanding to be judged. The natural sciences take verification for granted as an essential step in the process of discovery. Lonergan insists that such a step is the necessary goal of any inquiry whatsoever. We want to know what is the case, not simply what we think is the case.

To summarize, at the center of Lonergan's achievement, therefore, is a radically empirical response to the epistemological questions with which modern philosophy energetically struggled. By empirical I mean a focus on the actual, experiential operations of the thinking and knowing subject, not on the mythical "already-out-there" that is often taken by some forms of empiricism. The focus is on our understanding of our own experience, not on a theory of experience. We have seen that Lonergan shares with many modern philosophers, whether rationalists or empiricists, at least one thing: he begins with the subject. With Descartes, he commends a methodical approach that seeks clear and distinct ideas. With Kant, he affirms the necessity of investigating the conditions of the possibility of knowledge. With Hegel, he celebrates an inquiring intelligence that must never be satisfied with any form of obscurantism cloaked as intellectual modesty. With Hume, he recognizes the organizational and unifying power of the imagination in its encounter with sense data. But if Lonergan has made the turn to the subject and thus shares many of the characteristics of modern philosophy, there remains a decisive difference. The difference, and it is radical, is in Lonergan's starting point in the operations of the subject; our actual performance in cognition, rather than the contents of thought, holds the key to understanding our understanding. The doing, and the noticing what you are doing when you are doing it, is the thing.

The bewildering diversity of positions among philosophers today on the most basic epistemological questions is due in part, according to Lonergan, to a mistake about this concrete fact about you and me. Lonergan spends the first eight chapters of his book *Insight* to reveal to the reader, through examples drawn from mathematics, physics, chemistry, biology, common sense and the human sciences, that we do in fact have insights, that we do in fact understand. Readers are asked to attend not primarily to the content of the examples but to the operations of the intellect, and indeed to find their own examples, for the content of those examples in *Insight* are not the point of the book. Rather, they are all examples of a concrete matter of fact, the event of understanding, which is not the mere adherence to the rules of logic but something prior and more basic.[35]

Because he takes his stand on cognitional structure, Lonergan possesses an invariant base on which to build a philosophy. But this invariant structure is that which every knower, as knower, can personally grasp and affirm. Besides the data that is received through the senses there is also the data—what is given—in consciousness. The structure of operations is given and can be understood and known. This self-affirmation of the knower is a matter neither of subjectivism nor naive realism (the assumption that knowing is like looking at what is "already out there"). The self-affirmation of the knower eliminates the imagined prison of subjectivity ("How do I bridge the gap between what is out there to bring it in here, into my mind?") nor is there any need to imagine a simple brute fact to be looked at. Lonergan begins instead with the subject who, in the act of affirming himself or herself as a knower, is concomitantly affirming the existence of a reality irreducible to the activity that knows it.

Lonergan has identified the conditions of the possibility of knowing in the knowing subject's operations. Not only can these operations be known, but any attempt to deny their existence necessarily entails their existence. This is not a logical claim, but a statement of fact that one can affirm in experience. Self-knowledge is a rock to stand on, not a house of mirrors.

Practical Method

In this brief sketch of certain key figures in the history of modern philosophy, we have noticed not only a preoccupation with the subject, but a concomitant inability to deliver the knower out of the realm of the ideal and into the real. Now I would like to identify some of the concrete repercussions

---

35. Lonergan insists that "the deductive method alone is not enough. The fascination exerted by this method lies in its apparent promise of automatic results that are independent of the whims and fancies of the subject" (*Insight*, 433). See also ibid., 596, on interpretation and the limitations of the treatise: "A familiarity with the elements of logic can be obtained by a very modest effort and in a very short time. Until one has made notable progress in cognitional analysis, one is constantly tempted to mistake the rules of logic for the laws of thought. And as all reading involves interpreting, there follows automatically the imposition upon documents of meanings and implications that 'logically' they must possess but in fact do not bear."

of these epistemological problems for realms other than philosophic de-
bate. The most obvious and fundamental is, I believe, psychological, and
it manifests itself in the individual's loss of confidence and sense of being
at home in the world. It is indeed ironic that, although modern and post-
modern thought is preoccupied with the subject, a thoroughly empirical
self-knowledge continues to be elusive.

How can one respond to an incomplete turn to the subject in which
there is a failure to unite the knower and the known? There is the retreat
to common sense and a withdrawal from things intellectual, especially
philosophy. There is the surrender of one's personal autonomy to the experts: scientists, social planners, professional ethicists and the like. The
first response holds on tight to the pragmatic "facts" and methods proven
successful in the business of everyday life. Amidst the cacophony of philosophic voices, common sense scorns the thought that there may be a higher
viewpoint than its own. Theory becomes "just a theory" and researchers
are easily dismissed by the women and men of common sense who are intent on exposing projects that do not deliver a quick and obvious payback.
Lonergan calls this phenomenon general bias, and its social and historical
consequence is the social surd. Common sense believes itself to be omnicompetent and therefore is hostile toward insights that challenge the intellectual status quo, even if the situation it attempts to grasp is partly absurd.
When operating within common sense "[t]he insights that accumulate
have to be exactly in tune with the reality to be confronted and in some
measure controlled. The fragmentary and incoherent intelligibility of the
objective situation sets the standard to which common sense intelligence
must conform."[36] Because common sense is an indispensable set of skills,
behaviors and practical wisdom learned through repetition and imitation,
it does not give rein to the unrestricted desire to know which could advance the insights necessary for a higher viewpoint. Common sense tends
to imagine that absurdities that are woven into the social situation can be
understood, when in fact they are absurd—incapable of being understood.
The situation is complicated even further by the emergence of pseudothe-
ory. Because common sense does not possess an adequate understanding
of its own limitations, its bias against theory constructs a self-justification.
Intellectuals become the target of men and women of practical action who
see no value in the effete dwellers in the ivory tower.

The second response, one that is perhaps more rapidly debilitating, as-
serts that knowledge is at best a rare acquisition, even for the highly educated. If the really real is what can be known only by the methods of the natural

36. Ibid., 255.

sciences, then common sense appears to be not only common but also fundamentally false. Such an attitude, however, does not necessarily lead to a recognition of the priority of intelligence since the "science" in this viewpoint is really a kind of common sense into which citizens of a scientific culture are socialized.[37] Alienated from a world that seems impenetrable by intelligence and much too complex for the exercise of their own sovereign intellect to make much practical difference, this common sense eclecticism insists that insights and judgments are in reality mere figments of the imagination, not evidence of the eros of the mind. The alienated mind will consider that, if the great philosophic geniuses of modernity can't agree on whether we can know anything, can an average person hope to attain knowledge? Accordingly, knowledge reveals itself when scientists burrow below everyday experience to find the truth behind the appearances.

One who denies the power and efficacy of science would ironically seem to reveal a lack of common sense. Theory—scientific, philosophical or theological—begins when common sense description fails to account for certain relevant data, and this development toward a higher viewpoint is absolutely necessary if we are to respond to new questions. But in fact theory does not obviate the need for common sense because common sense remains the necessary way of getting on with the business of life. Common sense rests on insights and judgments that do indeed disclose the real. Lonergan expends great energy trying to convince the reader that the drive to understand requires recognition of the biases of common sense, and the entire plan of *Insight* has its foundation in the movement toward successive higher viewpoints. But Lonergan does not conceive the viewpoint of common sense as illusory. Only if common sense understands its own limits can the individual attain the confidence to be at home in the world. But the limitations of common sense must convert to the questions that promote a viewpoint that incorporates the necessity of common sense but does not accept its mistaken self-sufficiency.

More basic than Lonergan's affirmation of common sense as a form of knowing, however, is the self-affirmation of the knower. Both the person of common sense and the scientist must first have the confidence that knowledge is indeed possible. By presupposing past scientific achievement, science grows exponentially in its information and power, but this does not guarantee that its practitioners will have mastered the dynamics of their own intelligent and rational self-consciousness. In fact, just the opposite is frequently

---

37. "Opinions and attitudes that once were the oddity of a minority gradually spread through society to become the platitudes of politicians and journalists, the assumptions of legislators and educators, the uncontroverted nucleus of the common sense of a people" (ibid., 262).

true. Because of its overwhelming successes, especially as made manifest in technology, science appears to many scientists as self-contained, as having the muscle to vanquish a universal range of problems. Unless the scientist knows what she is doing when she is knowing, such a view of science as omnicompetent will seem highly plausible. But if she comes to understand and affirm the structure of her own cognition, there will eventually emerge an empirical residue from which science cannot formulate an explanation. A philosophy understood as the science of sciences is the consequence of that same drive for understanding that first gave rise to scientific inquiry. When one acknowledges the need to move to a higher viewpoint, the refusal to address questions that fall outside the horizon of natural science is merely an academically acceptable form of anti-intellectualism.

The negative repercussions of the failure to shift to a broader horizon now come into focus. The scientist, for example, may be tempted to disregard as unscientific and therefore merely emotional those ethical questions that emerge from her research. Or, on the common sense level, a moral resignation or complacency toward social disorder may set in. If the brilliant scientists can't figure it out, what am *I* supposed to do about it? Yet the dynamic character of the human spirit does not allow stagnation: we either acknowledge the unrestricted desire to know, and thereby move toward increasingly more comprehensive syntheses of knowledge, or we block it and thus cooperate in social decline. "In principle, other fields alone are competent to answer their proper questions. In fact, men in other fields do not triumph over all the various types of bias, to which polymorphic human consciousness is subject, unless they raise and answer successfully the further questions that belong to ever further fields."[38] A physicist, for example, who would dismiss the ancient question, "Why is there something rather than nothing?" in favor of an assertion of brute fact or mere givenness is not really "sticking to the facts" or "being scientific," but is instead making a prejudgment, imposing a concept onto reality rather than seeking intelligibility and ignoring the "empirical residue," the leftover data that should give rise to questions that cannot be answered within the horizon in which they were raised.

Without this dynamic and unrestricted movement toward a higher viewpoint, the more fundamental inquiry is missing. Lonergan's life's work was to supply such a radical inquiry by attending to the facts of cognition. Because the structure of human cognition is invariant, we possess the ground or Archimedean point against which to judge divergent philosophies and worldviews, and any denial or refutation of Lonergan's phenomenology of

38. Ibid., 765.

thinking and knowing demonstrates the truth of his thesis by involving itself in intelligent formulation and rational judgment. Lonergan is not asking you to trust him on this matter, as if to say, "This is what you do when you think!" He is merely inviting you to give his therapy a try.

A Few Words on the Authenticity of Belief

Throughout his works one can find Lonergan defending the rationality of belief.[39] A few elementary examples of this principle will help to show the essential complementarity between memory and intellect, the past and the present, tradition and innovation. Lonergan's analysis of belief is an alternative to the unrealistically skeptical bent of our recent heritage. As we shall see in chapter six, belief enters into the process of redemption.

Memory is an essential component of identity. Our connection to the past comprises much of our sense of self. Who I am when I wake up in the morning is who I remember myself to have been when I went to sleep the night before. Intellect, however, the capacity to understand and judge, is equally important. At least in one sense I am *not* the same person now as I was last week, insofar as I have learned from experiences and have changed because of them.

Most beliefs are items of memory—ideas we have inherited from the past which have been mediated by a myriad of people who themselves have inherited most of what they in turn handed on. These "traditions" (literally what is handed on, passed down) provide the basis for our thinking and acting; they are in fact not truths which we have personally verified but beliefs we have accepted. Imagine, for example, the sorts of things we "know" by the time we graduate from college. Ideally, most of our "knowledge" will make sense to us, fit together with other items acquired in our education, and provide a basis on which we will learn more in the future. But how much of it have we discovered for ourselves, and how much have we simply accepted on the word of another? Should we have doubted the readout on our calculators?

Well, maybe, but not as a rule. If there is, as we say, "good reason" to doubt, one would be unreasonable not to doubt. At this point, however, let us merely observe that, whatever the term "critical thinking" might mean, it surely should not include a requirement to doubt systematically from the start what one reads or hears or inherits. In fact, in many situations not believing can be an obstacle to learning. It is a good bet that the physics

---

39. See, for example, ibid., 725–40, and *Method*, 41–47.

professor does not hail as a critical thinker the first-year student who professes doubts about the veracity of general relativity theory.

We start out in life by believing. Launching an investigation from the right spot, like asking the right question, can mean the difference between success and failure. Contrary to Descartes, who recommended a starting point of strict and absolute doubt, the more true to life approach is to start where one in fact is, i.e., as one who by necessity holds innumerable beliefs, and move from there to raise questions, when necessary, about the relative adequacy or reasonableness of some of those beliefs. Newman counseled that it would be better to start by believing everything that has been proposed as true, then sift as one lives, rather than to begin by doubting all.[40] Lonergan agrees: "[T]he method of universal doubt is a leap in the dark."[41] This approach seems to be the way of human growth and development. Children begin by believing what they are told and gradually, as they gain experiences of life, sort, modify, retain or reject ideas and values that they have inherited. Should we lament that this happens? What parents do not want their children to believe them and *at the same time* to grow into reasonable—not naive or credulous—people responsible for their own intellectual lives?

An inclination to trust what one is told is not, of course, an implicit belief in the infallibility of one's source. We trust that the letter carrier is not holding back pieces of our mail or that the mechanic has not merely guessed that our brake shoes do not need changing, in spite of the fact that occasionally mail gets lost or mechanics are negligent. After getting directions from a stranger on the street, should we respond with the challenge, "Oh yeah? Prove it!" On the other hand, we don't assume that these directions cannot be wrong, either. Sometimes we are disappointed by directions, but we do not stop asking for them. Such common sense concerns make it clear, but the principle holds among scientists as well. Chemistry students don't begin by rediscovering the Periodic Table.

If we shift the focus from the individual to the group we observe that inherited beliefs and values hold an historical community together over time, providing it with meaning as well as guidance as it moves toward the future. In fact, trust in one's inheritance is a necessary (although certainly not sufficient) condition for contributing to the development of that tradition. As the twelfth century theologian Bernard of Chartres said, "[L]ike dwarfs standing on the shoulders of giants, we see farther than they."[42] We

40. Newman, *Essay in Aid*, 243.

41. Lonergan, *Insight*, 435. See the section in ibid., "Universal Doubt," 433–36.

42. Quoted by Chenu, *Nature, Man and Society*, 28n56.

also stand on the shoulders of average-sized people, who are in turn standing on others' shoulders, and so on. From birth, thanks to those who in a
variety of ways pass on to us their understanding of reality, we find ourselves
in a "world" or "horizon" of meaning and significance. No matter how we
may eventually judge the adequacy of our original horizon, the way we initially "make sense" of life is by inheriting beliefs from others.[43]

Within a horizon, particular ideas have meaning and seem credible,
while others do not. Differing horizons structure different ways of imagining
"the whole"—nature, humanity, the transcendent. Certain ideas from one horizon may not only seem incredible within another horizon, they are likely to
be simply meaningless. A neurotic New York intellectual needs psychoanaly-
sis, for example, but a Haitian possessed by a demon needs an exorcism.[44] If
this "sociology of knowledge" is correct, the term "unbeliever" is a misnomer
in the sense that it actually refers to people who are believers in something
other than the religion of those using the term. It is a designation dependent upon a particular religious horizon. The person whom a believer calls
an "unbeliever" does in fact believe *something* about life, destiny, meaning.
Moreover, they *believe* these things, they do not know them to be true. The
point is simply that the world does not divide into believers and unbelievers,
as if to imagine (as the modern mind often does) that knowers and believers
are separate groups. Everyone is a believer and a knower.

It is inevitable that we assume the basic truth of inherited beliefs. Historians, for example, learn from others—and believe—certain things about
the mentalities or horizons associated with particular times and places;
to know those mentalities is to have gone a long way toward an adequate
interpretation of the words and deeds of that era's personalities. Even the
outstanding innovators of an age must be understood as being, to a significant degree, reflections of their culture. Only when they assume as a
starting point a lifetime of accumulated insights and beliefs do historians
have a basis on which to advance in knowledge, correcting what may be
errors in their inherited knowledge and building on what is true.[45] Even the
attempt to grasp the impermanence of things human requires assumptions
about the way peoples of particular times and places thought and lived, assumptions that many historians understand and accept, but probably have
not verified for themselves. The more the historian's fund of knowledge,
acquired through belief, the more he can learn.

---

43. Lonergan, *Method,* 235–36.

44. The example is from Berger and Luckmann, *Social Construction,* 177.

45. Lonergan, *Method* 208–9.

Colloquial expression sometimes leads to confusion in matters of belief and doubt. Take, for example, the word "questioning" and cognates like "questionable." If we say that a claim is "questionable" we may mean we doubt its veracity. Asking questions about an idea, however, does not necessarily imply that the questioner is in a state of doubt concerning that idea. Investigating something by asking questions is not the same as doubting. Doubt is the state of mind in which one does not believe or assent to an idea proposed as true. However, questioning for the sake of understanding or verifying does not require the suspension of one's belief in the thing being investigated. One may or may not be in doubt when one inquires into a matter, and one may also change from belief to doubt or vice versa during the inquiry, but either state of mind is compatible with the dynamism of questioning. Difficulties in understanding, Newman once observed, look like but are not the same as doubts, just as ponies look like but are not the same as horses. Ten thousand ponies do not make one horse.[46] Memory and intellect, tradition and innovation, believing and discovering—both terms of these reciprocal pairs are necessary for human flourishing.

46. Quoted by Ward, *Life*, 250.

2

Conversion and Change

THE IMPORTANCE OF CHANGE made a significant entry into the intellectual horizon in the nineteenth century: the terms development, growth, process, and history were increasingly invoked. With Schelling and Hegel, history became a component of philosophy; Darwin formulated a theory of the evolution of biological species; with Newman, development emerged as an essential component in the study of religious doctrine. In Germany, historiography—the theory of how history should be written—introduced a method that has become an essential component of all scholarship.[1] Lonergan was educated in a Catholic tradition that had only timidly acknowledged change and development. The theological efforts at the turn of the twentieth century to integrate change failed to gain the support of the Catholic hierarchy in part because of a failure by many Modernist thinkers to recognize the element of judgment and so did not have a robust sense of the continuity and truth of doctrines.

Lonergan's efforts to tackle the problem of change in theology began even before his doctorate was started, in the midst of the Great Depression, with his study of economics.[2] Also at this time he began to develop a theory of history that would make sense of historical process, development within cultures and cultural pluralism.[3] These were early efforts; in *Insight*, Lonergan worked out a theory of emergent probability, a refinement

---

1. See Lonergan, *Early Works 2*, 241.

2. See Shute, *Early Economic Research*.

3. In the mid-to-late 1930s Lonergan produced six drafts of what came to be called in the final three versions an "Analytic Concept of History." It was an attempt to construct the social and historical categories necessary for the transposition of the doctrine of the redemption into modern, post-enlightenment thought. See Shute, *Dialectic of History*, 131–58. See also Crowe, *Lonergan*, 22–27, and Crowe, *Christ and History*, 166–70, esp. "Lonergan and History in General."

of Darwinian evolution that explains the intelligibility of development in natural processes. His work after *Insight* continued to aim at developing a method for theology that would integrate historicity with systematic analysis.[4] Lonergan's interest in change, development, and history, therefore, did not emerge late in his career, although it did continue to evolve after *Insight*. But throughout his career Lonergan located the root of change, as well as the obstacles to it, in the human being, the individual as he or she is situated in history and society.[5]

Intellectual, Moral and Religious Conversion

The center and source of change is the human person, a developing creature whose need for conversion is ongoing throughout life. The beginnings of human life are rooted in an attachment to sense—we hear and see and feel and smell our connection with the world, long before we do much thinking. Learning proceeds by trial and error, a self-correcting process.[6] As reason evolves, we have the task of overcoming our early life tendency to interpret all things according to physical sensitivity. We learn that correct understanding issues not in a body but in a "thing," a unity-identity-whole. A thing is not already out there now; a thing is what is correctly grasped by intelligence. It is identified by a common sense description or a theoretical explanation, but in either case a "thing" is not simply the data that comes through the senses. What comes through the senses is data to be understood; the understanding does not come through the senses, but grasps the meaning of the sense data.[7] Knowing the distinction between a thing and a body is a rare development in the individual; most people spontaneously conclude that what they imagine is a thing. What Lonergan calls intellectual conversion requires the change in the individual from thinking of knowledge as seeing what is "out there now" (analogous to an

---

4. As he worked to develop a method for theology that incorporated historical consciousness in the late 1950s, Lonergan explored the possibility of the "implicit/explicit" distinction for an explanation of doctrinal development, but he acknowledged that the distinction "is more valuable in systems of logic, ethics, and metaphysics than in the natural sciences . . . These limits will be ignored if the sole way of proceeding is just to render explicit what has been implicit before" (*Early Works* 2, 115). See also ibid., 577, as well as Crowe, *Lonergan*, 80–103, esp. "Experiments in Method."

5. Hence the need to explore the sociology of knowledge as the dynamic interaction between individual and society as a way of understanding the church in the world. We will return to this theme in the final chapter.

6. Lonergan, *Insight*, 197–98.

7. See ibid., 270–95.

intellectual "look") to what is known by the correct judgment of what is understood. The lack of intellectual conversion can distort what we know and impede what we are capable of knowing. The cure for one's confusion is often to be intellectually converted, which means coming to know what one is doing when one is knowing.

Intellectual conversion means coming to understand what we do when we think, judge and decide. In other words, intellectual conversion is a coming to understand understanding. Because theology is a particular instance of understanding, intellectual conversion is especially important in the theologian. Intellectual conversion establishes the possibility of reflecting accurately and fruitfully on the age-old matter of reason's relationship to faith. In this chapter we start with some historical background on the faith-reason relationship and then move to an account of intellectual conversion. We then discuss moral and religious conversion, especially as it affects the work of theology. Lonergan uses the word "conversion" to mean the transformations that can occur in the human subject intellectually, morally and religiously. For religious conversion, Lonergan uses the metaphor of "falling in love in an unrestricted way," that is, being in love with the infinite God. Moral conversion is a matter of making decisions based on what is truly good, not just for individuals or their groups, but for what Lonergan calls "the good of order." The term includes not only the common good of society but the whole of world process.[8]

Theology and Intellectual Conversion

Because Thomas Aquinas became such an important authority for Catholic theology after Pope Leo's late nineteenth century encyclical to place Aquinas at the center of Catholic education, most of the great Catholic theologians of the early twentieth century began their careers by studying his work, or at least some interpretation of his work. Although he did not begin with a study of Aquinas,[9] Lonergan eventually discovered that the way Aquinas was typically presented was in fact not what Aquinas actually held. In particular, Lonergan discovered that Aquinas's psychological analogy of the Trinity was grounded in an accurate grasp of the operations of human cognition. In other words, Aquinas understood what human beings do when they think, deliberate and judge, and he must have come to this knowledge about

8. "We know God insofar as we are collaborating with God in the work of the universe, and it makes much more specific and concrete our knowledge of God to attend to that" (*Early Works* 1, 134).

9. See Crowe, *Lonergan*, 1–38, and Liddy, *Transforming Light*, 3–90.

human thinking and knowing by paying attention to and understanding his own thinking and knowing.[10] Knowing what we human beings are doing when we are knowing is a powerful instrument: it can provide controls for any sort of knowing, in any science or form of inquiry. No matter how diverse the subject matter—from physics to biology to theology—the one thing that doesn't change is the fact that a human being is asking questions, thinking about data, and making judgments about what one understands. If theology is a type of thinking and not simply the repetition of traditional formulas, then theology will benefit from understanding human thinking. One of Lonergan's basic contributions is just that: he has drawn attention to thinking in a way that can provide an insight into insight. Knowing what one is doing when one is knowing enhances and clarifies all knowing, including the theological kind.

The self-knowledge that results from the "turn to the subject" in philosophy and theology is in sharp contrast to a style of Catholic theology, dominant in the first half of the twentieth century, which concerned itself in the first place with doctrinal propositions. As judgments of truth, doctrines carry meaning but they are not usually self-explanatory; sometimes they can appear as extrinsic to human beings and irrelevant to their spiritual lives. As scientific culture becomes increasingly sophisticated and as education struggles to keep up with a rapidly growing body of knowledge about the universe, the theologian's responsibility to mediate the Christian faith to that culture cannot be content merely to repeat biblical images or doctrinal formulas. There must be an effort to bring the light of understanding to what Christians receive in faith. In his early work on theological method Lonergan observed that the "fundamental problem at the present time is that there are all sorts of people who are at the peak of human culture in scientific fields and at the same time their ideas on religion are most elementary."[11] If religion moves further and further away from the mentality of the culture in which is exists, it will become less and less intelligible and so less and less effective in its task of individual and social transformation. An "extrinsic" theology, concerned to deduce logical conclusions from doctrinal premises, often seemed to leave the experience of concrete human living untouched. It is the age-old task of theology to ensure that the doctrinal beliefs and the authority that communicates them be legitimated. Those who hold religious beliefs as true must have reasons for doing so—reasons that make sense to them. Faith seeks understanding, and understanding depends for its context on the cultural presuppositions that inform the way of life of a

---

10. See Lonergan, *Verbum*, 2; see also Crowe, *Lonergan*, 39–57.

11. Lonergan, *Early Works 1*, 316.

particular people. For that reason, theology needs always to be redone in different ages, for differing cultures. The extrinsic approach of a classicist, ahistorical mentality lacks a sense of historical and cultural difference, lacks the need for change, and finally renders itself opaque.

Lonergan understands theology's role as the instrument for integrating religious knowledge within a cultural context. That task can only be accomplished empirically; it cannot be done by constructing a grand theoretical system, such as Hegel tried in the nineteenth century. Soren Kierkegaard quickly pointed out that Hegel had explained everything except the human individual.[12] As with Hegel, Lonergan's approach requires systematic understanding, but his project locates the need for system as well as system's obstacles within the developing individual, who is always within a particular cultural context. Intellectual conversion, knowing what we are doing when we are knowing, is something that has to happen in a person; it is not a set of ideas on a page. Because intellectual conversion makes a significant difference in the doing of theology, the conversion or "turning" to this self-knowledge will be of fundamental importance to the development and communication of the religion within a culture.

Self-knowledge requires an understanding of whether one is in the theoretical or the common sense pattern of experience. The mathematician in her office, concentrating on a problem, is in a different pattern of experience than when she is driving home, stopping at the grocery, or preparing supper. This "differentiation of consciousness" can only be fully grasped when it is an achievement within one's own consciousness. There are many forms of differentiation; the scientist makes the distinction between common sense and theory; she knows the difference between birds in the backyard and ornithology. But the common ground of both common sense and science is the self-understanding that knows oneself as operating in these different patterns of experience. In other words, besides the differentiation in consciousness of common sense and theory there is also the differentiation of both within what Lonergan calls "interiority."[13] Interiority is the understanding that both common sense and theory are both located in the fundamental cognitional acts that are operating in all patterns of experience. For example, as different as astrophysics is from conversing informally with a neighbor about the starry night, in both cases there are the operations of the human spirit paying attention, trying to understand, and wanting to understand correctly.

12. See Burrell, *Exercises*, 143–81.
13. On interiority, see Lonergan, *Insight*, 107.

To do their work well, theologians require a differentiated consciousness. When interpreting the texts and practices of a religious tradition such differentiation allows the scholar to distinguish symbolic expressions of meaning within their proper genres. Symbolic expression is not to be confused with theories of systematic theology. For example, in Genesis 3:8, God walks through the Garden of Eden in the cool of the evening, but this isn't a statement about God's physicality, or when Saint Paul wrote that Christ became a curse (Gal 3:13-14), he was not constructing a theory of Christ or of curses. He was expressing in a dramatic image the feeling in us that Christ's spiritual sacrifice communicates. On the other hand, when Aquinas answers whether it was necessary that God become human to save humanity, he starts with a distinction: it depends on what you mean by necessary. God, after all, can't be under some necessity or constraint that is external to God, otherwise, that constraining power would be God. In a systematic approach, a theoretical pattern of experience is implied: one in which things are to be understood in relation to other things and not as those things are immediately related to us.

The value of Lonergan's proposal to ground theology in the facts of human intentionality is verifiable. The method that he has developed is possible only because our own consciousness can be the object of our inquiry. Lonergan takes the turn to the subject in a thoroughly empirical way. As we have seen, his "Generalized Empirical Method," as he came to call it, is general because all human knowing exhibits the same basic pattern of operations but it is empirical because it is available to be understood and verified within human subjectivity. We can know what we are doing when we are knowing.

A Recurring Pattern

In each human being there is a need to obey the precepts that correspond to these operations of the human subject. The dynamic desire to know exhibits a recurring pattern of operations organized for the purpose of getting the point of the data of our experiences. There is, in other words, an intentionality built within human subjectivity. We need to pay attention to the data of our experience because we want to grasp the pattern or intelligibility within the data, and we want to make systematic connections among our experiences to expand and integrate our understanding. As we learn to ask the right questions we are rewarded with insights. When we understand, it brings joy because we are beings driven by an appetite, a desire to understand. If we were merely dreaming, or sketching the possibilities for a science fiction novel, any sufficiently interesting ideas would satisfy us. Most of the time, however, we need, not just any ideas, but true ones. No matter the occasion or question, no matter how controversial the issue, we can't get through a day without making judgments about what is true or false, probable or dubious, more or less adequate, good or bad.

Our desire to understand is a significant clue to answering the question, what does it mean to be human? Few of us are willing to say that we do not at least try to make sense of things and ideas, or that it doesn't matter whether these ideas are correct or not. In other words, if we refuse to claim that we are regularly silly and perpetually out of touch, then we have acknowledged that there are norms or standards within us. To be true to ourselves is to be true to these standards. When we fail, and know it, we also receive confirmation and an encouragement to pay more attention or think more intelligently or be more reasonable in out judgments or repent of our moral failures.[14]

The natural sciences, of course, are the great tools of our age that have unlocked many secrets of the physical world. The intelligibility of the universe is without doubt deep and mysterious; and there is evidence to suggest that the human person is one of the world's great mysteries. At the heart of the human mystery is love; it is the reality that our minds ultimately serve. This mystery is best described not as an achievement but as a gift. Although we choose many things in this life, we cannot choose what God has destined for us; there are diverse (multi-cultural) ways of being human but we cannot choose what it ultimately means to be human.

Love, Intelligence and Change

Lonergan understands religious conversion as being in love in an unconditional way—being in love with God. That love, flooding our hearts by the power of the Holy Spirit, which is given to us (Rom 5:5), is the source and summit of all love. Conversion, therefore, is not a matter of turning toward God so that God can then approve of our willingness to change. The gospel mandate is to "turn around" or "change the way you think." One turns from one way of thought and life and toward another, to escape a more limited horizon and enter a broader one. Conversion is itself a gift. The translation of *metanoia* is often "repentance" because human beings are sinners and for

14. "There is a responsibility to intelligence or reasonableness, and it is neglected when one overlooks the inadequacy of answers and, no less, when one withholds a qualified assent when further relevant questions are not made available" (Lonergan, "Post-Hegelian," 206–7).

them to be healed they must first accept the grace of repentance. And so, religious conversion is the Holy Spirit flooding the human heart with divine love. Saint Paul's metaphor, a favorite of Lonergan's, is exactly right: flood waters are not requested or merited, and they are not to be argued with. The notion of "reform" is not radical enough to do justice to the reality that the apostle identifies. God's love is less a matter of reform and more akin to being remade: "So whoever is in Christ is a new creation; the old things have passed away; behold new things have come" (2 Cor 5:17). The goal of human longing, as well as the power to remake us is God's love.

Common sense language about conversion often describes the human person as composed of both "head and heart." But what is the link between them? Lonergan's systematic presentation integrates intellectual, moral and religious development. Intellect moves toward the discovery of the world through inquiry, from experience through understanding and judging the truth of that understanding, and deciding. The process involves more than questions of fact and value; it leads to the question of God. In addition to development from inquiry to knowledge and decision, there is the opposite movement from God's love to judgments of value, through new understandings and new experiences. In other words, besides searching, learning and achieving, there is also the fact that religious conversion is a grace that orients and promotes our thinking and acting. God's love, mediated through affectivity and values and belief, can initiate a transformation in the questions we ask, the openness of our quest, the reasonableness of our judgments and the moral responsibility of our actions.[15] The power of love, in other words, enlightens our minds and puts us to work. Let's look at an example.

C. P. Ellis was a high school dropout and an "exalted cyclops" of the Ku Klux Klan who, after an unlikely transformation in his understanding of what is true and good, became a member of the Durham, North Carolina Human Relations Council, laboring for the betterment of both black and white working people. The story he told to Studs Terkel is one of profound conversion and enlightenment.

Although he had long worked at low-wage jobs, it became increasingly difficult for Ellis to support his family. As his bitterness grew, Ellis decided to follow his father's example and join the Ku Klux Klan. "I didn't know who to blame. I tried to find somebody. I began to blame it on black people. I had to hate somebody."[16] Eventually, he began to realize that

15. For the two ways of achievement and heritage, see Lonergan, "Natural Right," esp. 180–81.

16. Terkel, *American Dreams*, 200–211.

black people were struggling for the same basic dignity and opportunity that poor whites like himself wanted. "I found out they're people just like me. They cried, they cussed, they prayed, they had desires. Just like myself. Thank God, I got to the point where I can look past labels. But at that time, my mind was closed."[17]

It happened that Ellis was elected as co-chair of a school committee. The other co-chair to be elected was an activist black woman. After serving on the committee with this woman, Ellis began to rethink his assumptions. As fellow-klansmen accused him of betraying the white race, his self-examination intensified.

> Am I doin' right? Am I doin' wrong? Here I am all of a sudden makin' an about-face and tryin' to deal with my feelin's, my heart. My mind was beginnin' to open up. I was beginnin' to see what was right and what was wrong." Ellis concluded his story by pointing out his new ability, the fruit of his conversion, to understand what he previously could not grasp: 'since I changed, I've set down and listened to tapes of Martin Luther King. I listen to it and tears come to my eyes 'cause I know what he's sayin' now. I know what's happenin.'[18]

There are internal standards, "imperatives" that correspond to our basic operations of experience, understanding, judging and deciding. "Am I doin' right? Am I doin' wrong?" Note, however, the order of Ellis's change. The real desire of his heart—love, not hatred—became known to his mind. Ellis's heart did not change because he was thinking clearly; rather, he began to think clearly because his heart was changed. The movement was reversed—the gift transformed his ability to do what is right, to know what is true and to ask the right questions. Hatred had made him stupid. Love now made him smart.

Theology and Conversion

Self-knowledge is a religious value because God has given us human beings the responsibility to create ourselves by freely thinking, deciding, believing and acting. What we become results from the use, misuse or neglect of these God-given gifts. If we do not take responsibility for our lives, we will probably conform to opinions we do not examine, thinking what others think,

17. Ibid.
18. Ibid.

doing what others do, and never asking what is true or false, good or bad. Lonergan called this lack of responsibility "drifting."[19]

We have another example from the journalist Studs Terkel, whose encounter with a cab driver during the war in Vietnam provides an example of what Lonergan calls "drifting" and reveals what is at stake when one is a stranger to one's own knowing, believing and acting.

> During the Christmas bombings of North Vietnam during that war, the Saint Louis cabby, weaving his way through traffic, was offering six-o'clock commentary.
>
> 'We gotta do it. We have no choice.'
>
> 'Why?'
>
> 'We can't be a pitiful, helpless giant. We gotta show 'em we're number one.'
>
> 'Are you number one?'
>
> A pause. 'I'm number nothin'.' He recounts a litany of personal troubles, grievances, and disasters. . .Wearied by this turn of conversation, he addresses the rear-view mirror: 'Did you hear Bob Hope last night? He said . . .'[20]

Terkel's insightful commentary on the encounter focuses on the cabby's lack of confidence in himself as one who can responsibly know, believe or act, and points to the deleterious consequences of this irresponsibility for the common good of society.

> Forfeiting their own life experience, their native intelligence, their personal pride, they allow more celebrated surrogates, whose imaginations may be no larger than theirs, to think for them, to speak for them, to be for them in the name of the greater good. Conditioned toward being 'nobody,' they look toward 'somebody' for the answer. It is not what the American town meeting was all about.[21]

Responsible faith, like responsible citizenship, is impossible if we abdicate our intellectual, moral and spiritual powers. Lonergan reminded his readers that Jesus forbade us to cover our light with a basket or to hide our talents in a napkin (Matt 5:14; 25:14–30).

---

19. Lonergan, *Method*, 36–41.

20. Terkel, *American Dreams*, xxiv.

21. Ibid.

Theology, like other forms of exploration, should be a process of discovery conducted by people who have some sense of their own powers and purposes. The student of theology is first of all a wayfarer, a pilgrim on a journey. The goal of the pilgrimage is insight into God's creative and saving presence revealed in the natural world and in human history. Theological wayfarers should also be "sovereign" over their own discovery: sovereign not in the sense of having authority over others, nor in the sense that they are isolated or independent of all authority, but rather in the sense that thinking or knowing or believing or deciding is not a matter of passive reception. Even when you recognize that you do not know something but have come to believe the testimony of another, you are taking responsibility for your assent to another's testimony. If, for example, your physician tells you that you should take a particular medicine, you may be exercising your sovereignty by believing the physician and following the advice. No one can believe for you; others can advise and persuade you, but the tasks of thinking, judging, believing, deciding, and acting are yours alone; they cannot be transferred to a stand-in.

There are social and historical implications. Taking responsibility for your beliefs, decisions and actions is not, however, the same as an individualism which sets up a false choice between commitment to the community and personal faith. Christians who take responsibility for their faith are part of a historical community that has transmitted the faith to them; apart from that tradition Christianity is simply not available. Moreover, Christians need the help of the community if their faith is to deepen. Without that community and the wisdom of its tradition, personal faith can quickly degenerate into a confused mélange of clichés. On the other hand, commitment to the church, like commitment to the larger society, is not the abdication of personal responsibility. Terkel's comment on the cabby's distortion of the ideals of American citizenship highlights the fact that drifting along with the herd destroys community in the long run. The common good—the good of order—requires the conversion of individuals.

Feelings: A Vehicle of Conversion

The opening of C. P. Ellis's heart was palpable: There were feelings of unrest while he was a Klansman, as well as the feelings of peace after his conversion, a conscience at peace with itself—he could sleep at night! Feelings, or what used to be called the "affections," carried these messages. The affections are not here-today-and-gone-tomorrow emotions, like anger or fatigue, but deep-seated and long-lasting feelings that signal the basic direction of one's life. Ellis's conversion was accompanied by distinct changes in these feelings. (Several times during Terkel's interview, he wept as he recalled his life story.)

What we learn through our feelings is rarely conveyed without the concrete, the personal, the imaginable. For C. P. Ellis, his personal contact with the black activist woman who co-chaired the school committee made the difference. It is much easier to hate an abstraction such as a racial stereotype than it is a real person. Through personal encounter Ellis discovered a common humanity that knew no color barrier.

The capacity to love establishes a new horizon, a new way of viewing the world and our place in it. Just as the stingy person has difficulty recognizing an act of generosity in another, so the loveless person is inclined to interpret acts of love as something less—as some sort of self-interest or a mere chemical event in the brain or as a cover for a hidden agenda. The meaningfulness and truth of the various elements of the Christian religion, therefore, are most fully understood within the horizon made available in religious conversion. Religious stories, imagery and symbolism are the language of love.[22]

Our hearts are on the move, in search of something to satisfy their deepest desires. Lonergan calls religious conversion the call to holiness, which is "other-worldly fulfillment, joy, peace, bliss. In Christian experience these are the fruits of being in love with a mysterious, uncomprehended God."[23] Whether we are able to name this ultimate goal of our longing or not, it is true for all of humanity that, as Augustine came to see, our hearts will remain restless until they rest in the cause and goal of human desire.

The skill with which one discerns the goal of the heart's desire will be educated or built up by a commitment to the wisdom tradition that communicates, through story and image, precept and example, the ways in which our ancestors in this quest have differentiated between illusory objects of desire and the real thing. We may be born with a desire for God, but we are certainly not born with the skills we need to find God. Those skills are available in religion. Although it may be possible to find God through personal trial and error without much help from the past experiences encoded in the great wisdom traditions, it is surely the harder, less secure way. Sin, illusion and self-deception all conspire to send us off track. The vagaries of life tend to make our path to God anything but simple and direct; all the more reason to seek as much guidance as we can get from the community of faith, both present and past.

22. Lonergan, *Method*, 115–18.
23. Ibid., 242.

The Role of Conversion in Theological Method

We have seen that objectivity is a matter of authentic subjectivity. Loner-gan's completion of the turn to the subject rejects the naïve assumption that objectivity results from careful looking at the object. Lonergan's position—a verifiable one—is that the subject who does the attending and thinking and judging is of central concern in any effort to be objective. It is only by a careful analysis of human subjectivity that "subjectivism"—the imposition of biased perspectives on what one is trying to understand—can be avoided or corrected.

Today, theological method is enriched by a variety of intellectual disciplines, especially history and the human sciences (anthropology, psychology, sociology). But how to orchestrate the contributions of these sciences is today an urgent task for which there is no consensus.[24] The conviction behind this book is that Lonergan has discovered a powerful tool and the consensus needed will be a matter of working out the implications of his method.

Method, of course, is not a formula that functions automatically. Scholars, including theologians, sometimes differ in their interpretations and judgments. In the writing of history, for example, what Lonergan calls "perspectivism" is the notion that the differences among historians need not be considered the result of the distortions of bias but emerge from the variety and individuality of the historians themselves.

> They may investigate the same area, but they ask different questions. Where the questions are similar, the implicit, defining contexts of suppositions and implications are not identical. Some may take for granted what others labor to prove. Discoveries can be equivalent, expressed in different terms, and so leading to different sequences of further questions.[25]

On the other hand, some differences have to do with the intellectual, moral or religious horizon of the interpreter. In every case, the task of the scholar is growth in understanding through the self-correcting process of learning. There are "differences arising from personal inadequacy, from obtuseness, oversights, a lack of skill or thoroughness."[26] Whether the example is the writing of history or some other specialization in theology, the differences in interpretation are in the interpreters. In some cases, the differences will be complementary and open to discovery, development, and correction;

24. See Tracy, *Blessed Rage*, 3–21.
25. Lonergan, *Method*, 217.
26. Ibid.

in other cases, the root of the differences will be the interpreter's distorted horizon, to be corrected only by some sort of conversion.

There are many examples in Christian history of the explicit call for conversion to achieve an adequate interpretation. The anonymous author of the great fourteenth century mystical treatise *The Cloud of Unknowing* insists that the merely curious, those who are not "determined to follow Christ perfectly," should not be given the book to read because it "will mean nothing" to them.[27] Religious conversion transforms what we are able to know and so, through belief, encourages intellectual conversion. "[A]mong the values discerned by the eye of love is the value of believing the truths taught by the religious tradition, and in such tradition and belief are the seeds of intellectual conversion."[28] As we have seen, without belief, there is little or no chance of progress in understanding.

The theological specialization that Lonergan names "Dialectic" is the process of sorting through conflicts in interpretation and determining their roots within differing horizons.[29] If the differences and disagreements can be traced back to the presence or lack of intellectual, moral or religious conversion, then the only resolution is one's conversion to the process of human authenticity. The three-fold conversion then becomes the foundation for theological method. The specialization that Lonergan names "Foundations" depends on the conversion of the scholar, but this does not imply that the converted thinker's authenticity is "some pure quality, some serene freedom from all oversights, all misunderstandings, all mistakes, all sins."[30] The theologian is in the world of time and space, a sinner and an historically limited thinker. Foundations does, however, mean that the process is an ongoing movement to correct ourselves by acknowledging what is true and good "even in the lives and thoughts of opponents" while at the same time learning about the mistakes, misunderstandings and evil "even in those with whom [we are] allied."[31]

Those who love can recognize love and the realities that love discloses. Conversion calls for the transformation of the whole human person, and not just an act of will, so that the act of faith is not irrational. And yet, faith is a gift and not a logical deduction. Religious believing differs from other types of belief in one important aspect. Religious beliefs refer finally to the reality of God's unrestricted love. A gift rather than an achievement, this love establishes a new horizon, a new way of viewing the world and our place in it.

27. Spearing, *Cloud of Unknowing*, 52.

28. Lonergan, *Method*, 243.

29. Ibid., 235–66.

30. Ibid., 252.

31. Ibid., 252– 53.

3

The Drama of Religion and the Theory of Theology

IN THIS BRIEF CHAPTER we will explore the distinction between two realms of meaning: common sense and theory. By imagining a few ordinary examples, we will clarify the fact that common sense and theory complement one another, and that theory sometimes corrects misleading impressions of common sense.

Sometimes people in the same room cannot agree on whether the space is cold or warm. One person, who has just been running, finds the room too warm. Another, who has been sitting in an air-conditioned building for two hours, thinks the room is cold. It would be silly to ask the question, "Who's right?" because the words "warm" and "cold" function here as expressions of how the people feel. Imagine a third person, a physicist, who overhears the two people debating whether the room were cold or warm; she tries to settle the argument by saying, "Here, I've got a thermometer: let's find out scientifically." A thermometer, of course, is an even sillier response to the disputed question. Why? Because "cold" and "warm" in this situation are expressions of the temperature of the air in the classroom *as it affects those people*. The words are expressions of how they relate to the air in the room, not what the temperature of the room happens to be. The thermometer's reading would indicate not how the air in the room feels to anyone, but the relation of the air's temperature to a standard scale of measurement, how the air is related to other things in the environment, such as the mercury in the thermometer. Just as the physicist cannot settle the dispute with a measurement of temperature, neither can she measure the temperature of a thing by announcing that it is "warm" or "cold."

We are dealing with two different types of thinking here: common sense thinking, which attends to *things as they relate to us* (a warm or cold room) and theory, which shifts from common sense to *things as they relate to other things* (twenty-three degrees centigrade on the thermometer). To illustrate the difference between common sense and theory, touch something metal and notice how it feels; then touch something wooden in the same place. The metal feels cooler on the hand, but does the metal have a lower temperature than the wood? That is a different kind of question, a *theoretical* question, because it is asking about the relationship of one thing to another—the relationship of the metal to a standardized index of measurement. Metal *feels* cooler to them because it conducts heat out of their hands more quickly. As it relates *to us*, metal is cooler; as it relates *to wood*, it is the same temperature.[1]

Try to think of your own examples of the difference between common sense and theory. Here are a few practice questions. Does the sun rise in the east and set in the west? When dropped from a certain height, does a heavy thing—say, a cannon ball—fall faster than a lighter thing such as a billiard ball? What is the difference between experiencing anger and studying the psychology of anger?

What Is Theory?

By now it should be clear that, for Lonergan, "theoretical" does not mean "hypothetical" or "as if." The word is sometimes used that way, but here we mean something more precise: "theory" refers to an explanation of the way things are related to other things, regardless of the way these things are related to us. In this sense of the word, all scientific explanations are theoretical, but that does not mean that they are in doubt or that we merely suppose them to be true. When we are concerned with theoretical questions we are in what Lonergan calls the intellectual pattern of experience.[2]

The intellectual pattern of experience heads toward an understanding of a thing or event or set of phenomena; how the thing under investigation affects our lives or makes us feel, once we shift into the intellectual pattern, is irrelevant to our inquiry. For example, we may ask how bombs work. Bombs have been used for evil and destructive purposes for hundreds of years, and the very thought of them can make us wince, especially those who have directly experienced their violent force. It is possible, however, to set aside the emotional impact that the thought of a bomb may have on us, and to ask how it works. As Robert Oppenheimer watched the first test explosion of a nuclear weapon in the New Mexico desert, he quoted Krishna's words to Arguna in the *Bagavad Gita*: "I am become death, the

---

1. See Lonergan, *Insight*, 196–31, and *Method*, 81–96, section 9, "Realms of Meaning" and "Stages of Meaning."

2. On intellectual conversion, see Lonergan, *Method*, 238.

shatterer of worlds."[3] In the *Gita*, Krishna is trying to persuade Arguna to do his duty, no matter the cost. We can be sure that during the scientific work at Los Alamos, it was not poetry or feeling that was foremost in the physicist's mind. At the test site, however, what focused Oppenheimer's attention was not a technical problem in physics, but rather the more general issue of how the bomb relates to humanity. Is it good, bad, helpful, harmful, beautiful, ugly, necessary, superfluous? For a moment, Oppenheimer stopped thinking about equations that explain how the bomb works and expressed, in the quotation from a Hindu scripture, his complex feelings about this weapon he helped invent.

Theory Begins in the Drama of Life

Let's look at a few of the more important characteristics of theoretical inquiry in the intellectual pattern of experience. First, theoretical knowledge begins in the dramatic pattern of everyday life. Someone may get great pleasure from looking at and listening to birds, but if he becomes serious about this hobby he may also want to study the science that studies birds. Serious bird watchers study such things as habitat, patterns of migration, color patterns, mating behaviors. In other words, they learn about ways in which these characteristics are interrelated and not just how birds affect them when they look at or hear them. As a non-serious bird watcher, I certainly appreciate the beauty of the occasional bird that flies into my yard, and I take great pleasure in its appearance and song, but that experience is limited to how the bird relates to me. I usually know nothing about its name, species, habitat or activities; I know little about how any of this information is systematically related.

Imagine a non-serious bird watcher like myself who becomes curious about the hummingbird's ability to remain suspended in mid-air for long periods. Questions begin to arise: how fast must his wings beat? How long is the expected lifespan of such a rapidly moving creature? By raising these questions I am initiating a move from one realm of meaning (common sense) to another (theory) and my own pattern of experience shifts from the dramatic to the intellectual. The answers to these questions will require, not common sense, but theory, because I am now inquiring not about the bird as it relates to me but about the relationship between the bird's wing speed and its lifespan.

Of course, one need not pursue ornithology to enjoy watching the birds in the backyard. If I do not find out how lifespan and wing speed are related,

3. See Davis, *Lawrence*, 239.

I can still marvel at the tiny thing as it drinks the red nectar in the feeder near my window. But it is that marvel that encouraged the questions to arise in the first place. Science grows out of ordinary observation and description; common sense is the matrix out of which is born the drive toward theoretical inquiry. Concern for the way a thing or event is related to us is the starting point for theoretical inquiry. Questioning how things are related to one another begins in our experience of how things are related to us.

We Need Both Theory and Common Sense

In daily life most of us shift back and forth between the dramatic and the intellectual patterns of experience quite easily and without adverting to the change. Both patterns are necessary for human living. While theory serves to answer questions that can be asked but not answered within a common sense viewpoint, common sense serves to focus intelligence on the concrete, particular and ever changing situations of life. When my sixty-five-year-old uncle built a new house, he hired a landscape expert to determine what kinds of trees should be planted in the yard. The landscaper knew a great deal about trees, but because he was in business he also knew that theoretical knowledge of trees is often only part of his concern. When my uncle asked what sorts of trees should be planted he replied, "Well, at your age, I'd suggest fast-growing ones!" It wasn't the most tactful answer, but it was right in the context. Instead of explaining the qualities of any particular tree in itself, or the affinity of a particular tree with the climate, the wildlife, the soil, or the neighborhood, he went directly to the question of trees as they relate to my uncle's particular situation. The landscaper showed himself to be experienced not only with trees, but with the needs of his customers as well. Theory universalizes insights while differences in time and place, culture and circumstance, custom and tradition, perpetuate the need for common sense; theory will never eliminate the need for common sense.

Common sense is not something that we can do without once we have learned to be "scientific." At the same time, however, theory has become just as indispensable; we cannot solve many of our contemporary problems with common sense alone. Theory, in other words, is not an irrelevant, ivory tower preoccupation of an intellectual elite. Imagine that you are a nurse and your mother gets sick. She is admitted to the hospital, but the physicians are not sure what is wrong. You are naturally worried about your mother; her pain causes you great mental and emotional stress. However, because you have been trained as a health care provider, you decide to set that worry and anxiety aside for a few hours and go to the hospital's library to research the various possible maladies being discussed by your mother's physicians. While reading and thinking about these things, your attention is focused on the interrelationships of the various systems of the body, on your mother's symptoms, on her medical history, on patients you have known with similar problems. Your focus of attention is not your relationship to your mother but the disease that afflicts her. All the while, you try as best you can to remain in the intellectual pattern of experience so that you might answer the question, what is wrong with her? You know, at least implicitly, that an answer to that question is to be found in the realm of meaning that we are calling "theory."

The next day you are back at her bedside, thinking about her, your relationship with her, how important she is in your life, how to make her more comfortable. You have shifted back to the dramatic pattern of experience, confronting your mother's illness as it is related to you. You are again operating in the "common sense" realm of meaning.[4]

Notice that in these ordinary examples, there is no necessary conflict between the two realms of meaning or the corresponding patterns of experience. The point is not that one is truly being intelligent when one sets aside things as they are related to us. Successful action often requires that we learn the concrete situation of a particular person, community or culture; we cannot do without the specialized intelligence of common sense. However, in the dramatic pattern of experience questions can arise that cannot be answered within that pattern, or through its common sense responses. Instead of merely wishing for a smoother ride, the mechanic opened the hood and started to think like a mechanic, while the nurse set aside her anxiety and went to the library.

Common Sense, Theory and Truth

A theoretical explanation of some thing or event does not necessarily overturn its common sense description as false. A view of things as they relate to us has its own meaning and significance. It would be pedantic and just plain silly to correct people who talk about the sun setting in the west by reminding them of the structure of the solar system. As it relates to us earthlings,

---

4. The movie *Lorenzo's Oil* is an excellent illustration of the distinction we are making here. Lorenzo is a boy stricken with a rare disease for which there is no treatment. After an initial period of deep grief and agony, the father, a well-educated man, decides to do his own research to find a treatment for his son. Several things had to be balanced in this most stressful time, but the management of the situation was possible only because the father could shift back and forth from his grief as a parent to the detached perspective of the medical researcher.

it *does* set in the west; as the sun relates to the earth and the other planets, however, "to set" and "west" simply have no meaning. The key to knowing when to use phrases like "sets in the west" correctly is in knowing whether or not one is in the intellectual pattern of experience.

On the other hand, there are times when our common sense misleads us; in these cases, if we are to follow our natural desire to understand, our common sense will require correction from a theoretical angle of analysis. Earlier in this chapter I asked you to think about the difference between common sense and theory using the example of two falling bodies of differing weight. Students of physics know that falling bodies drop at the same rate of acceleration regardless of weight, but that is not the spontaneous image that our common sense provides for us. Imagination jumps to the conclusion that heavier things drop faster; weight, however, is not a factor in the acceleration rate. In this case, theory not only complements but corrects common sense.

Shifting from common sense to theory, for those not accustomed to differentiating these two realms of meaning, will often not seem like the right approach. One characteristic of common sense is its stubborn tendency to think it can handle any question. This is especially the case when the theoretical dimension of some state of affairs seems not to promise immediate or practical results. Moreover, theories are often beyond our understanding, and so we are tempted to conclude that they make no sense. There is a big difference, however, between admitting that one does not understand the theory and claiming that the theory makes no sense. In many cases conversion into the realm of theory makes the difference between understanding and failing to understand. Awareness of the different realms of meaning, like awareness of what constitutes knowing, brings with it a heightened critical control over of thinking.

Theology and Theory

Just as ornithology might seem like drudgery to one who takes no pleasure in watching birds, so theology might appear quite uninviting or even irrelevant if one lacked interest in its originating religious concerns. Although theology has sometimes become sterile and detached from Christian life and religious affections, it need not take that alienating route. All theology, no matter in what religion, has its roots in a transformative experience of the divine or the "sacred" whose meaning is conveyed in rituals, symbols, images and stories. Just as all natural science originated in a common sense encounter with the physical world, so too the gradual shift toward theory emerged from within the early Christians' ongoing attempts to understand more fully the experience of the risen Christ in their midst.

To claim, therefore, that theology sometimes requires a shift from the common sense symbolic expressions of religious experience to the more abstract and less immediate formulations of theory does not imply that the believer's experience of God and the symbols of that experience are to be left behind. Symbolic expression is a permanent feature of religion; faith cannot do without this realm of meaning. Imagine, if you can, the liturgy in abstract theological language: no biblical imagery, no ritualized gestures, no feeling-laden hymns, no stories, no Christian symbolism. For the vast majority of worshippers, it would utterly fail to communicate the transforming message of the gospel.

Interiority

If the move from one realm to another can be implicit, still it is not necessarily so. Indeed, the standpoint of this chapter is one within which the difference is explicit. In what realm of meaning must we be to talk about the distinction between common sense and theory? Common sense tends to think it can solve all problems, answer all questions. The person within a dramatic pattern of experience must either dismiss as irrelevant the questions it cannot answer or shift into an intellectual pattern, thus recognizing the limitations of common sense. But does theory encompass both theory and common sense?

New questions arise out of the fact that there are these two distinct realms of meaning. How can we account for them? How can we acknowledge the concrete common sense knowledge of our particular world or horizon while at the same time recognizing that there are important, even urgent questions that common sense can answer? The realm of meaning within which both common sense and theory can be recognized is called by Lonergan "interiority." Just as some questions that arise within the horizon of common sense can be answered only by way of a shift to theory, so too some questions about the relationship between common sense and theory can only be clearly addressed from a standpoint that includes both. This chapter, in other words, could not have been written from a common sense or a theoretical point of view, since its theme has to do not with theory alone, nor with common sense alone, but rather with the relationship between the two and their residence, therefore, in a larger horizon of meaning. To put it very succinctly, interiority is the realm of meaning from within which we take explicit notice of the fact that we operate in different realms of meaning.

Interiority is the realm from within which we identify and distinguish the operations of common sense and of theory in ourselves.[5]

The word "interiority," like the word "subjectivity," should not imply a retreat from the "objectivity" of science nor from the practical affairs of daily life. The spatial metaphor, suggesting the "interior" of the person as distinct from the "exterior," should not be allowed to throw us off track here. Interiority is the standpoint that allows for an awareness of these different realms and their interrelations. Its most basic element and moving force is the human drive to understand—the intentionality of the human spirit at work in the world. That drive is more likely to approach its goal if the inquirer is aware that there are different realms of meaning, that common sense is not capable of answering all the relevant questions, and that the maintenance of the intellectual pattern of experience requires concentrated effort since it is not the spontaneous pattern of daily living.

Conclusion

The difference between theoretical and common sense understanding has to do not only with the thing we are trying to understand, but with ourselves, with our way of attending to it, with our attitude, our intention, our angle of inquiry. Conflicts between common sense and theory must be resolved on the level of interiority. Theory alone tends to denigrate the symbols of common sense, and sometimes reads into the symbol what is not there. Common sense religion can be tempted to dismiss theory as a "head trip," abstract and irrelevant to piety, devotion, and real love.[6] Some dismiss theology in its theoretical or systematic form as the unwarranted invasion of reason into matters of faith. Theology, it is sometimes said, should be biblical and should never go beyond what scripture says.

The shift to theory shows that the development of doctrine is inevitable. The communication of the gospel evokes something more than mere repetition of biblical or other common sense expressions. In the next chapter we will appeal to the distinctions we have illustrated here in order to come to a better understanding of what Christians mean when they think and speak about the central reality of their faith.

5. On interiority, see Lonergan, *Method*, 81–86 and 257–66.

6. See ibid., 114–15 and 350–51.

4

God and Creation

LONERGAN'S UNDERSTANDING OF GOD's relationship to the universe is in line with that of Aquinas, who famously insisted that we can know that God exists through our understanding of creation, but we cannot know what God is. We know, therefore, that "God by his intelligence moves all things to their proper ends; for God causes every event and applies every agent and uses every operation inasmuch as he is the cause of the order of the universe."[1] In this chapter we shall focus on the incomprehensible mystery of God who is at the same time the Creator and Conserver of the universe. This approach employs certain basic skills necessary for theology to do its job of seeking a better understanding of the content of faith because Christian revelation presents the startling view of God as actively saving the world from evil through personal and loving involvement. We begin with the spirit of inquiry itself and note that the question of God reveals the core human experience of self-transcendence, an orientation toward unconditional intelligibility and love. Second, we present the doctrine of creation as the basis for the claim that we cannot know what God is. The distinction between God and creation means that God, who is not a being within the world, is therefore incomprehensible. Knowing *that*, however, opens up the possibility of a better understanding of God's relation to the world. Knowing what we don't know is an enrichment in our understanding of the unknowable and also improves our understanding of how the unknowable God is related to the world.

Thirdly, we ask what we are doing when we talk about God. We will explain what it means to say that religious language—speech about God—is always analogical or metaphorical, never univocal. Finally, in light of the doctrine of creation and our analogical language about God, we will

---

1. Lonergan, *Insight*, 687.

return to the Christian vision of God's active presence and ask *how* God is active in the world.

Self-transcendence

An orientation toward mystery is built into our beings as self-transcendent; that claim is as ancient as the sacred scriptures of humanity. The orientation manifests itself in the form of inquiry. The question of God, Lonergan insists, is constitutive of our humanity.[2] Human authenticity is a matter of being true to this self-transcendence, a reaching beyond what we know now, or are doing now or love now. Human beings are "on the move" cognitively, morally and religiously as they seek to go beyond themselves to live an ever more authentic life. When we know something we go beyond what we were before we knew it; we are different to the degree that our new knowledge changes us. When we decide to act in order to advance the good or when we repent of our failures and seek healing and forgiveness, we go beyond what we were before our decision and action. When we fall in love with God—when we experience love in an unconditional way—we go beyond our previous selves by catching on to the love that is the source and ultimate meaning of the universe. Often this experience of being in love with God precedes and motivates moral and cognitive self-transcendence. But as experience, being in love with God is what Lonergan calls the "infrastructure." Experience provides the data about which we wonder and ask questions.[3]

Religious traditions provide the language with which to think in an explicit way about religious experience. Traditions are normally communicated through the symbol systems of a particular religious culture, but as we have seen, beyond the symbols of any tradition there are potential questions to be raised regarding the meaning of those symbols and the meaning of our desire to understand them. When we consider the value of our coming to self-knowledge cognitively, morally and religiously, the question of the ultimate meaning of the universe arises. And as part of that universe, the self-transcending human being can be understood systematically within the physical, chemical, biological and social meanings that constitute human communities and their histories. As Lonergan asks, "is the universe on our side, or are we just gamblers and, if we are gamblers, are we not perhaps fools, individually struggling for authenticity and collectively endeavoring to snatch progress from the ever mounting welter of decline?"[4]

2. Lonergan, *Method*, 103.
3. See Lonergan, "Religious Experience," 113–28.
4. Lonergan, *Method*, 102.

The questions we ask lead us to the question of the ultimate meaning and ground of our desire to know and act and love. The question of God is the question of whether or not there is an ultimate ground to our desire for self-transcendence and authenticity. In other words, are we living within a friendly universe?[5] These are inevitable questions; they can be dodged or dismissed or answered in despair rather than faith. But they are the questions that make us human.

> Could the world be mediated by questions for intelligence if it did not have an intelligent ground? Could the world's facticity be reconciled with its intelligibility if it did not have a necessary ground? Is it with man that morality emerges in the universe so that the universe is amoral and alien to man, or is the ground of the universe a moral being? Such questions invite answers and, as the questions intend, so too the answers can reveal an intelligent, necessary, moral ground of the universe.[6]

Lonergan is asking us to discover within the experience of our own consciousness that God is implied in all questioning.

Creation out of Nothing

The *Confessions* of Augustine of Hippo is one of the classics that articulates a great mind's desire to understand the hungry human heart. But Augustine had problems thinking and talking about his religious experience.

> I imagined you Lord, who are infinite in every possible respect, surrounding and penetrating [creation] in its every part, like a sea extending in all directions through immense space, a single unlimited sea which held within itself a sponge as vast as one could imagine but still finite, and the sponge soaked in every fiber of itself by the boundless sea.[7]

The young Roman from North Africa could not understand how God could be without a body. Even though he did not imagine that God had anything like a human body, still Augustine could not seem to do without an image

---

5. "Faith places human efforts in a friendly universe; it reveals an ultimate significance in human achievement; it strengthens new undertakings with confidence" (Ibid., 117).

6. Ibid., 342. See also *Insight*, 703, where Lonergan notes that the universal viewpoint of proportionate metaphysics issues in "questions that cannot be dodged."

7. Augustine, *Confessions*, Book 7, sections 5 and 7.

of God as a material reality diffused in some way throughout the universe. God, it seemed to him, must be extended in space.

> For whatever I conceived as devoid of such spatial character seemed to me to be nothing, absolutely nothing, not even so much as an empty space. For if a body is removed from a place, and the place remains empty of any body whatsoever, whether earthly, watery, airy, or celestial, yet there remains that empty space, as it were a spacious nothing.[8]

So it seemed to Augustine that if something is real, it must be a body in some sense, extended in space, and the space itself is a body of sorts—it exists whether there are bodily things in it or not. How can anything, even God, not consist of material stuff? Augustine's imagination simply could not give up some picture of God as diffused in all things, just as the sun's light penetrates the air. On the other hand, if God were indeed material, he would then be susceptible of change and corruption; but this would make God inferior to a God who was not changeable or corruptible.[9] Augustine had long before rejected the idea that God had a human-like body with arms and legs and nose etc.; the Manichean religion to which he belonged for nine years had derided what they claimed was this "catholic" idea of God, and Augustine's acceptance of their judgment prevented him for a time from taking the Christian position seriously.

His inability to think of God as non-material was a formidable difficulty for this brilliant but struggling seeker. Lonergan notes that "[f]or years, . . . Saint Augustine was unable to grasp that the real could be anything but a body."[10] But while he puzzled over these difficulties, Augustine did not advert to the very power that made his inquiry possible. The human mind itself is proof of the non-corporeal nature of something very real, but he did not yet know himself well enough at this time. "I did not perceive that the mental power by which I formed these images was no such corporeal substance."[11] In other words, there was a reality more intimate to Augustine than anything else—something that he experienced continually—that would have provided an example of a non-bodily reality. And so it is with God, an unimaginable mystery that makes everything possible. With the help of philosophers of the neo-Platonic tradition, Augustine eventually came to understand that God isn't a body.

8. Ibid., Book 7, section 1.

9. See ibid., Book 5, section 10.

10. *Insight*, 437.

11. Augustine, *Confessions*, Book 7, section 1.

Augustine's eventual recognition of the non-material nature of God provided the basis for further insights, such as the notion that creation is "out of nothing."[12] Through his struggle to understand whether God was made out of material stuff, Augustine grasped the notion of space as linked to that of time—these categories that have no meaning apart from their existence in the material universe. Augustine tells the reader that the question, "what did God do before he made heaven and earth?" is a serious question and does not deserve the mocking joke that was often given in response: "He was preparing hell. . .for those prying into such deep subjects." Augustine's answer to the query is minimal but of utmost importance. "I know that no creature was made before any creation took place."[13]

Well, yes—that's logical. But notice the implications of this simple observation. Since time does not exist until creation comes into being, it makes no sense to ask what God did "before" God created. The question rests on a mistaken presumption that God operates within a reality—time and space—that was always already there as God's "field of operations," so to speak. The notion of creation, however, means that God, the source of all that is, creates space and time along with everything else that is not God. There is no "before" for the Creator Who creates time, and everything in it, out of nothing, and so is not within time.

We note again how important the differentiation of consciousness is to the development of Christian understanding. The dramatic and highly symbolic genres of the biblical narratives communicate meanings that are later explored and developed in the theological traditions that interpret and apply the teachings of the bible in changing historical and cultural circumstances. The Bible is a record of God's revelation to the people of Israel and through them to humanity; that record, however, is expressed variously in symbolic stories, historical narrative, poetry, law and other literary forms. The meanings carried by these forms raise questions that the texts themselves do not answer. For example, the start of the poem of creation in Genesis 1 presents God as bringing order out of chaotic waters. In the stories of creation the divine concern is primarily for the people who will be related to God in the covenant and so the focus of the biblical writer in this poem of creation is on God's making the world habitable for human beings. Notice that while the text is clear in its affirmation that God created the heavens and the earth, it also says that "when" God created the earth, it was a formless wasteland, an abyss, a chaos. The question thus arises,

12. Ibid., Book 11, section 12.

13. Ibid. Augustine here takes the phrase "heaven and earth" to mean all that has been created.

before God brought order out of chaos, was the chaotic wasteland already there? By the nature of its literary form, the text does not raise—and therefore does not answer—the question, where did that chaos come from? The text and subsequent reflection on it within the biblical tradition does make it clear, however, that God is the Creator of "the heavens and the earth," an expression of totality. In the language of the Bible, the phrase "created the heavens and the earth" means that God is the Creator of everything. There are no existent things outside of what God created.

Without a differentiated consciousness that distinguishes between symbolic and theoretical realms of meaning, there could be no development of Christian theology. The original symbolic expressions and the limitations of their genres must be understood in order to affirm the belief in creation out of nothing. God did not use pre-existing material to form the universe. In Genesis 1 it is God's "word" that effects creation: "God said" is a refrain that occurs throughout poem. A word is the expression of what its speaker intends; it comes forth through an act of intelligence, not necessity. The poem's other refrain makes it clear that God considers what He has made to be good. In the mythology of some Gnostics, however, the good god of salvation—the god who supposedly sent Jesus with secret knowledge about how to escape the evil clutches of the material world—is not the Creator. The Creator god was at war with the good savior god. These myths, therefore, denied the goodness of the material creation as well as the ancient Hebrew belief in the unity of the Creator and Savior.[14] In their response to these false teachings the early Christian theologians insisted that the Christian understanding of God must include the notion of creation *ex nihilo*, out of nothing. Irenaeus, one of the most important of the early theologians (he was writing before the year 200 CE) had the Valentinian Gnostics and their complex mythologies as his target when he links God's revealed love for us with the all-encompassing creation; he wants to eliminate the possibility of interpreting the scriptures from a gnostic view that separates the Creator from the redeemer. This early expression of the Christian understanding of creation means that nothing ever existed—not even a pre-existing, chaotic raw material—outside the creative and redemptive authority of the one God.

Irenaeus illustrates the early Christian conviction that God is "the all," as the wisdom book of Sirach says; nothing is outside of God's freely intended creation. Irenaeus also shows us a glimpse of the development of the doctrine of creation. The sixth century BCE author of Genesis 1 was not asking the same questions as those of the second century CE Christian

14. On Irenaeus's symbolic/narrative retelling of Christian teaching in response to the gnostic mythology, see Loewe, *Lex Crucis*, 15–70.

theologians; still, when circumstances evoked them, those questions had to be raised and answered. By the second century Christian writers understood that loyalty to the biblical texts and to their experience of God in Christ required that they interpret Genesis 1 to mean creation "out of nothing." The biblical accounts of creation, understood within their literary and historical contexts, reveal Genesis 1 as a poem written after the Israelites returned from exile in the sixth century BCE; it is not a philosophical or scientific statement. The poem's meaning, however, has been interpreted within a more philosophical context to mean creation "out of nothing." This transposition from symbolic poetry to abstract statement took generations of reflection on God's revealed word in scripture.

The Distinction between Creator and Creation

God is the Creator—a simple enough claim on the surface of things. But when misunderstood, few claims are as loaded with implications and few claims bring in its wake so much theological confusion. To put the issue briefly before we explore the details, as the intelligibility and thus cause of all beings, God is *not one of* those beings. In the words of Thomas Aquinas, God "lacks anything that is merely creaturely."[15] In contrast to creatures, God is not a composite of things that come together. God, in other words, can be called "simple." When speaking of the created world, Aquinas employed the Aristotelian concept of "form and matter" as a structural explanation for the fact that we find many instances of the same kind of thing. There are many dogs, for example, but they are all dogs. For Aristotle, all beings are a composite of form (what makes a thing the sort of thing it happens to be) and matter (the principle that makes an abstract "form" to be an individual thing). Lassie is a composite of dog "nature" (form) and the principle of individuation (matter). She is not an abstract, immaterial nature (doghood) nor is she an undifferentiated, unformed mass of matter (no such thing exists—matter has to be this or that *sort* of matter). According to this Aristotelian way of thinking, everything in the world—everything that has existence—is such a composite.

Aquinas employs this composite Aristotelian "ontology" but he does so within the Christian vision of the Creator-creature distinction. In other words, the composition does not apply to God. While every being is a composite of form and matter, God's essence or "form" *is* God's existence. God is therefore "simple" rather than a composite or complex, as beings are. God is the pure act of *to-be*, the Cause of all that exists. Aquinas points

15. Aquinas, *Summa,* Ia, Q.13.

to Exodus 3, the famous story of the appearance of God to Moses. God tells Moses that he has witnessed the oppression of the Israelites and intends to liberate them from their Egyptian masters. Aquinas interprets the name God gives him—a form of the Hebrew verb "to be"—as most appropriate for God because God is the cause of all particular beings having existence. God *is*, and so whatever is shares in that existing that is God. This interpretation places supreme importance on the distinction between Creator and all creatures. God is pure action, the pure act of existing, while creatures—all things that have being—exist only as partial and imperfect participants in the Creator's existing.[16]

The distinction is radical and unlike any other distinction, but as we shall see in more detail, this does not imply "distance" or any sort of alienation between God and creatures. God is, rather, at once the Wholly Other, incomparable Creator of all that is, and the most intimate thing about any creature. The Creator is supremely intimate with creatures by sheer virtue of their being created; Aquinas can therefore claim that "existence is more intimately and profoundly interior to things than anything else."[17] God is metaphorically "closer" to the creature than the creature is to itself.

The distinction between Creator and creature also means that creation did not have to be. There was nothing necessary about the fact that there is something rather than nothing; there could have been nothing. Without creation, God's greatness would not be in any way diminished and with creation God's greatness is not increased. There is no necessity in God to create. The distinction is not between this sort of being and that, but rather the difference between *the fact* that there is anything at all and *the possibility* of there not having been anything other than God. We can now begin to understand why Christian theology is in no way hostile to the natural sciences. The distinction means that the Christian teaching on creation is not a scientific claim, not a description of what came before the "Big Bang" or the emergence of galaxies or the biological evolution of life on earth. These processes take place over time and are events within what we are calling creation. As a precise term in Christian theology, creation is simply the relation of what exists to the pure act that creates it and sustains it in existence.

Creation out of nothing is a vitally important notion for Christian theology but it is not always an easy one to talk about. The modern imagination tends to picture God as building the universe out of raw materials (perhaps the abyss of Genesis 1:1) and, having built it, existing separated from it. This is in part due to the fact that the amazingly successful discoveries of modern

16. Ibid., Ia, Q.13, A.11.
17. Ibid., Ia, Q.8, A.1.

science were often uncritically mixed together with religious skepticism. For many modern thinkers (starting in the seventeenth century), progress was science and it was liberation from the dominant religious traditions of Europe. The Enlightenment philosophers imagined they had no need of the God hypothesis in order to explain the mechanistic world; what they imagined not needing was a very great person or thing that would intervene in that mechanical world.

God and the World

The Jewish, Christian and Islamic traditions claim that God is present and involved in every aspect of reality, and especially in the life of God's people. There are two truths about God's relationship to the world that stand out in the scriptures: (1) God is active in the world sustaining it in being—the opposite of a distant, uninvolved deity, a passive observer. In theological language, God is immanent. Yet (2) God is always free, never forced or coerced to create or to redeem, as if God were part of the universe obeying laws that coerce God's will. In theological language, God is transcendent.

According to the symbolic biblical narratives, the Lord of all creation made the world for human beings to inhabit. God called Abraham out of his native territory and into a new land flowing with milk and honey, promising to make of him a great nation (Gen 12:1–3). God appeared to Moses, identified himself as a faithful presence (YHWH = "I am") and commanded him to lead the enslaved Hebrews out of Egypt and back to the land that had been promised to them (Exod 1–15). Within this redemptive drama God forms a people by establishing a covenant lived out according that relationship (Exod 19–20). In the land God raised up mighty leaders, and eventually kings, to govern the people in God's name (1–2 Sam, 1–2 Kings). When the people broke the covenant, God sent prophets to indict their wickedness, exhort them to reform, warn them of consequences if they didn't, and affirm once again that God is the redeemer. In the Psalms, the songs of worship in ancient Israel and later the "prayer book" of the Christians, humanity calls out to God with praise but also with anxiety and petitions to awaken God to our peril. Jesus continues this covenant tradition by doing what God has done in the history of Israel: teaching people to pray, healing their infirmities, forgiving their sins and exhorting them to find and live God's reign. In Jesus' ministry, death and resurrection, the Creator and Redeemer is revealed in the flesh—an involvement of God in the world more intimate than can ever have been anticipated.

I have very briefly summarized a biblical narrative as it has been traditionally presented. What I now want to call to our attention is the symbolic forms that operate within the texts from which we draw this narrative. In doing so we will want to notice the human subject's reception of these forms. In other words, the type of consciousness that understands symbolic forms must be one that can grasp the meanings carried by those forms. Biblical metaphors operate within symbolic consciousness. The Bible is not a philosophical argument regarding the nature and attributes of God but rather a collection of dramatic narratives, poetry, history, law, wisdom and prophecy almost always having to do with God's creating and redeeming action in the world. God's sovereignty extends not only over God's wholly good creation but also over the evil that threatens it. God's opposition to evil is a key for interpreting much of the Bible.[18] The divine struggle against evil is symbolically and metaphorically communicated in these stories by images such as God's "anger." Although the biblical picture of God is often "anthropomorphic," that is, constructed by using human characteristics such as bodiliness, emotion and so forth, the philosophical question of whether there are emotions in God is not being asked in these biblical texts. For example, our ability to recognize the dramatic pattern of experience in the Bible helps us to get what is meant by references to God's anger: it does not mean that God has this emotion; rather, it refers to the human experience of knowing that sin is in opposition to God.

We see the same dramatic and symbolic consciousness operative in the New Testament. Saint Paul refers several times to the wrath of God in order to continue the Hebrew scriptures' presentation of human sin and its consequences. In his indictment of Gentile evildoers, those outside of the revelation given to the Jews, Paul states, "The wrath of God is indeed being revealed from heaven against every impiety and wickedness of those who suppress the truth by their wickedness" (Rom 1:18). As is true of the Old Testament texts that present the same image, Paul is concerned not with the inner emotions of God but rather with human behavior and the need to be faithful to the covenant relationship God has established with humanity.

The biblical tradition, therefore, presents God as deeply and passionately involved in this world. God sustains all that God creates and salvages creation when people lose the way divinely established for them. In the Bible God's activity in the world is not a past event but an ongoing reality—indeed, the most fundamental reality of every being at every moment. In the dramatic narratives and symbolic poetry of the Bible, God's response to humanity is steadfast, unchanging love. God's necessarily unchanging love

18. See Levenson, *Creation*.

is directed to a necessarily changing humanity. In an earlier chapter we have noticed that symbols are capable of holding seemingly contradictory meanings together. The mixed imagery is of an unchanging yet ever-active God always present to humanity in need of salvation. The Bible's overall focus is on God's relationship to us and not on God apart from that relationship. We do learn about God from the Bible, of course, but the truths being communicated are expressed functionally and linked to the divine purpose of salvaging human beings.

Analogy and God Talk

Throughout Lonergan's writings we find reference to a principle from Vatican Council I's constitution on Divine Revelation, *Dei Filius* that affirms the possibility of improving our understanding through analogy of the revealed mysteries. But as we have seen, for Lonergan, understanding is not certitude, "for by faith one is already certain." Nor does it mean "demonstration, for the mysteries cannot be demonstrated."[19] In addition to his profound reflections on God as Cause of all, a principle that informs a great deal of his writings, Thomas Aquinas also produced highly skilled examples of the proper use of language to name God. This section summarizes a few of his key insights into theological language, especially those that help to clarify the Christian "distinction" between Creator and creation.

The meanings of words in a book are primarily determined by the way they are used in larger contexts of sentences and paragraphs and chapters. When we use a word in different contexts but mean essentially the same thing by it, we use it univocally. Jack is healthy; Martha is healthy. The word "healthy" is being used *univocally*; it has the same meaning in both sentences. When we use a word to mean something essentially different in each case, we are using the word *equivocally*. "He saw the saw in the toolbox." The captain of the ship is stern and the ship has a stern. The word "stern" has completely different meanings in each sentence. Then there are jokes that depend on our knowing that some words can be used equivocally: "'Go to the back of the ship,' the captain ordered sternly."

Language and our ability to communicate, however, would be sorely impoverished if words were limited to univocal or strictly equivocal uses. Fortunately, that is not the case. Consider the word "healthy" again. There is a category of "health foods" in the market. Are these foods "healthy" the way Jack or Martha are healthy? Well, no, but neither are the foods "healthy"

19. Lonergan, *Verbum*, 219.

in a completely unrelated way, either. They are healthy by analogy.[20] In the ordinary use of language we quite frequently use words analogously.

Analogical use of language employs terms in somewhat different ways in order to capture some meaning that is unavailable in either univocal or strictly equivocal uses. In the analogical use of a word there is similarity to the primary meaning of the term but also—and mostly—dissimilarity. Broccoli has something to do with health but it doesn't exercise, get physical check-ups or reduce stress as healthy people do. Orange juice doesn't skip rope and broccoli doesn't swim laps. There are many ways in which these foods are not physically fit, which is the primary sense of the word "healthy." Yet, these foods might have something to do with Jack or Martha's health: they might help to cause it. So, we call these foods "healthy." And if you hear someone say that "low cholesterol is healthy," you'd know that the word "healthy" is analogous to Jack or Martha's "health," except this time you might notice that the low cholesterol could be considered not a cause of health but a sign of it. In this example the same word can be used analogously in two different ways.

Language about God is never univocal because God is not a creature. Yet if we speak strictly equivocally about God we might as well not say anything—what we say wouldn't have any meaning. Naming God, therefore, is always analogous. We know God through what God has made or done—through creation and revelation—but we obviously do not consider God *to be* as a creature. God is rather the meaning and cause of all that is. God is the answer to the question, "why is there anything at all?" As existing and thus participating in God as their ultimate cause, all things possess certain perfections only in a defective or limited way. Take the words "good" and "goodness" as an example. "God is Goodness" is a perfectly true theological claim. Creatures are also good; as created by God—as participants in God—they share in that goodness. God's goodness causes our existence. So, we don't know fully what we mean when we say "goodness" because the primary referent or fullness of that term's meaning is Goodness in the highest sense—God—who is unknowable. So, "God is good," or "God is Goodness Itself," are analogical claims. In its analogous usage the word possesses a similarity with the reality of goodness as we experience it in creatures but it *mostly* displays difference.

Because we can always use analogous terms such as wise, good, or beautiful "in a more comprehensive way,"[21] the proper use of such names for

---

20. The example of "health" is taken from Aquinas, *Summa*, Ia, Q.13, A.10, who got it from Aristotle. I have modernized the illustrations.

21. Burrell, *God and Action*, 70.

God does not presuppose a transcendent meaning available to us. In other words, there is always a greater wisdom or truth or beauty than any that may be encountered in creation. That is why Aquinas held that, although it is perfectly true to say that God is wise, God is most properly said to be not wise, but Wisdom Itself. This grammatical note does not mean we have the concept "wisdom" already settled. There are no adequate concepts for God, only analogous ones; the claim "God is wisdom" does not supply information about what God is. Such information, as we have seen, is strictly not available to human intelligence.

Despite his principle that we cannot know what God is, Aquinas maintained that it is possible to use both concrete and abstract names for God. Let us return for a moment to Aristotle's notion of form and matter. Lassie and Rover are both dogs, but they are not the same dog. They share a dog nature (form) but that nature is individualized in two numerically different dogs. Form alone is an abstract concept with no reality in the natural world whereas matter alone is simply the potential for an abstract form to become an individual instance of that form. Neither form nor matter exists independently of the other. "Doghood" becomes Rover, this barking animal at the door, when form (dog nature) becomes individuated in matter. Creatures, therefore, are composites of form and matter. Such a composite is named a "substance," something that exists in itself and not in another, and substances have attributes or "accidents" that exist in another and not in themselves. In the phrase "a white horse," for example, "whiteness" is "accidental" and thus has no existence apart from its being, in this case, "a white horse." Apart from its existence as a particular horse, whiteness is an abstraction, not an actual being.[22]

Aquinas understood that talk about God, the source of all being, must not imply that God is a being in the world—in other words, a composite. One way of correcting this erroneous inclination in theological speech is to attribute to God abstract words such as wisdom, goodness and truth. But the abstractions must not imply that the word "God" is merely a name for an abstraction, for God is not only real but, as the Cause of all, the most real. Aquinas, therefore, recommends that we not only use abstract terms but also concrete ones as well—God is Goodness *and* God is good; God is Wisdom *and* God is wise—to make clear that God is real—but in an unknowable way, as the cause of existence.

These multiple cautions and qualifications should alert us to the fact that, if analogical use of language is inescapable, it is also, when used to name God, dangerous. It can easily conjure up a false image of God as the most

22. Aquinas, *Summa*, Ia, Q.13, A.1, ad.2.

powerful being in the universe. We must continually invoke our corrective principle that we do not know what God is if we are to avoid the "Supreme Being" idolatry. Analogy is merely a way of using language to point in a direction, not a theological scope for peeking inside the divine nature. Again, the unknowability of what God is must control what our imaginations propose to us when we use analogy. We only know what God is not. We come to the notion of God's unknowable "transcendence" or otherness by exploring the range and limitations of human language about God. God is not the "perfect being," nor "the biggest thing around."[23] The distinction between Creator and creation helps us to avoid making idols by reminding us constantly that we do not know the "essence" or "nature" of God, and should not try to imagine it. God's essence is not picturable; but to know that it is not picturable and that God is incomprehensible, is to know a very important thing. When speaking analogously of God, in other words, we are not really saying much. "God is wisdom," for example, means that any instance of wisdom that we might encounter in this world is not an adequate expression of God's wisdom but merely a participation in the supreme wisdom of God—but what that supreme wisdom is we don't know because it is identical with what God is, and therefore unknowable. Analogies of God, therefore, cannot serve to build up a picture or concept of a Supreme Being.

God is the pure act of existence, and we cannot know what it means to exist.[24] The analogy that we use for knowledge of God is that between Creator and creature—between a thing (all things) existing and the "universal source of existence." The analogical knowledge is on the level of judgment, not understanding—knowledge *that* rather than knowledge (understanding) *of* God. Being is not a possession or a doing; it is simply what it says—existing. So, there is no resemblance between God and creatures if we are talking about *what* God is. God is incommensurate as "the measure of all things, inasmuch as the nearer things come to God, the more fully they exist."[25] The notion that God is pure act serves Aquinas as the prime analogue for action itself. We do not know what goodness means, because the prime analogue of goodness is the unknowable God; so we do not know what action means, and for the same reason. We know what creaturely action is, but we also know that creatures are not their own reason for being and, therefore, acting.

23. This is David Burrell's phrase. See his *Friendship*, 115–20, for a critique of "perfect being" theologies. See also his "Analogy of Being," 53–66.

24. Burrell, *God and Action*, 51.

25. Ibid., 52.

Does God Change?

This discussion of theological language should help us to understand why the Christian tradition does not attribute "change" to God. As the pure act of *to-be*, God possesses existence in a way that does not involve the potential for change, achievement, or temporal sequence. To use the language of change when speaking about what God is would mean the reduction of God from the Cause of all to something caused, a creature. If we remind ourselves that knowing is not like looking, we will be more cautious here. There is nothing to see or to picture in this relation of "causality."[26] As we have noted, religious common sense normally communicates using symbols, which are usually received and understood in a common sense way through feelings. The religious response to the biblical symbol of God's wrath is not meaningless or "merely emotional." The metaphor can communicate the way things are with us when sin distorts the image of God according to which we were created. The language must be corrected, however, when a shift in perspective asks about what this metaphor might tell us about God apart from our experience of sin.

When applied to God the word "unchanging" does not mean uninvolved or passive, as it does when we apply it to creatures. Aquinas's claim that we cannot know what God is turns out to be "a simple a matter of logic. . . . It has nothing whatsoever to do with a personal or cultural predilection for the enduring over the novel."[27] God is the cause of all that has existence, all that acts, all that has being. Notice how vigilant we must be to eliminate confusions in thought that creep in because of our natural (and generally good) tendency to use our imaginations. God is the cause and governor of all being, ". . .down even to the quivering leaves on the trees," as Augustine says[28] but this fact does not require a God who changes in the divine nature itself. "A causes B" is a relation of dependence, as Lonergan has pointed out, "not an imaginable 'influence' occupying the space intermediate between A and B. It is not a change in A, for the fire does not change when it ceases to cook the potatoes and begins to cook the steak."[29]

Knowing that God is beyond our understanding—what is often called "negative knowledge of God"—is not simply a negation of what we thought we knew about God. Knowing what God *is not* enriches our understanding, just as Socrates, who knew he didn't know what justice is,

26. See ibid., 131–34, and Burrell, *Exercises*, 116–17.

27. Burrell, *God and Action*, 15.

28. Augustine, *Confessions*, Book 7, section 6.

29. Lonergan, *Insight*, 663.

was therefore wiser than those who thought they knew but were mistaken. Nonetheless, such knowledge does not give us a concept of God, or imply that we can finally know what God's nature is. Knowledge that your friend is not a drug-abuser, or that your doctor is not an impostor constitute very important information! To have and benefit from this information you don't have to comprehend the mystery that is your friend, nor do you have to know what it means to be a heart surgeon. Still, that negative knowledge is extremely valuable.

To characterize a human being as unchanging could be an insult, implying a complete lack of involvement. Strictly speaking, if you were unchanging, you would be inactive, passive, inert, unconcerned, dead. You wouldn't exist. If we take the Bible's meaning seriously, however, we know that the theologian's refusal to speak of change in God cannot imply that God is indifferent and unchanging toward creation. This is not what the traditional claim means. On the contrary, the God of love and redemption, the God of the Bible who redeems Israel from Egypt and raises Jesus from the dead and generally fights against evil, is not a distant or uninterested Absolute. God is rather the pure act of dynamic, free self-communication whose (metaphorical) passion for humanity is beyond all reckoning. Any talk of the God of Abraham, Isaac and Jacob, the God of Moses and the prophets, the God of Jesus, would have to affirm that God is active indeed. The pure act of *to-be* is in no way a passive or static being. And yet, God is not in need of something that can be supplied only in time, for that would make God a being in and of the world. And such a being would not be the Creator God that Jews, Christians and Muslims worship.

Conclusion: The Constant God of Love

If we insist on a picture of the holy mystery that is God, we may one day be surprised to learn that we cannot square it with what we have come to know about the world. The traditional insistence on the incomprehensibility of God is an advantage to Christian thinking because it provides Christians maximum freedom to mediate the gospel in changing times and diverse cultures. The principle of God's unknowability reminds us that current images, schemes, views and ways of thinking cannot inform us of what we cannot know. This protects Christianity from collapsing into the cultures in which it necessarily expresses itself. Feminist theologies have recently drawn attention to the advantages of this "negative knowledge of God," as it is sometimes called. For example, the incomprehensibility of God reminds us to resist the myth of male superiority by an appeal to the fact that God cannot be known as male; indeed, what God is cannot be known at all. The feminist critique can do its work of correcting the ways we communicate about God on the symbolic level while avoiding any reduction of God in the imagination.

While theology resists such idolatry by calling to mind the limitations of our symbols, the religious imagination is always seeking to express the experience of the personal God intimately related to us in the processes of creation and redemption. Christians must communicate the mysteries of faith in fresh ways to meet the circumstances of their times and places; there must be progress, growth and development in the Christian life and doctrine. In his book on the development of doctrine John Henry Newman famously noted that "to live is to change, and to be perfect is to have changed often."[30] God's loving action, however, remains constant and ever beyond our ability to understand. Lonergan's lifelong efforts to introduce historical consciousness into Catholic theology was intended to clarify the relationship between God's providential love and the free human response to it. The many and rapid changes we are experiencing, he insisted, are changes "not in God's self-disclosure or our faith, but in our culture."[31] The clarity he brought to thinking about God places the need for change where it must ever be: on us.

---

30. Newman, *Essay on Development*, 63.
31. Lonergan, "Future," 163.

5

A Theology of Grace and Freedom

FRIENDS OF MINE OCCASIONALLY indulge in a long-standing dispute. The one is committed to the Christian faith and often debates with her friend regarding the importance of her religion. Human beings are arrogant to think that they have any ability to effect solutions to the world's enormous and complex problems. Instead, they should place their trust in God and not in human powers. Her friend, on the other hand, insists that the fate of the world is up to human beings. We, not God, have the responsibility to end war, reverse the effects of environmental degradation, fight racism and sexism, curb economic exploitation and eliminate other forms of oppression and hatred. Religious people, he believes, shirk their responsibility by appealing to God for help; they should be doing something to change the world, not whining to some distant and dubious deity to intervene and clean up the mess that we human beings have created for ourselves.

On the surface, the views of these friends are opposites. For one, God is the only solution to the world's woeful state of affairs; for the other, if there is to be an end to the evils of this life, it must come from human effort. Both tacitly agree, however, that God's grace and human effort are mutually exclusive options. Either God lifts human beings out of the mire in which our own stupidity and malice have landed us, or we do it for ourselves. Salvation is either our own work or it is God's.

This either/or presupposition imagines God and humanity as two beings alongside one another, each working to salvage the world. Only God is up to the task of doing so, one thinks. For the other, if there were such a powerful being, it should not be counted on to do anything. After all, God's track record isn't good—look at the mess the world is still in! So if we want to change the world we must do it ourselves.

Neither position squares with the great Christian tradition of the theology of grace and freedom. Both friends assume that there is competition between divine grace and human freedom, but is this true? What follows is an exploration, following Lonergan's pioneering work, of some of the key historical moments in the theology of grace. After a brief look at the biblical data we turn to Augustine of Hippo. We then note Lonergan's retrieval of a linguistic innovation by the thirteenth-century Chancellor of the University of Paris that made it possible to think about grace while maintaining the integrity of human freedom. Finally, in the twentieth century we turn to a summary of the way Lonergan transposed the medieval synthesis into a contemporary subject-centered theory of the way in which grace operates within the free human person.[1] The purpose of Lonergan's study *Grace and Freedom* was to show that a theology of grace does not—and must not—force a choice between divine assistance and human effort, but rather seeks to understand how God works in and through the intelligent and responsible behavior of human beings.

Augustine's Drama of Grace and Freedom

One cannot read far in the Bible without noticing two fundamental claims. First, God exercises power and authority over all things, including human behavior. Second, people are held responsible to God for what they do. The Bible simultaneously insists that humans are dependent on God, and that they are responsible. In the centuries after the age of the apostles Augustine of Hippo (354–430 CE), a convert to Catholic Christianity and a bishop in North Africa, was the first great theorist of the relationship between human freedom and divine providence. His thinking stressed that grace (1) is absolutely gratuitous (a free gift from God to humanity and never something that is earned or that God owes), (2) heals the damage to human freedom that results from sin, and (3) raises human nature to a reality that goes beyond what was originally given in creation. The full expression of Augustine's theology of grace, which has had a profound influence on the history of theology, was occasioned by the preaching of the British reformer Pelagius who was distressed at the moral laxity of so many Christians after Constantine liberated the faith from imperial persecution.

To acquire an understanding of the dispute between Augustine and Pelagius, it is necessary to enter the world that Pelagius and Augustine

---

1. Lonergan's doctoral dissertation on grace and freedom in Aquinas set up the historical development not only of the question through the centuries prior to Aquinas but within Aquinas's own thought. The methodological example of Lonergan's dissertation, written in the early 1940s, is important for its integration of an historical analysis of the sources, to avoid the "endless vices of anachronism" (Lonergan, *Grace*, 7).

inhabited. That world was shaped by the still-fresh memory of the sufferings of the Christian martyrs. After the Emperor Constantine in the early fourth century had allowed freedom of worship, the heroic courage of those willing to follow Christ in an act of self-sacrificing love was now no longer required to be Christian. Pelagius was shocked by the ease with which new Christians entered the church and claimed the name of Christian, a name that had cost the martyrs so much. Constantine's prohibition of persecution, following a very severe attack on the Christians by the former Emperor Diocletian, meant it was suddenly no longer difficult or risky to be a Christian. Monasticism—"white martyrdom" as it came to be known—was an effort to regain that sense of complete self-sacrifice displayed by the martyrs. Monks were to imitate Christ not by shedding their blood but by a life-long process of self-giving through celibacy, fasting and other forms of asceticism. The monk Pelagius, in other words, was very concerned about the church being flooded with people for whom being Christian was a good idea but for reasons that were not focused on the heart of the gospel call to conversion. Pelagius promoted a more authentic way of life within the church and stressed human freedom and responsibility.

While visiting Rome, Pelagius had heard the following words of Augustine's *Confessions*, quoted by a bishop: "Give me the grace to do as you command, and command me to do what you will."[2] Pelagius took Augustine's prayer to be an unhealthy denial of the power of free will and thus a threat to the principle of moral responsibility and the reform Pelagius desired. Robert Markus summarizes the anxiety caused by the new freedom of the Christian in Roman culture.

> The heated debates in Western Europe around the year 400 on the meaning of perfection had their roots in the uncertainty about what it meant to be a genuine Christian in a society of fashionable Christianity. In a world in which outward conformity with the religion of the establishment was hard to distinguish from real commitment, the call to authentic Christianity often took the form of conversion to some form of the ascetic life.[3]

Augustine himself was strongly attracted to the ascetic ideal and in fact formed a monastic community soon after his baptism. However, in contrast to Pelagius, whose rigorous views placed a premium on human willpower, Augustine's own moral struggles helped him to understand that without grace there is ultimately no freedom. Left to their own devices, people are prisoners of their own moral powerlessness.

2. Augustine, *Confessions*, Book 10, section 29.
3. Markus, "From Rome," 67.

The problem, Augustine argues, was that the bonds in which he was imprisoned were imposed by his own will.[4] When he was young he used to pray that the chains of lust be removed from his heart, but not right away! Augustine's self-deprecating comment reveals his awareness of the two necessary elements in the story of salvation: human freedom and divine grace. Freedom without grace is not effectively free, and yet grace without freedom would leave the human will out of the equation. What Augustine wanted was an authentic liberation of his human will, a solution that did not compromise his freedom but rather restored it.

Although his mother was a staunch Christian, Augustine himself did not embrace Christianity until he was thirty-three years old. At a certain point in his spiritual journey Augustine accepted what God has revealed in Christ but his response to that reality was not forthcoming. It was, he said, as if he were heavy with sleep, unable to awaken. Finally Augustine discovered that the solution to this inner turmoil is to be found only in God's grace. In the Confessions the figure of Lady Continence asks Augustine, "Why do you try to stand in your own strength and fail? Cast yourself upon God and have no fear. He will not shrink away and let you fall. Cast yourself upon Him without fear, for he will welcome you and cure you of your ills."[5] And so it came to pass: Augustine turned his life over to God in that paradoxical surrender whereby the strength of his freedom was restored.

Many years after Augustine's conversion, Pelagius came to Rome preaching a message of moral reform. Augustine observed in the monk's teachings a lack of appreciation for humanity's absolute dependence on God. Augustine had come to realize in his own struggles that the human being is to God as the infant is to her mother's breast.[6] While this image dramatically presents the need for grace, it does not suggest how the milk of unearned grace is integrated with the human powers of reasoning and choosing. When God acts in the human person, how can those human powers resist being completely overcome by God? Can we continue to speak of human freedom in such a graced state?

Perhaps the most famous line from Francis Ford Coppola's great film *The Godfather* comes from Don Vito Corleone as he explains how he would persuade a movie producer to give his godson an acting role in an upcoming production. "I'm going to make him an offer he can't refuse." The "offer" that Vito Corleone makes, of course, severely diminishes the receiving party's freedom because it comes with a not-so-subtle threat of violence. In

4. Augustine, *Confessions*, Book 8, section 5.

5. Ibid., Book 8, section 11.

6. Ibid., Book 2. Section 3.

the context of the film, two human wills, both corrupted by sin, compete for dominance. One wins at the expense of the other; for one will to be done, the other must be diminished. The mobster in the movie is not really making an offer that might be accepted or refused; he is simply reducing the other's freedom. It is a sheer matter of force and not persuasion.

In contrast to the Godfather's offer that cannot be refused, Augustine speaks of God's grace as a "congruous call," the divine influence on human will that operates within and according to the God-given nature of human freedom. Human freedom is from God and oriented to God before it can be opposed to God. God persuades and enables the sinner to turn away freely from sin and toward God. The Creator of human freedom, works not in competition or by coercion, but through the mystery of a gracious liberation of our God-given desires. Neither human freedom nor divine providence is left out of Augustine's theology of grace. In his growing dissatisfaction with Pelagius's teachings, however, Augustine became ever more wary of the tendency to give credit to human freedom independent of grace. Augustine insisted that only *because* of God's grace do we have the freedom to achieve our divinely intended goal, our full participation in the life of God. God's grace gives us freedom and restores it when we distort and weaken it by sin.

One of Augustine's scriptural sources was Paul's teaching about the love poured into our hearts by the Holy Spirit (Rom 5:5). Pelagius's moral rigor replaced this loving God with something like a drill sergeant: God expects us to shape up and has given us the freedom to do just that. Monks and moral teachers such as Pelagius were certainly right to find in the New Testament the call to moral conversion; in their insistence on our obligation to turn from sin and toward God, they were responding to a central theme in the teaching of Jesus and the early Christian tradition. But the development of Christian thought is driven by new questions arising out of new circumstances or challenges to the faith. The New Testament writers do not raise the question that came to the fore in the dispute between Pelagius and Augustine: when God bestows grace on the human soul, is that gift given to those who, independent of grace, merited it or at least were disposed to receive it?[7] For Augustine, love itself—the longing built into the human heart—is a gift of God's love that is directed to God as to its goal. We come from, are made for, and return to God. The entire drama of grace and freedom is God's gift of love.

After Augustine, the problem that remained for the medieval theologians to work out was this: if all is grace, then how do we distinguish between the grace that heals us of the wound of sin and the grace that elevates

---

7. See Lonergan, *Grace*, 4.

us to the state of being worthy to share in the divine life? The ancient notion of salvation as deification (*theosis*) is the elevation of human nature, apart from the fact of sin. How are the two actions of grace related?

The Medieval Synthesis

One of the most important developments in the theology of grace occurs in the thirteenth century. Augustine's reflections on grace were in a psychological key; his own experiences, combined with his training in classical rhetoric, gave his work a persuasive force that continues to ring true. The rhetorical and symbolic horizon within which Augustine and the rest of the early Fathers usually wrote, however, is not the only possible horizon. A new theological situation emerged and the rise of new questions, stimulated by changing cultural circumstances. By the twelfth century, as a result of increased trade and the rise of European cities there emerged a humanistic renaissance, a cultural movement that sought to explore all aspects of what it means to be human. In this new climate, which witnessed the birth of the European universities, theologians again turned their attention to the problem of reconciling grace and freedom. This time, however, the circumstances dictated a shift in perspective—from Augustinian rhetoric to medieval metaphysics.

To understand this change in mental perspective, we have noted that the human person is capable of a shift from the "dramatic" to the "theoretical" pattern of experience. As we have seen, Lonergan calls this a shift in the stages of meaning. The dramatic pattern is intent upon things as they affect us: the aesthetic pleasure of the bird watcher, the care and concern of one who cares for a sick parent, or the experience of the first disciples upon encountering the Risen Lord. Augustine's concerns reflect the dramatic pattern of consciousness; he wanted to understand the ways in which God's grace affected him in his own particular situation. His *Confessions* tells the dramatic story of how in one soul God's grace overcame the weight of his sin and transformed his life. We have discussed the intellectual pattern of experience as preoccupied with the relationship of things to other things: the ornithologist measuring a bird's wing speed and relating that to its life span, or the health care professional researching possible causes of a disease, or Athanasius, defender of the creed of Nicea, formulating a proposition to express the relationship between the Father and the Son.

Thanks to the reintroduction of Aristotle's metaphysics to Christian Europe in the twelfth century by Arab scholars, the theology of the medieval scholastics shifted from a dramatic to an intellectual pattern of experience.

Aristotle's philosophy, unlike that of Plato which had been the dominant influence on Christian theology before the Middle Ages, was systematic; its ideas were linked together by mutually related meanings. Following Aristotle, the medieval scholastics now wanted an explanation—a theory—of God's grace operating within human freedom. Thomas Aquinas (1224-1274) was the greatest representative of this new age in which much of theology shifted from a monastic style of prayerful reflection on the symbols of sacred scripture to a more "scholastic" or theoretical style. A new intellectual pattern of inquiry was emerging from the ferment of cultural change in the cities and their new universities. This change in theological method signaled the rise of what would today be called a "systematic" theology in which the meanings of precisely defined technical terms were now determined not by their symbolic and experiential force but by their relations with other such terms linked within a system.

In this changed context, the focus of theological work on the reality of grace was not psychological but metaphysical. In other words, the question posed had to do not so much with the human drama of grace in the concrete circumstances of life as with an explanation of how this reality called "grace" works within the human person who continues to be free. The breakthrough in this effort was made possible by the invention of a technical term—"the supernatural"—credited to Philip the Chancellor, a predecessor of Aquinas at the University of Paris.[8]

The term "supernatural" is fraught with potential misunderstanding. To clarify how it functioned in the thirteenth century, consider first that, in one sense, absolutely every good thing is given by God. To bring this home you need only realize that the next breath you take, the next beat of your heart, the very fact that you *have* a heart and lungs, is due to God's creative and sustaining favor. But if all is grace, what was Augustine talking about when he described his conversion? For example, how could the theologians speak of the transforming gift of continence in Augustine without, on the one hand, imagining it as an alien divine "stuff" added from outside, imposing on his freedom or, on the other, reducing it to a simple matter of human effort? Philip and the theologians like Aquinas who followed in the thirteenth century invoked the term "supernatural" to denote the realm of grace, where "nature" is the realm of created things and agents. The theorem of the supernatural liberated the theologians to talk about nature within its own realm, apart from any consideration of grace. This is not to say that we ever find the realm of nature in the concrete as separated from grace, but it

8. For a succinct statement on the shift to theory in the doctrine of grace, see Lonergan, *Method*, 309–10.

does mean that there can be a vigorous examination of creation according to its own laws, tendencies and modes of operation. But as we have seen in the chapter on God and Creation, none of these laws, tendencies and modes of operation apply to their Creator. The word "nature" is an abstraction, as is "supernatural," because it does not correspond to any actual human being's lived situation. A purely natural human being would be sinless, and (other than Jesus) that is not a human being in the world.

The systematic relation of the terms "nature" and "supernatural" means that they can and must be distinguished but not separated without a loss of understanding. Philip's definition of "the supernatural" did not add anything new to what the tradition had known all along about the need for God's healing grace. It did, however, allow the theologians to give full attention to the way in which human nature works without continually worrying about how a higher power might be altering it. The laws of human freedom, or any other laws of creation, simply do not apply to God, the maker of free agents. As their source, God is not within that created order. The term "supernatural" created a distinction that allowed for an uninhibited inquiry into the workings of the world, including human nature, because it eliminated the mistaken desire to place divine grace and human effort on the same level. In the human realm, people do not cease to operate in a human way when they receive God's grace. In fact, it is just the opposite: we cannot be fully human without the cooperation of God's grace.[9]

Philip's term "supernatural," therefore, has nothing whatsoever to do with a layer of divine favor separable from the built-in and divinely intended goal of every human life. This misreading of the medieval idea of the supernatural, popular in the nineteenth and early twentieth centuries, imagined that grace has its own powers which, when conferred, are added on top of those of a self-sufficient human nature. This misinterpretation presented human nature as having a natural end or goal that fell short of God; grace was above nature, and was added on to or external to our natural way of being human. What is lost in this view is an understanding of the very destiny of the human being, which is God alone, our elevation to a share in divine life. Human longing, the deepest desire of the human heart, finds its destiny in God. Without that destiny, desire might function in partial ways to aid us during our allotted time, but finally, there is no "finality," no goal, no end to the journey. It is this destiny—this *telos* or target inscribed on the human heart—that gives life its desire and inclination toward God.

The "extrinsic" misreading of the term "the supernatural" is linked to Augustine's key insight regarding the unearned, unmerited gift-like quality

9. See Lonergan, *Grace*, 303–15, esp. "The Theory of Cooperation."

of grace. The unmerited quality of grace—grace as a pure gift—led some to picture human deliberation, choice and action as operating independently of God's saving grace. Grace is then imagined as added on to an already complete human nature.

By the thirteenth century the theologians in the West had accepted the essential elements of Augustine's critique of the Pelagians. In continuity with this tradition, Aquinas taught that the natural desire for God is not enough to heal us of the effects of sin.[10] To be healed of our alienation from God and other people we need a new and higher principle of action and being. When God provides what we need, the human desire for God is graced with the means for its own fulfillment. The divine friendship makes it possible for human beings to achieve the end for which they are made. The graced human being, then, is thoroughly human; God not only respects and preserves the integrity of human freedom but causes it. Freedom, weakened by sin, is liberated to be fully itself. God's grace becomes the principle of action in the converted human being, in whom there is human freedom precisely because of the action of grace.[11]

Human nature, with its reason, freedom and natural desire for God, is completed by faith, hope and charity, the three "theological virtues," so called because they are God's gifts which transform our living and orient us toward the properly human end God intends for us. Grace is not, therefore, something that is added onto an already complete nature but is that divine friendship which makes it possible for our natural desire to reach its goal. God is not increased by creation, nor diminished without it. The distinction between God and creation is itself a part of creation and therefore does not determine what is possible for God. To put this simply, God has freely made the distinction, which exists, along with the rest of creation, to express God's glory. The world is not the given reality within which God operates; creation is not something that happens in an already-there world. Rather, all of creation, including the very fact that there is anything other than God (the distinction between God and the world), is as it is because God freely made it that way.

The free human act is always that of a creature with a God-given goal or end. Freedom does not, therefore, include the power to choose our end. That has been given already by the Creator; God our goal draws us into a

10. Lonergan's view is that, although a world order without grace is hypothetically possible for God, in fact the actual world order is oriented by natural desire to know God, which can only be fulfilled by grace. See Lonergan, "Natural Desire," 81–91. See also "Supernatural Order," 53–255. For an historical study of the problematic notion of "pure nature" in modern theology, see Duffy, *Graced Horizon*.

11. See Stebbins, *Divine Initiative*, 87–89.

full participation in the life of the Holy Trinity. The divine action of drawing or luring the human being into the divine life, therefore, must never be
imagined as in competition with our own human desires. Only a distorted
human desire, which leads to sin and therefore alienation from God, is contrary to this pull of grace.

Scholasticism Degenerates

If Aquinas marks the highpoint of the medieval theology of grace, the
theological tradition after Aquinas developed an unfortunate tendency,
beginning with Duns Scotus (1264–1308), to imagine competition between
Creator and creature. God's assistance was conceived as external to the creature's will. Scotus downplayed the intelligibility of God's creation: he insisted
that human reason cannot know nearly as much about God's purposes as
earlier generations had supposed. In other words, the goal built into created
things—the teleology of creation—is detached from creation's intelligibility.
The result was a separation of intellect and will and the implication of an
arbitrary freedom. With the downgrading of intellect came the upgrading
of a freedom detached from its intelligibility.[12]

Scotus thought of the human will as the absolute origin of choices;
freedom is utterly autonomous to the point of severing it from intellect. This
makes God's will arbitrary—we cannot begin to understand why God does
what in fact God does. Such presumptions created serious problems for an
understanding of grace and freedom. Within Scotus's theological horizon
(which became increasingly common in theology after the thirteenth century and is often identified as nominalism) the language of grace will conjure
up pictures of two very unequal agents: the human being and a powerful
not-to-be-denied Being. In other words, if you think of your freedom and
God's grace as in any way on the same level with regard to choosing the goal
of human life, then you have (perhaps unwittingly) reduced God's activity in
the world to creaturely action.[13] The picture creates a pseudo-problem and
cannot do justice to the theological question of grace and freedom because
it presupposes Duns Scotus's notion that we are not only free to cooperate
with God but we are also free to choose our destiny. Such a notion does
not adequately take into account the implications of the doctrine of creation
that we have discussed in the previous chapter. If all of creation is naturally

12. On Scotus's presupposition that the will is free to choose its end, see Lonergan,
Grace, 420n. See also Burrell, "Aquinas and Scotus," 105–29.

13. On the confusion that the "anthropomorphic fallacy" causes, see *Grace*, 322–24
and 446.

inclined toward its Creator, each creature according to its particular nature, then human freedom is called to God as the fulfillment of its desire.[14] Human freedom is not arbitrary and the God-given orientation to divine mystery is not chosen; that orientation can only be frustrated by sin, which David Burrell aptly describes as "a holding back from letting oneself be caught up into the full dynamics of action."[15]

Any position that fails to recognize the human person's natural desire to know God does not recognize the need to think about grace without imagining it as interfering with human thinking, deciding and acting. It was to avoid this confusion that the term "supernatural," as Philip and Thomas Aquinas used it, was conceived. "The supernatural," properly understood, causes the Scotist conundrum to vanish; once one realizes that there is no created analogue to God's causing, human freedom and divine grace can never be in competition. The term, when not distorted into an image of something added on to human nature in some external fashion, will correct the tendency of the imagination to picture God's actions in the world, and on our freedom, as being an alternative to or functioning alongside of natural human powers. As created, freedom operates within the universe governed by God's eternal and unfathomable wisdom, but as true human freedom it works according to its own integral nature. God is not an external agent whose involvement in human affairs signals our enslavement. God's saving grace is liberation of what is authentically human; our freedom and our dependence on God's grace increase proportionately.

Having eliminated any competitive version of the grace-freedom relationship, freedom is best understood as "being for love." We come from and are meant to return to God, our Source and Fulfillment. God does not make us an offer we can't refuse—but by drawing us into a relationship of love and friendship.

This relationship requires freedom; the human person must be free to respond in love to God's invitation to a new life. Love, mercy, forgiveness—these realities simply cannot exist without freedom. God is the author of human freedom Who draws the free creature toward the ultimate Good, which is God alone. God, in other words, is our own deepest desire, the cause and ultimate target of the desires of the human heart. As our end, given in our beginning, God calls us out of our own egoism and into the life of love.

Our love for God is a gift of God's love for us. This means that our response to God is not that of mere gratitude toward a superior but is rather

14. See Lonergan, *Early Works 1*, 43.

15. Burrell, *Freedom*, 125.

one of authentic and free response in love. Jesus says in the gospel of John that he call his disciples not servants but friends (John 15:7–17). We are made to be friends of God and our lives are oriented toward that unchosen, already given goal. This friendship is what Saint Paul speaks of when he says that if anyone is in Christ he is a new creation (2 Cor 5:17). Anything in contradiction to this love, anything that prevents us from loving fully, blocks our becoming a new creation.

A Contemporary Transposition

As the zenith of thirteenth century scholasticism, Thomas Aquinas brought systematic order to Christian teachings that had evolved over centuries. As is true of all thinkers, however, Aquinas's horizon was limited. The centuries following the thirteenth saw massive cultural upheavals. The scientific revolution changed thinking about the natural world while historical consciousness revealed the fact of substantial change in matters that were thought to be changeless. Finally, there is the modern attention to the human subject whose operations intend the objects on which science and historical analysis centered.[16]

In a cultural climate that places great stock in the experience of the person, Lonergan's approach to grace and freedom integrates psychological, sociological and historical insights that have emerged in the modern period. Lonergan retains the great metaphysical achievement of Aquinas while integrating Augustine's interest in the psychological experience of grace within a modern and post-modern context. His transposition to this new cultural situation means that we recognize the human person as a project, a being in process, and so grace and freedom operate within the context of human development. Quentin Quenell, commenting on Lonergan's theology of grace, puts it this way: "We do not begin [life] in possession of the development which only living itself can furnish us with. We begin as a self which is the center of its own universe and only gradually do we come to perceive another self which we could—and know we should—become."[17] Our growing awareness of the self we should become—and our means of becoming it—is the operation of God's grace in our lives. Lonergan illustrates the project of self-making by noting that "each of us is engaged in publishing the one and only edition of ourselves."[18] This developmental process is free and yet is also completely within and a part of the world governed by God's

16. See Lonergan, "Mission," 27–28.

17. Quenell, "Grace," 171.

18. Lonergan, "The Subject," 83.

providential care. Being in love with God—a state of being that is itself a gift of God's love for us—propels and directs our development toward authentic living. To speak paradoxically, grace makes us willing to live in a state of free, loving openness to God's will in all things.

What moves us is what we love—and what we love has been given to us as a gift. We are more likely to love one who has loved us first. Love requires that we ask questions about how to live. Being in love with God is not a vague emotion; it is a trajectory, at the heart of an individual's project of self-making, toward ultimate truth, goodness and beauty, which can be nothing but God. God's gift of love is felt in the nagging discomfort we feel when we cannot understand something that we know is important to get right. God's love produces the shame we feel when we violate our consciences. Divine love creates the deep longing we have for what is true, good, and beautiful. But "love" here does not necessarily have a romantic connotation; sometimes there is little feeling that accompanies it. At times, love will take the form of a dogged persistence in the tasks that must be performed if we are to remain true to ourselves, which means true to the gift of God's love. In these existential experiences God is not operating as an external force but rather is acting upon us as the very drive that propels us toward a more authentic life.[19]

Conclusion

You may have seen the New Yorker cartoon of a man kneeling at his bedside, praying, "I asked You, in the nicest possible way, to make me a better person, but apparently You couldn't be bothered."[20] The picture evokes a smile because it is obvious that something is missing in the theological understanding of the man on his knees. We can supply that missing insight as follows: grace is the divine initiative becoming actual in our intelligent and free responses. The heart flooded with God's love enkindles the mind and sends us into the world to act according to the gift. With the help of divine friendship, we are able to do what we could not otherwise do. We are not God's puppets but rather agents seeking to come to that end for which we have been created.

Reason and human freedom do not have to be compromised in order to affirm the necessity of grace to achieve human fulfillment; it resides in the soul as its divinely intended goal and not as one option among many.

19. See the index references in Lonergan, *Method* to "Love," 390, and "Being-in-love with God" in Lonergan, *Second Collection*, 285.

20. J. B. Handelsman, Cartoonist. *The New Yorker*, September 14, 1998.

The horizon of one's whole being, the satisfaction of one's desires, doesn't take away our freedom but rather makes it possible, builds on it and thus raises it up. God's love for us, which is often experienced as our loving God and our neighbor, enables, empowers, and therefore gives freedom. "Where the Spirit of the Lord is," Paul claimed, "there is freedom" (2 Cor 3:17). The Spirit of love—the bond of Trinitarian love that unites the Father and the Son—is the source and fulfillment of human freedom. We have freedom so that we may grow in the bond of charity, so that we may share in the very life of God.

6

Redemption

THE FUNDAMENTAL GOODNESS OF God's creation is recognized by all
three of the Abrahamic religions: Judaism, Christianity and Islam. The
religious vision of the world as a good creation, however, is not blindness to evil in the world; such a vision springs from the conviction that
the Creator is utterly good, and so that which issues from God is also
good. The governance of this creation provides an order for the world
through laws natural to it. Plenty of things are not right with the world:
nations are at war, people are enslaved or oppressed or starve. Evil is a
fact, and it causes many to wonder whether a God of beauty and order
and joy is merely an illusion.

Lonergan raises the question, what kind of fact *is* evil?[1] Where does
it come from, if not from God, whom the creed identifies as "the maker of
all things visible and invisible"? Could there be an Evil God? Surely not, for
then God would not be the maker of all things. Let's think again. The devil,
you say? But is the devil not a creature? If so, he is good—or at least good as
made by the good God, like you and me. If the devil is not a creature, then
there is no devil. Terry Gilliam's delightful film "Time Bandits" includes a
scene in which the Devil is criticizing God's creation as inefficient and ri-
diculous. One of his demon lieutenants naively asks the Devil whether he
himself is not a creature. Instead of answering, the Devil simply points his
finger at the demon, who then evaporates in a puff of smoke. When you
have no intellectual defense, only power remains.

Lonergan's position is in line with the ancient Augustinian notion
that evil is no created thing at all. Recall Saint Augustine's struggle with
the dualism of the Manichees. Mani taught that creation is a tragic mistake resulting from a war between the forces of Light and the forces of
Darkness. Physical, material bodies are used by the Darkness to ensnare
souls, who, as particles or sparks of Light, have their real home in the

1. Lonergan, *Insight*, 710–18.

94

Light. Augustine eventually figured out that the Manichees did not know what they were talking about regarding scientific issues such as the phases of the moon, and their confusion in this realm of knowledge led him to doubt their religious teachings as well.

If creation is good, as Augustine came to understand, then evil is the privation of good. Evil is the word for what's missing. Like blindness, which is a privation of the capacity for sight that should by nature belong to a person or other sighted animals, evil is the lack of what ought to exist but doesn't. Evil is a fact like blindness or darkness are facts: the fact of deprivation, of something missing. Blindness is not, however, a thing that might be studied by physiologists or physicians. To call blindness "no thing" does not thereby make the blind to see.

Physical evils such as the pain that results from an unintended injury or illness are not evils in the fullest sense; they are evils only by analogy. They are "like" moral evil only in the sense that they are deprivations. A limp is the lack of a normal or healthy stride and results, perhaps, from a defect in the leg, not from the leg itself. A tumor, as a material thing, is good because it is a dimension of created being. Still, the blindness, derangement or other malady that results from the tumor deprives the body of some function. All sensitive beings eventually lose functions that are created to be temporary, and that loss often entails pain. God's creation of a world in which there are sensitive beings results in the reality of pain. If evil is not a created thing, then it must be that God allows physical evil so that the universe can evolve as it is intended. We in fact have this kind of world: the kind in which some things diminish, suffer deprivations and eventual extinction, for other things to come into being and flourish. The interconnectedness of things and their mutual dependency—the sort of systemic relationships that natural scientists study and that Lonergan explained as "emergent probability"[2]—reveal that the world we have, the only one that we know about, is one in which there will be loss and deprivation as conditions for the evolution of the world. From this angle, biological death is simply part of the natural processes of life.

What Lonergan added to this traditional Christian understanding of the fact of evil is his analysis of human consciousness and its need for development. On the level of theory he proposed an explanatory account of the roots of moral failure within the developing human person.

2. On emergent probability, see Lonergan, *Insight*, 126–62.

Moral Evil

Just as there is deprivation in the aspects of the world studied by natural science, so too there is moral deprivation in human relationships; this is evil in the fullest and most proper sense. We learn to make our way through life by correcting our mistakes. To be human is to be a creature who, through mind and heart, is meant to bring goodness into the world, to extend and develop the good creation by contributing to the human community's efforts to bring about authentic progress. As we bring more good into the already good creation, or as we refuse to do so, we are at the same time also creating ourselves. Becoming human is an achievement of thought, decision and action. Sin is the breakdown of that development.

Sin introduces moral evil into the world and impedes our participation in the good of order. The world requires our personal growth and development so that we might make our contributions to social order and historical progress. What *should be* in the world *is not* when we refuse to fulfill our human potential; sin is in that sense inhuman. If you think about what might be called particular sins you will notice that one can speak of them as failures. Most generally, sin is the failure to love in some way. Violence, for example, is the failure to be at peace, and greed is the failure to share. These failures deprive the world of some good, which is now poorer because it lacks what God intended to bring into being through human contributions. And those failures make similar ones more likely in the future: violence leads to more violence, for how are we to stop those who would harm us? Greed can become a social habit, or even an institution justified by false theories of the "goodness" of selfishness and the "evil" of generosity. The corruption of consumer behavior through mendacious advertising allies with the perverse attempt to satisfy the heart's longing with an accumulation of superfluous products.

To speak of evil as a lack, a privation, does not minimize the suffering that it produces. Of course, human beings make relatively innocent mistakes because learning is a matter of trial and error. But when we refuse to try, to learn, to act—when we refuse to obey the transcendental precepts—then we have in a sense refused the gift of life. In our passivity, we sit out the game and refuse to make our contribution to God's world-in-the-making. In other words, we contribute to the disorder of the world; some goodness and meaning are missing because of our resistance to the divine pull of our destiny. Authentic human living is an instrument of God's ongoing creative and redemptive activity. An attentive, intelligent, reasonable and responsible life promotes progress while evil results from our failure to develop.

An example of the refusal to be intelligent is found in Primo Levi, *Survival at Auschwitz*. Levi reached out to break off an icicle—he had been without water for some time—but the guard would not allow him to have the ice. When Levi asked a guard "why," the reply was, "*Hier is kein warum*," "Here, there is no *why*."[3] In other words, there in the concentration camp, the place that best symbolizes the absurdities of the twentieth century, meaning has been banished along with all sense of truth or goodness or purpose. Evil lacks being, and so lacks intelligibility. Evil makes no sense. Drifting through life, thoughtlessly obeying the ever-changing common opinion of one's social group, following the crowd, accepting the unstable and often oppressive standards of "the way things are," is not only the construction of an utterly passive life, but the encouragement for others to do the same. Here we don't ask *why*. But is that the way it must be?

Is it enough for individuals to recognize evil and to avoid it? I some-times hear people say that life on earth is a test devised by God to see if we can do just that. The Christian notion of redemption often suffers from such reduced understanding. The biblical witnesses as well as the great theological traditions of Christianity do not justify a view of salvation in Christ as passing a test; they do not justify a strategy whereby we "wait it out" making the best of life until we can join the race car driver Dale Earnhart who, according to the bumper sticker, has "gone to race in a better place." To wait without working to improve the world is to be inclined toward conformity to the surd, the "false fact" of evil in the world.[4]

Passivity cannot be justified by some version of "the myth of the way things are." The parables of Jesus call this myth into question. To imagine that the social surd is an aspect of reality to be understood is to encourage the development of ideologies that can make the uprooting of evil that much more difficult.[5] How can you explain what has no intelligibility? What is needed is what Lonergan has called the "inverse insight" that recognizes, not that evil is intelligible, but precisely the opposite, that evil is the social surd, that which possesses no intelligibility.[6] And yet, such an insight is truly an enrichment of our knowledge which sets us on the path to a greater understanding of what the solution requires. If we know that the social surd is indeed absurd, then we will not try to maintain it with phony theories that have presupposed "the myth of the way things are," the mistake that we must accept and

---

3. Levi, *Survival*, 29.
4. Lonergan, *Understanding*, 236.
5. Lonergan, *Insight*, 196–269.
6. Ibid., 43–50, 709, 711.

explain even the irrationalities that have become objectified in institutions and customs, rather than work to achieve what should be.

Bias

If nothing ever impeded the human desire to know—if there were no obstacles to the drive to understand all of being—then the world of human relationships and the institutions created by and determining them would be quite different from the way we experience them. There is no denying that the desire is too often partially blocked or derailed. In his analysis of human development Lonergan has identified three basic ways in which attentive, intelligent, reasonable and responsible living breaks down. The three breakdowns fall under the category of bias.

The biases impede authenticity by discouraging intelligent, reasonable and responsible behavior. Individual Bias encourages us to choose what seems to be satisfying at the time at the expense of what is good in the long run. Individual bias can often promote the bias of one's group. The love of self, family, company or country is good, but one's identification with an institution or association or church or ethnic group or political party can encourage a blind spot. The good of the group is not the entire good or the only good worth promoting. Examples of group bias are easy to find. The history of revolutions reveals a pattern whereby oppressed groups, when they manage to overthrow their oppressors, can assume their former enemies' role as the new oppressors by recreating similar structures that had formerly kept them in subjugation. The oppressed are now the oppressors.

In addition to Group Bias and complicating it is what Lonergan calls General Bias. The common sense of a culture—the common knowledge and know-how of a people, what "everybody knows"—tends to see itself as the final arbiter of what is intelligent. Recall that in our discussion of drama and theory we noted that theory treats things as they are related to one another. The solar system, for example, rather than the morning sun's location in the east, explains why we see the sun rise in the east every morning. General bias ignores the distinction and tries to solve problems by insisting that they must be understood if at all in terms of things as related to us; in other words, general bias insists that all problems be solved by some form of common sense. Specialized theoretical knowledge is, from the horizon of this bias, "ivory tower" speculations. The expression "purely academic" in this context usually means "holding no practical value," which is to imply, "with no value at all." If a theory cannot show an immediate practical value or usefulness, there is little hope that a better understanding of the problems will receive a proper hearing from those who are determined to judge everything from a perspective that derides theory. Common sense, in other words, sometimes devolves into common nonsense.

When analysis of the religious, cultural, or political complexities of the strategy are given insufficient attention, general bias is at work. General bias is not absent in those inhabitants of the "ivory tower" that common sense often derides.[7] In the universities, traditional educational and research basics can be sacrificed in favor of seemingly more practical, technique-oriented courses of study. Competing philosophies within the academy can appear to have no resolution, but this stalemate is no matter to common sense: their divergences don't seem to make a difference in the practical affairs of the world and so do not garner much thought or attention. After all, many forms of common sense tell us that philosophy is "subjective," a mere matter of opinion. And opinion cannot be judged to be true or false. But there is no disputing the right way to check blood pressure or to balance accounting ledgers and schools can show with numerical data their success in training their students in the demands of nursing or business skills. These sorts of issues are practical matters.

We are led to ask, what makes conversion happen? Is religion relevant to conversion? The middle-class comfort in which so much religion finds itself in the United States today would suggest that, at least, the needed individual and social transformation is not an automatic consequence of religion. America seems to be replete with religious décor in retail sales, politics, and leisure activities, but in practice religion is often tamed, domesticated and put to service to help the economy or the latest political election. Jesus' birthday boosts retail sales in November and December as family credit card debt climbs; opinion polls show the phrase "family values" to be an attention-getting slogan for a candidate's electoral campaign in times of cultural uncertainty or confusion. The complex question of cultural decline does not receive much meaningful public discussion in an age of rapid fire images, personal attacks and misleading sound bites. In such circumstances, inattentive, unintelligent, unreasonable and irresponsible thought and action find fertile soil.

In the case of each kind of bias there is a failure to be intelligent, reasonable, responsible. The reasonable solution consequently does not find its way into the concrete situation. Some form of the myth of the way things are is often in the background, a myth that discourages intelligence, reason and

7. On theoretical bias, see Doyle, "Vatican II."

responsibility to protect a particular good at the expense of the common good or the good of order.[8]

But if human beings are free, is it possible that we might so abuse that freedom that we utterly destroy ourselves and thus thwart God's intention to make us God's lovers? The Christian faith insists that God can and does bring good out of evil. We do not name *evil* a mystery in the same sense that we name *God* a mystery. Evil is instead a problem in the sense that there is a solution to it.

We commonly use the word mystery to identify what we do not understand. The crucial difference between the incomprehensible mystery of God and the problem of evil is this: we cannot understand evil since it is not understandable—it is rather irrational or absurd. As the Nazi soldier pointed out to Primo Levi what he had already experienced many times, here in this concentration camp, here where the order of human relationships has been distorted into massive suffering and death, your "why," expressing the distinctively human drive to understand, will be utterly frustrated: there is simply no meaning to be understood here. Evil makes no sense because it contradicts God's intention whereas God's intelligent intention is incomprehensible because it is completely intelligible, and therefore transcends the reach of human intelligence. Evil is not a mystery that we must submit to and accept as if it were fate. Whereas submission to the mystery of God increases our understanding, love, and freedom, submission to evil enslaves us to a stupid and hate-filled way of life.

But *how* does God bring good out of evil? First, we should notice that this conviction of faith does not say that evil is an illusion even if it is correct to say that evil is *no thing*. Lonergan calls evil a "false fact" because it is in the world but it contradicts God's intention for the world. Second, we must recall what it means to say that God is incomprehensible: it means that what God does for the sake of our salvation can be shown to be "fitting" for our condition, but that fitting intelligibility does not extend to a complete explanation. Complete understanding belongs only to God—or better put, God *is* complete understanding. To put it colloquially, we human beings are on a "need to know" basis: what we need to know are the truths and their implications in human living that are necessary for our salvation. We need to know and appropriate the teachings, ministry, death and resurrection of Christ. God can bring good out of evil, and we have been given the example of Christ as its ultimate expression. The solution remains a mystery in God but it is the solution to the *problem* of evil.

---

8. Lonergan, *Insight*, 254–57.

The situation is not hopelessly mired in biases of one sort or another. In addition to the discouraging myth of the way things are, there is also a counter-pull toward the good and the true. There is, in other words, the force of the *telos* of human life that we discussed in earlier chapters, a built-in desire to understand, to know, to love: a desire for God. Religion when it is working well serves to encourage our pilgrimage toward this *telos*. For Christians, the cross of Jesus is the prime encouragement to break the fetters of bias and sin. Rather than indulge a passive waiting for a reward in the afterlife, Jesus' example is God's way of saying something much more interesting and life-giving. What Lonergan called "the law of the cross" is the solution provided by God to solve the problem of evil.

The Law of the Cross[9]

The great tradition of Christian faith, contrary to some recent aberrant expressions, understands redemption to be in history, not merely at the end of history. Salvation in Christ has to do with peace and social order, not simply with an individual's afterlife. And yet, it is not rare to encounter an inauthentic reading of the New Testament teaching concerning the "Second Coming of Christ." Lonergan noted that such a misinterpretation tended to make Christians passive in the face of the social ills of the day.[10] Views of history that result from this passivity are an open invitation to theories of society and history that provide less than adequate explanations. Lonergan's soteriology locates the solution to evil in the self-sacrificial love of Jesus Christ for the world. In Jesus' free acceptance of suffering, he communicated his refusal to protect himself from the evil of those who sought his life if such self-protection would mean the perpetuation of the world of alienation, violence and oppression that constitutes the disharmony of the human race. But what good did it do us that one courageous and virtuous man said to the violence? How can one man's heroism have the cosmic consequences that Christians claim for it?

There are several ways that the documents of the New Testament express the importance of the cross. His death is a sacrifice, a ransom (an image of commercial exchange), and a priestly intercession. We are talking about symbols here: Jesus was not actually a sacrificial victim burned on the Jerusalem altar; he was not actually a debt paid to someone holding sinners as ransom; nor was Jesus a priest. These varied expressions are symbols

9. The magisterial treatment of Lonergan's soteriology is Loewe, *Lex Crucis*, 283–368.

10. Lonergan, *Papers 1958*, 76.

taken from the world of the early Christian Church that, in Lonergan's view, all point to a basic claim: that in some way Jesus' death on the cross brings salvation to the world.[11] The role of theology is to explain through analogy how this can happen.

Lonergan argues that the mystery of the cross has to do with the transformation of evil into good, for God can do this, and in fact does it through the law of the cross. Love motivates Christ to accept evil without retaliation, to bear the burden of suffering that results from others' evil act. That loving response—not hatred or retaliation but self-sacrifice—is transformative. Jesus raised from the dead is the hope of those who follow in this path of love whereby the cycle of retaliation can be broken. Death accepted in love—death to the old way of retaliation and the escalation of hatred in response to offenses—is transformed by God into new life, not just for Jesus at that time but for us in the form of a promise. Faith in the resurrection is the fundamental horizon from which the entire New Testament was written, which makes the Christian scriptures a testament to hope in the sense that none of these documents would have been produced had the disciples of the crucified Christ not experienced his resurrection.[12] The cross is not the end of the story.

And yet, the cross is the instrument. Through the New Testament images that affect us on the level of common sense symbolism, we are moved to accept God's solution to the problem of evil. The complete solution will engage every level of reality (physical, chemical, sensitive, psychic, spiritual), and thus will require the natural and human sciences that contribute to our knowledge of every aspect of reality. Hence the need to co-operate with anyone willing to combat evil: humanists, scientists, members of other religions and no religion. As a divine mystery, no one can prove as a philosophical necessity that God has delivered the solution to the problem of evil in the cross and resurrection of Jesus. The "paschal mystery" is not a logical deduction but it does fit our situation.[13] The Christian faith is that nothing will break the cycle of hatred and retaliation other than to call a halt to irrationality: people grasp at what they think they deserve, they strike back, take revenge, refuse to forgive, ignore solutions that require

11. Lonergan's heuristic (philosophical) presentation of the structure of the solution to the problem of evil is in *Insight*, 740–51. His systematic presentation of "the law of the cross" is in Thesis 17 of *De Verbo Incarnato*, to be included in Volume 9 of the *Collected Works*. For an excellent summary, see Loewe, "Law of the Cross," 162–74 and Loewe, *Lex Crucis*, 283–86.

12. On the interpretation of the resurrection as a matter of hope, see Meyer, *Critical Realism*, 120–21.

13. See Lonergan, "The Notion of Fittingness," 507–33.

self-denial. The Christian alternative is the love exemplified in Christ's life, death and resurrection.

But if Christ is our exemplar, if we are to be "conformed to the image of Christ" (Rom 8), then what about the cross? In what sense is the cross intended for me? It is not about denying the desires that make us human but rather about our transformation, our conversion into the new life of resurrection, a life in which these desires are fulfilled. Masochistic imitation of someone's suffering does no good; only love is transformative. Christ's crucifixion points toward a way of life that resists "business as usual" in the world; these images are not life-giving if we imagine them as denigrating authentic human desire. When we deny the ego's inclination to selfishness, for example, or when we repent of our failures, the result is joy in renewed life.

The same point can be made when we consider the matter from God's perspective. The cross is not the will of a bloodthirsty, irrational or sadistic God, as the theory of penal substitution suggests. The interpretation of the cross as penal substitution imagines that God must punish, and so (for some weird or cruel reason) decides to punish the one person who is completely innocent. But what sense does this make? Is such a theory fitting our condition? Does it change us from being stupid to intelligent, from being irresponsible to responsible? Does it create in us a new horizon from which we understand how to be lovingly in the world? Does it change the world itself? No, the meaning of the cross is not punishment but love. Jesus doesn't suffer God's punishment; he suffers the consequences of human evil. When evil causes good choices to be repaid with suffering, then the person who does not back down, who does what needs to be done in spite of the cost, will be sure to suffer. The value of the cross, in other words, is not "out there" in the suffering of a man but rather is the expressed meaning of that suffering which the images of the New Testament communicate.

Conversion is what happens when those images effect the kind of transformation that can transform one's horizon so that the effects of sin can be reversed and the future can open onto one of solidarity and love rather than hatred and violence. The symbolic communication of the cross touches the whole person through the feelings. It is one thing to know in a very passive and non-committal way—acknowledging a truth unaccompanied by any impulse to do something about it. More than a mere notional acknowledgement of information is needed. One needs a "real" apprehension of the reality, a knowledge of what is the case that poses a challenge, in the depths of the soul, to respond in some way. The cross as a symbol communicates several things: the horror of human sin, the love of God for a sinful world, and the sense of needing to follow in Christ's pattern of self-sacrifice in love.

Knowledge alone will not transform us because sin weakens human intentionality, both intellectual and moral. Bias, prejudice, hatreds, traditional suspicions, business as usual, drifting, believing the myth of the way things are—these obstacles to change can only be broken through by an affective symbol that moves us as whole people, that gives us not just information but the courage and the persistence to make radical changes. That is why the cross and resurrection are symbols. Christ's death and resurrection tell us that innocent people suffer because of sin. We are social beings in solidarity with one another for good or ill, and so we inevitably either encourage or discourage one another in the pull toward authentic life.

The world, because of sin, is partly constituted by absurd ideas and practices, the concrete expressions of inattention, unintelligence, irrationality and irresponsibility. When taken to be "the way things are," as if they must be that way, if many are convinced by this status quo myth, then the chances that things will change grow very slim. In other words, the violation of the transcendental precepts can become institutionalized, structural evils. Racism leads to slavery and discrimination; misogyny can exclude women from opportunities for education and leadership. Laissez-faire economic practice can generate theories that blame the poor for their plight. If common sense is the only criterion for decisions, we make things worse by overlooking the solutions that are only available from theoretical perspectives. That oversight will push the cycle of decline one step further. Phony action, accepted as common sense behavior, promotes the pseudo-theories to justify itself.[14] Every problem has a structure that its solution must meet. Christian faith is grounded in the belief that the example of Christ has changed the real world, the world mediated by meaning. Lonergan calls the solution "the law of the cross."

The law of the cross in us is expressed in living the three theological virtues: faith, hope and charity made necessary by the fact of evil.[15] Charity undercuts the cycle of evil. Self-sacrificing love refuses to allow the violence and oppression to be ultimately victorious. We must then hope that this charity is worth it, otherwise we would despair. Faith is the basis of the other two virtues; believing in the solution provides some understanding of the truth of God as related to us. Without that belief, there is little hope that an individual will discover the solution to the problem of evil.

The mystery will also communicate affectively, through feeling; its symbols will bring the head and the heart together and direct the whole

14. Such a situation Lonergan calls the "Longer Cycle" of decline. See *Insight*, 618–56 and 709–52.

15. See Loewe, "Law of the Cross."

human person toward God.[16] As we have seen, Lonergan understands the three conversions to be linked. One who is in love in an unrestricted manner is one who surrenders in love to God, "the basic fulfillment of our conscious intentionality."[17] The religiously converted subject will respond to the imagery of the New Testament that reveals the self-sacrificial love of Jesus and God's unconditional love of humanity. That entails the building up of communal solidarity because the meaning of Jesus has to be communicated if it is to accomplish its goal of the good or order. The outer word comes first in the incarnate meaning of Jesus, then in the mediation of the experience of the disciples in kerygma (preaching) and then in the documents of the New Testament, then in the subsequent tradition.[18]

Through the grace that is given to us through the cross, change is possible. But "through the cross" should not be taken to imply an external or magical process. God effects salvation by the transformation of our intentionality. Grace is necessary for change but the change is really in us. God could have saved us in a different way but in fact chose to do so this way because it fits our condition as "symbolic animals," as creatures who respond in more than simply intellectual ways. The church's job is then to communicate the symbol and its meanings in a way that extends the effects of the death and resurrection of Jesus to those who have ears to hear. The role of theology as systematic is then to ensure that the communication of the law of the cross makes sense within the context of the other truths about God and God's relationship to the universe of being, a task that assists in the communication of the message as faith illuminates reason.

16. *Insight*, 745.

17. *Method*, 104–5.

18. On the inner and outer words, see *Method*, 112–15.

7

God with Us: Incarnation and Divine Transcendence

LONERGAN TAUGHT CHRISTOLOGY AT the Gregorian University in Rome within the required neo-scholastic structure of the day, a structure that he found to be "impossible."[1] As William Loewe and others have shown, Lonergan's insights will continue to be relevant into the future as they are extracted from that outmoded form.[2] In this chapter I intend to communicate some of those insights in a readable way that encourages readers to take the time and effort to explore Lonergan's work in Christology. The scholasticism that disappeared after the Second Vatican Council need not obscure his enduring achievement.

As we have seen in the previous chapter, the God of Christian faith is revealed in the event of Jesus Christ, crucified and risen from the dead. Reflection on this liberating and redeeming grace of the Christ event among the early Christians raised questions about the precise identity of this Jesus of Nazareth. In this chapter, therefore, we explore the meaningfulness of the doctrine of the Incarnation. To anticipate, we want to show, contrary to many of the pictures that suggest themselves to our imagination, that only a truly transcendent God can be incarnate in a fully human being. As we have articulated in chapter 4, "God and Creation," the transcendence of God turns out not to be an obstacle to the affirmation that Jesus Christ is the incarnation of God but a necessary presupposition for it. We will be headed toward the idea that a proper understanding of God's transcendence allows for God to become completely human without ceasing to be the uncreated, unchanging divine Mystery. Along the way we will explore the development of the early disciples' experience of Jesus and how that experience quickly became a cause for serious intellectual struggles. The first concern was to identify the relationship of Jesus to God; the second

1. See Quenell, "Scholasticism."

2. See Crowe, *Christ and History*, for the historical development of Lonergan's work on Christology.

was to work out language to talk about Jesus as fully God and fully human. In other words, the two questions were: (1) who is Jesus, and (2) how can Jesus be both God and human?

Jesus' Own Experience

Lonergan's Christology takes very seriously the implications of the Council of Chalcedon's insistence that Jesus was like us in all things except sin. As sin is the failure of self-transcendence, our understanding of Jesus' experience will be analogous to our own experience of self-transcendence. Lonergan makes the point regarding the importance of the humanity of Jesus:

> We can know nothing about the divinity of Jesus apart from his humanity. For this reason the basic emphasis must be on his humanity and it is only therefore by trying to under-stand this humanity that we will ever reach an understanding of his divinity.[3]

For this reason, it is important to be clear that Jesus had the task of human development and he came to know in a human way. That is why Lonergan insisted that "[i]f we are to think of Jesus as truly a man we have to think of him as a historical being, as growing in wisdom, age, and grace in a determinate social and cultural milieu, as developing from below as other human beings and from above on analogy of religious development."[4] We have been discussing that human way as self-transcendence. To appreci-ate Jesus' experience, as well as the development of the doctrines about that experience, we must have an accurate grasp of our own. "It is in the progressive clarification of Christian experience and in the continuous exercise of spiritual discernment in the Christian community that Chris-tological doctrine developed."[5]

Christian faith insists that Jesus was a human being. Today such an insistence may strike us as strangely unnecessary, yet the early centuries of Christological development as well as the seminary textbooks of Catholic theology through the first half of the twentieth century make it clear that the implications of the claim that Jesus was fully human was not always ap-preciated. The way we interpret the impact he had on his disciples and on the world, starts with this simple acknowledgment. Jesus grew in his human self-transcendence, and in that way, began his response to God's call to love.

3. Lonergan, *Ontological*, 108.
4. Lonergan, "Christology Today," 82.
5. Ibid., 88.

Jesus had faith in God and responded to God's love with a self-sacrificing human love that embodied the very mystery of God as Love Itself. "He learned obedience through suffering," Hebrews 5:7 tells us. If human beings make themselves through their thinking and deciding and acting, then Jesus shared that task with the rest of us. He developed and grew not just in body but in intellect and spirit. He also inherited the wisdom and understanding of the Jewish traditions in which he was raised. All human beings experience these two trajectories, from below as we learn and from above, receiving the gifts of a religious culture that already exists. From below, we seek true understandings of our experiences; as we learn for ourselves the way the world works, we grow in wisdom and knowledge. But we also benefit in this development from the wisdom and knowledge of past human achievements that have been handed on to us. As we have already seen, most of what we learn is not knowledge that we ourselves generate through our own experiences; most of what we know we in fact have by believing. In this regard, Jesus was no exception: he had faith in the God about whom he learned from his Jewish faith. The history of philosophies and religions in the ancient Mediterranean world reveals, amidst all the diversity of teaching and practice, a common search for the true nature of things. Jesus sought within his own tradition to deepen his understanding of the truth about reality and the way of life grounded in that reality. People in the ancient Mediterranean world, like people today, joined religions to burn away the fog of illusion so that conditions for living a good life would emerge.

Jesus was a man on fire with the question of how to live. He shared the human need to "fit" into the true nature of things and not simply the way things were. To be human, however, means to be located, to be human in this time and place, learning this culture and these beliefs. His quest for wisdom, in other words, did not begin in a vacuum. As a faithful Jew of the first century, Jesus studied the Jewish scriptures and the oral teaching about it in the synagogues; his search led him to deepen his understanding of his Jewish tradition. Jesus probably apprenticed himself to a baptizer named John whose reform movement aimed to prepare the Jewish people for the imminent coming of the reign of God. John had some characteristics that were similar to a religious party known as the Essenes, Jews so dissatisfied with the way in which the Temple was being run that they decided to establish their own community in the desert near the Dead Sea, there to await God's coming reform. But unlike the Essenes, John and Jesus remained in society, like the Hebrew prophets, to encourage social and religious change.

In the course of a human life, the knowledge one inherits helps to prepare us for the knowledge that we discover for ourselves; likewise, the knowledge that we discover helps to verify or correct the knowledge that we inherit. It is like driving on a two-way street with an occasional fender-bender or, in some cases, serious collisions. As we have seen in the chapter on redemption, the crucifixion of Jesus represents his fatal collision with the Romans who controlled the land of Israel at the time, with the assistance of some of the Jewish authorities who were trying to keep the nation together under the strain of occupation. Jesus' quest to announce God's kingdom and to fulfill his God-given mission opposed their efforts. Those leaders interpreted Jesus to be a messianic pretender with the potential to lead a dangerous political rebellion, and thus he appeared as a threat to the fragile status quo. When the Romans executed him, the disciples were disillusioned and lost—perhaps some were in utter despair. Then, something happened to convince them that his death was not the end of the story. Their experience of him as in some sense alive and exalted by God—that his life was not a tragic mistake but a life-giving sacrifice—sent them out to communicate the message that in imitation of him was God's offer of redemption.

Jesus and the First Disciples

The first disciples experienced the crucified Jesus as in some sense alive, exalted, raised from the dead; they understood this glorified Jesus as the source of their liberation, the true meaning of their lives. A fundamental assumption of the Christian faith is that the experience of the first disciples is in continuity with the meanings about him that we find in the New Testament. Beginning with the preaching and liturgy of the early church, the first followers of Jesus found themselves spontaneously worshiping Jesus as the risen and exalted Christ.[6] It is the disciples' experience of Jesus as communicated in the gospels, rather than scholarly reconstructions of what Jesus probably did or said, that express God's revelation. Scholarly reconstructions have contributed enormously to our understanding of Jesus and his Jewish context. Historical inquiry into what Jesus might really have said or done helps theologians to control the meanings that they discern in the evangelists' religious portraits of Jesus. However, a theology of Jesus—a "Christology"—cannot be developed merely from historical reconstructions.[7]

As far as we know, Jesus never wrote anything; all that we know of him has been handed down by the church in the form of written

6. "Spontaneously" is used here in the sense that all the early witnesses portray the early church as worshipping Jesus from the beginning of its experience of Jesus as risen or exalted. See Hurtado, *Lord Jesus Christ*.

7. See Loewe, "From the Humanity."

scriptures—especially the gospels—and the traditions of church practice such as worship and theological reflection. In the nineteenth century there began what has been called a quest for the historical Jesus in order to distinguish the words and actions of the Jesus of history from the theological interpretations of him that the early church produced. Many were motivated in this quest by a deep hostility to Christianity. And yet, their basic question was historically relevant: do the four gospels present, in every case, the very words and deeds of Jesus? No, the four gospels are, in fact, symbolically expressed religious interpretations of Jesus and not eyewitness accounts of what he did and said. Starting in the late eighteenth century with Hermann Reimarus, who employed newly developed tools for historical research, scholars probed the Christian scriptures to determine the difference between the actual words and actions of Jesus and the religiously motivated elaborations, additions, selections and arrangements of the materials handed on from those who knew and listened to him. These written gospels represent the third in a three-stage process beginning with the words and actions of Jesus himself, followed by the preaching of his disciples and motivated by the resurrection experience of Jesus as no longer dead but alive in a new way.

The written gospels are virtually the only sources that anyone has for trying to distinguish between the historical Jesus and the resurrection-inspired portrait of Jesus in the New Testament. The nineteenth century quest for the historical Jesus ended in a good deal of skepticism about the possibility of recovering very much of the actual words or attitudes of Jesus. However, a new quest began in the middle of the twentieth century, with much more positive results: the tools developed by scholars to determine the contexts, literary forms and editorial strategies found in the four gospels gave new confidence that certain basic information about the historical Jesus could be found.

The quest to differentiate Jesus' own words and deeds from the theological contributions of the early church continues, but by the start of the twenty-first century it had become much more obvious that the religious and philosophical presuppositions of the historical researcher has a great impact on the final evaluation of the significance of the results of the research, if not on the results themselves. Theologians have come to recognize two things. (1) We cannot return to a naïve, pre-critical time when one blithely assumed that the gospels are eye-witness accounts of what Jesus did and said. Critical history and literary analysis has proven its value and importance in so many areas of scholarship that it would be an irrational flight from understanding to ignore these tools for study developed over the past two hundred years. (2) By itself, however, the results of the historical and literary criticism of the New Testament cannot provide a foundation for presenting a Christian understanding of Jesus because the meaning of Jesus is to be discerned in the impact his life, death and resurrection had on his disciples, and that impact is manifest in signs of self-transcendence. In other words, Christians judge that the early witnesses to Jesus are true not just historically but as manifestations of converted discipleship. In every generation theologians must ask the question: which forms of expression will allow for the possibility of hearing God's word? The first followers of Jesus, in their efforts to communicate the gospel, implicitly asked this same question. The basic message about Jesus in the New Testament has been judged by the community of believers to be the real, authentic Jesus.

As the disciples' memory of Jesus is brought to bear on new situations in the life of local churches, that memory is shaped by preaching, liturgy, letters and finally the ancient biographical narratives of Jesus called "gospels." This "shaping" of the memory of Jesus is driven by the experience *as well as* by the new questions being raised about the meaning of the experience within new and diverse contexts. There was no immediate unity of doctrine or worship or church structure among the diverse communities of the early church; there was, however, the unity created by what has been called "the event of Jesus Christ," that is, the life, ministry and death of Jesus interpreted in light of the resurrection experience of the first disciples and those whom they converted to the Jesus movement.[8] The meaning of any event is always within a context, but the same meaning can be communicated within other contexts; it can be carried from one "location," so to speak, to another. Lonergan calls this process whereby a consistent meaning is represented in a new context "transposition."

Jesus and his first disciples were Jews. The Jesus movement begins within a diverse first century Judaism. The consistent meanings about Jesus to be found among the various literary forms and symbols of the early Christian writings were transposed in diverse ways for diverse audiences. As an example, we can point to the gospel writer John's transposition of what might have been Jesus' own wisdom based teaching into a wisdom pattern of descending/ascending savior figures. Another example is Luke's presentation of Jesus as a Hellenistic philosopher.[9] Similar themes emerge within diverse genres and symbolic forms. In the gospel of Matthew Jesus assures his disciples that he will remain "with them." From the start of the gospel, when he is given the name "Emmanuel" ("God is with us"), to the end of the text in which the Risen Christ promises that "I will be with you

---

8. See Knox, *The Early Church*, 44–50.

9. See Johnson, *Sacra Pagina*.

to the end of the age" (Matt 28:20), the continuing presence of Jesus within the community is a fundamental claim about his continuing salvific presence among those who follow him. Within a very different narrative and theological context, the gospel according to John accentuates not only the continuing presence of Jesus among the disciples but the need for those disciples to "abide" in Jesus (see, for example, John 15:1–10).[10] The authors and their audiences determined the ways in which the message of and about Jesus was put into language. The common event of Jesus, received by the early Christians, was presented in a variety of symbolic ways in the gospels and other texts of the New Testament. The forms of presentation are very different but they point toward the common meaning of Jesus' continuing presence within the community of his followers.

The experience of the Risen Christ, therefore, prompted the need to communicate the meaning of Jesus in different contexts or "paradigms." In the Hellenistic paradigm of the ancient Mediterranean world, there was resistance to the idea that a savior figure could be both divine and human. And so, since only the divine is the source of salvation there arose the question, was Jesus human? Many who took for granted Hellenistic ideas of salvation asked in bewilderment, how could he be fully human if he really was a divine Savior? So, in the early stages of reflection on the meaning of Jesus, the communities had to deal with two basic questions: (1) How can Christians talk about Jesus in his relationship to God, and (2) How could Jesus be human if he was also divine? The theological recovery of Jesus' humanity challenged a widespread image of Jesus as divine with a human appearance. This discredited position sent some in the direction of reducing Jesus' identity to simply a man. Lonergan worked to transpose the ancient dogmas in a way that allowed for the incorporation of modern exegetical and psychological insights.

Development to the Council of Nicea (325 CE)

Lonergan's interpretation of the early church's struggle to understand and articulate Jesus' identity proceeds by way of a dialectical analysis. Lonergan examines the intellectual horizon of the early thinkers to determine the stages of meaning within which the various thinkers were operating. Those limited to common sense symbolism could express the meaning of Jesus only in imagery, leaving questions unasked and unanswered. Those who took their stand on the level of the idea transcended the limits of the imagery, but there remained the question of truth. It required what Lonergan calls the

10. For the theme of abiding in the Gospel of John, see Kinlaw, *Christ*.

"dogmatic realism" of the Council of Nicea to answer the truth question. The meaning and truth of the symbolic communication of the biblical witness could only be grasped by an expansion of the intellectual horizon by defenders of Nicea like Athanasius. The following section will expand on this basic dialectical structure of Lonergan's Christology.[11]

The disciples' experience of the Christ event was one thing and their articulation of it another. Whenever we want to talk about something, we search for the right words, but where do those words come from? Most of the time they already exist. Ordinary things and activities and ideas are the words we must use to talk about new things, and commonly this poses no difficulty for our efforts at communication. We typically understand new things by comparing them to things we already know. We say, "It was like . . ." or "It's the same as . . ." or "Like that, only . . ." We compare two different things and then we qualify them to note the difference between what we already knew and what we have just learned by way of the comparison. Jesus' example will help to make the point. "The kingdom of God is like a mustard seed that a person took and sowed in a field." So, we know what a mustard seed is; now, how is the kingdom *like* that seed that is sown? "It is the smallest of all the seeds, yet when full-grown it is the largest of plants. It becomes a large bush, and the 'birds of the sky come and dwell in its branches'" (Matt 13:31). The kingdom is like the sowing and growing of this seed, but there is much that this agricultural activity does not share with the kingdom of God. Growth and surprise seem to be elements of this symbol of the kingdom, and when this parable is grouped with others that speak of the kingdom, our understanding of Jesus' teaching improves. The images, concepts and language are secondary; the point is to understand, and understanding is prior to the expressions and irreducible to them.

Religious words typically are taken from speech about ordinary things in the world, or of ideas that already exist, but they are qualified in some way to make them serve a new purpose. And so it was at the beginning of the Jesus movement: the disciples used already existing words, images, and ideas from Judaism or from the wider Hellenistic culture that they might use to talk about their experience of new life in Christ. The writer of the gospel of Matthew, for example, drew on Old Testament themes and Jewish apocalyptic imagery to present Jesus as the new Moses while, as we have seen, John appealed to the Jewish model of Wisdom to talk about Jesus and Luke drew upon the Hellenistic philosopher/disciple model to illustrate the meaning of Jesus and his relationship to the church. In every case, however, the older image needed some sort of qualification, updating or correction. For Matthew,

11. See Lonergan, *Triune God: Doctrines*, 199–255.

Jesus is not simply *another* Moses, but the new, better, transcendent Moses; perhaps Matthew even intended to suggest that Jesus was also the new Torah or Covenant itself. For John, the appearance of Wisdom as it functioned in the Jewish wisdom tradition was not sufficient for communicating his understanding of Jesus; and so, the theme of "abiding" was added to the model of wisdom as we have it in the Old Testament scriptures as a way of expressing God's permanent indwelling of God's Spirit in Jesus. And Luke must qualify his philosopher model, of course, by telling the story of Jesus' death on a Roman cross—something that didn't enter into the typical ancient philosopher's biography. Old concepts, models, and images took on new meanings when they were qualified or altered in various ways to indicate what was new in Jesus' life, ministry, death and resurrection.

The process of employing inherited images to talk about the meaning and significance of Jesus continued in subsequent centuries, after the writings of the New Testament were complete (by the early second century). However, because the use of inherited images or concepts to communicate some meaning cannot be adequately expressed by them, a new question arises: where does the inherited notion of the Logos limp? What qualification or alteration needed to be made to do justice to what is different about Christianity's understanding of Jesus as the Logos or Word of God? The "emanation" of the Logos from God that the inherited Hellenistic concept of the logos brings with it leaves important questions unanswered. So, early thinkers advance the cause of Christian theology by bringing the experience of the Risen Christ into dialogue with Hellenistic philosophy, the process of clarifying the difference between Jesus and the Middle Platonic/Stoic Logos was just beginning.

For example, one question that arises from the use of Hellenistic logos models is whether God can relate directly to the world. Does God need an intermediary to interact with the world? Is God constrained or forced, in some way, to hire this subordinate Logos? Is God's transcendence one of distance from the world, as in Hellenistic thought? Or is God's transcendence such that, without ceasing to be unchanging, God can become flesh?

The doctrine of the Logos as the intelligibility of the natural world was not the only influential idea that Christian thinkers took from ancient Stoicism. Most people have heard of an aspect of Stoicism's moral teaching that emphasizes the unemotional acceptance of suffering as a way of dealing with pain and disappointment in life. A "stoical" attitude recommends a pragmatic acceptance of what one cannot change. But a less well-known dimension of Stoic teaching had to do with its notion of reality. Everything that is real, the Stoics thought, was material; their criterion for determining whether something was real as opposed to an illusion was whether it was made out of physical stuff. Such stuff might be big and heavy or light and invisible, but if it was real, it was material. If it isn't material, it isn't real.

This stoic materialist way of thinking was a significant influence on a North African rhetorician and lawyer by the name of Tertullian (d. 222 CE) who wrote a very important work of theology. [12] Lonergan identifies Tertullian's Stoic materialism as the source of his subordinationist interpretation of the claim that the Father and the Son are of the same divine substance. His concern was to state what is distinctive in the Christian understanding of God as one and also three. Tertullian was opposing a Christian thinker named Praxeus who, according to Tertullian, so emphasized the unity in God that he presented the Incarnation as though the Father had become human and suffered on the cross. Tertullian understood that the Christian experience of Christ did not violate the Jewish insistence on the unity of God; there is only one God, not many gods, as in pagan polytheism. At the same time, however, Tertullian did not want to say that God the Father suffered on the cross. But how can such an idea be put into words? How is it possible to talk about the one God whose Logos/Son became human and died on the cross and whose Spirit was sent into the world, without turning the one God into two or three gods?

Tertullian insisted that the Father and the Son were of the same substance and yet, if one is not to imply that the Father was crucified, the Son must also be really distinct from the Father. However, in Tertullian's way of imagining it, this inner word of God became a Son only at the moment of creation; prior to its coming forth as God's speech, it was not distinct from the Father. After the Word/Son goes out of God, the Spirit follows from the same Father after the fashion of a material thing going out of its material source. The sun, for example, puts out rays; a plant puts down roots. The divine "going out" is imagined, spatially and temporally, and this Stoic materialist conception leads Tertullian to subordinate or make inferior the Son to the Father. A reality that comes to be, however, is inferior to one that has no beginning. For Tertullian to speak of Father and Son as being "of the same substance," therefore, did not imply what the creed of Nicea, professed by Christians to this day, will later term *homoousios*, consubstantial or "one in being." Tertullian inherited language that he knew was inadequate to resist Praxeus's interpretation of the Christian experience of God in Christ. Tertullian sought new ways of using the language of his culture but he also took for granted the Stoic materialist assumptions about the meaning of the

---

12. On Lonergan's interpretation of Tertullian and the influence of Stoic materialism, see *Triune God: Doctrines*, 95–107, and Lonergan, "Origins," 244–48.

word "real," and so could not speak of the Logos without making it inferior to the Father. The Logos and Spirit occupy lower (subordinate) ranks than that of the Father, even if the three share the same substance.

The challenge to the early church remained: how to talk of this new experience of God using language that had some currency in the cultures of the ancient Mediterranean world without simply reducing this new experience of the exalted Christ to the meanings that the inherited models, images and concepts previously held? If Stoic materialism encouraged a pictorial presentation of God such that the Son and the Spirit could not but be imagined as subordinate or inferior, a shift in philosophical assumptions about what makes something real would offer a valuable improvement for Christian theology. The forms of Plato's thought that thrived in Egypt in the third century provided such a corrective to Stoicism's presumption that to be real is to be a body. Platonic thinking values the immaterial over the material. In fact, the Platonic assumption is that what is real is ideal. The blueprints of a house, for example, are more real than the brick and mortar house built according to the blueprints. Unlike Tertullian's view that if something is real it has to be material, the Platonic school at Alexandria emphasized the superiority of *spiritual*—in the sense of non-material—reality. Where Tertullian thought of God as a fine, invisible, stretched-out stuff, the theologians in Alexandria in the third century, such as Clement and his brilliant pupil Origen, insisted that it would be absurd and sacrilegious to imagine God as made of matter.

Still, the "idealists" such as Origen did not thereby solve the question of whether the Word of God is subordinate to the Father. Why not? If the idea rather than any material thing is really real, then the idea of God the Father will be different from the idea of God the Word. The Father as ideal source will be superior to His Word, even if they share the same essence or nature. So, we come back to one of Lonergan's basic questions: what is the real? Is it matter? Is it an idea? Or is it something else?

Arius and the Council of Nicea (324 CE)

During the middle of the fourth century an Egyptian priest by the name of Athanasius was being hunted as an outlaw of the Roman Empire. "As the imperial police raced up the Nile to arrest him, Athanasius had his oarsmen reverse their course. As the police passed shouting had they seen Athanasius, he replied, yes, he is quite close. The police sailed upstream as Athanasius returned to hiding in Alexandria itself (where he was the exiled bishop)."[13]

13. Davis, *First Seven*, 102.

Several years before this amusing incident, a Council had met in the small town of Nicea near Constantinople in 324 CE. Eventually that Council was considered by the Christian Church as a key moment in the development of its thinking about God and Christ. This meeting of bishops mostly from the eastern parts of the Roman Empire faced a challenge from a priest, also from Alexandria, by the name of Arius. Against his views, the bishops gathered at Nicea declared that the Son of God made flesh in Jesus of Nazareth was *homoousios*—one in being—with the Father. After the Council many bishops were uneasy with the term because it seemed to imply a denial of the obvious "three" acknowledged by almost all of the sources of Christian faith and practice (the New Testament, worship and religious instruction): the reality of God is Father, Son and Spirit.

The wily priest Athanasius became a staunch defender of the conclusions of the Council of Nicea. He became an outlaw in the empire because those conclusions regarding the Father/Son relationship were not immediately accepted; indeed, certain emperors who followed Constantine (the emperor who called the bishops together in 324) inclined more toward the position of those who preferred a different way of talking about the relationship. Almost forty years after the Council (and having endured significant calumny and persecution), Athanasius was still trying to unite similarly minded Christians who instinctively understood that the three must not be reduced to insignificance in favor of the unity of being that is shared by Father and Son. Athanasius went about his task of persuasion by asking questions of those who could not agree to the new, non-biblical word *homoousios*: What do you mean by saying that there are three in God? Do you mean three gods? Or do you mean that there is one God but three modes of being the one God? He wanted to sort through the confusion surrounding the term that had become so controversial. Athanasius fought for decades, sometimes from exile, to defend this word *homoousios*, often while being hunted by the civil authorities.

Athanasius reports Arius's teaching that God is not only unchangeable and beyond all creaturely characteristics but also that God was in the beginning alone and therefore not a Father because He had no Son. God's desire to create the world first required that God make a being who would participate in God's Wisdom and thereby create the world. This being is called the Son, and his creation in time causes God to become a Father. In Arius's theology, therefore, the Word of God who had become flesh in Jesus of Nazareth was a creature who came into existence at a particular time. Arius is claiming that the *Word* or *Logos* of God spoken of in the scriptures and the Christian tradition is a creature. This creature is unlike (*anomoios*) God in nature or essence, a lower nature, even though it is certainly higher than any other creature. Later, within the history of the human race, this Word also effects God's salvaging of sinful humanity.

Arius inherited the intellectual traditions that dominated the school at Alexandria where he was trained as a theologian. As we have seen above, the shift to a Platonic way of thinking that Origen represents insisted on the utterly spiritual reality of God and rejected as inadequate any imagery that would imply that God is changeable. Such Platonism was clearly an improvement over the Stoic materialist assumptions about reality, but the particular version of Plato's thinking that Origen and (later) Arius had adopted also came with its own limitations. According to this Middle Platonist hierarchy of beings, God was imagined at the top of that pyramid. Just below God is God's Logos or Dyad, the craftsman whom God fashioned to be the architect of the rest of creation.[14]

Arius interpreted certain biblical passages in such a way that they fit this hierarchy that placed the Logos subordinate to the Father. It is true that, on the surface at least, various biblical texts do seem to imply that the Word of God is created. Proverbs 8:22, for example, reads, "The Lord begot me, the first-born of his ways, the forerunner of his prodigies of long ago; from of old I was poured forth, at the first, before the earth." There is also the saying of Jesus in John 14:28: "You heard me tell you, 'I am going away and I will come back to you.' If you loved me, you would rejoice that I am going to the Father; for the Father is greater than I." In response to Arius's interpretation of such texts Athanasius cited texts like Jesus' words in John 10:30: "The Father and I are one" and in John 14:10: "Do you not believe that I am in the Father and the Father is in me? The words that I speak to you I do not speak on my own. The Father who dwells in me is doing his works. Believe me that I am in the Father and the Father is in me, or else, believe because of the works themselves."

Lonergan appealed to Athanasius's strictly logical understanding of *homoousios*: what is true of the Father is true of the Son, except that the Father is not the Son.[15] The claim of Arius—that the Logos is a creature and thus inferior to God—was judged by the bishops at Nicea to be at odds with the Christian experience of salvation in Christ because only God saves. There is, for example, the scribes' dismay at hearing Jesus declare that the paralytic child's sins are forgiven: "He is blaspheming. Who but God alone can forgive sins?" (Mark 2:7).[16] Athanasius insisted that

14. On Arius, see Lonergan, *Triune God: Doctrines*, 137–71.

15. Ibid., 191–99 and Lonergan, "Origins," 251.

16. Although there were many "Judaisms" at the time of Jesus, the dominant Christian tradition came to insist on the identity of the Creator and Savior.

Arius's interpretation of the scriptures was his own and did not agree with the faith of the church. Arius seems to have imposed the Middle-Platonic concept of a subordinate Logos on any scriptural language of equality regarding the relationship between Jesus and the Father. Whatever might have been the influences on him,[17] Arius's idea was that God cannot conduct business directly with the world; instead, God had to make and commission an inferior or subordinate being, "the Son of God," to accomplish God's will. Arius affirmed the transcendence of God, but he thought of this transcendence in a way that did not allow the possibility that the utterly unknowable and transcendent God, the maker of heaven and earth, might be incarnate and known as a human being. Arius's version of the incarnate Logos seems to have been conceived as an intermediary being, neither *homoousios* with human beings nor *homoousios* with the Father. That is why Athanasius spent his long life in exile dodging the authorities and promoting Nicea's judgment. He understood that, as Lonergan put it, that controversial word *homoousios* "is not speculation regarding the essence of the Son. It is a rule about predication."[18]

The Question Shifts

"This was not putting the matter in a careful way." That is Lonergan's evaluation of an image used by Gregory of Nyssa to express the relationship in Jesus of divinity and humanity. The image "compared Christ's humanity, assumed by his divinity, with a drop of water immersed in the sea."[19] Although he opposed Apollinaris's position, Gregory's image reveals how difficult it is to break free of all images when trying to articulate the actual relationship. After Nicea, whose term *homoousios* remained highly controversial for many decades, a new question emerged—one that can be more properly called "Christological." If Nicea focused on the relationship of Father and Son, or God and God's Word, subsequent controversies and councils turned to the question of the relationship of the divine and the human in the one Christ. Let us spend some extended discussion on the doctrine of Apollinaris, bishop of Laodecea, whose thought was formally rejected in 381 CE by the First Council of Constantinople. Apollinaris is an important figure in the early development of Christology because many subsequent efforts to downgrade Christ's humanity stem from Apollinaris. His Christology is an exemplar of a problem that continues to mar the

17. On the influences on Arius, see Williams, *Heresy and Tradition*.

18. Lonergan, *Early Works 3*, 116.

19. Lonergan, *Incarnate*, 259.

understanding of many Christians: that Jesus could not have been fully human. Like Athanasius, Apollinaris became a very enthusiastic cheerleader
for the homoousios of Nicea. In his estimation, the Son of God was "one
in being" with the Father and he could tolerate no resistance to it. But his
staunch defense of the language of Nicea came with an assumption that
Athanasius did not draw. Apollinaris assumed that *homoousios* implied the
replacement of Jesus' human mind with the divine mind. After the union
of human and divine in Christ, in other words, Jesus was no longer making human decisions or thinking as human beings think. His life was now
controlled by God in a way that eliminated human freedom. God could
not, Apollinaris thought, allow the human mind of Jesus to operate while
Jesus was one in being with the Father. Why not?

Apollinaris held that the principle of animation or of movement in
Jesus did not have to be a human soul or mind—in fact, it couldn't be such
a fallible and weak thing. The Word of God, the scriptures tell us, "became
flesh" (John 1) and Apollinaris takes this word "flesh" in a strict sense to
exclude any human mind or soul. The Logos or Word moved the flesh of
Jesus, and that was enough to call him fully human or *homoousios* with human beings. The logic of Apollinaris's argument is difficult to fault, but the
premise—that one can be a human being without a human mind—is not.
Without our human minds, are we not simply animals? With all due respect
for animals—and humans have often shown appalling disrespect for God's
non-human creatures—still, there does seem to be something missing in
any account of what makes us human if we leave out the distinctiveness of
our thinking and deciding.

Like other pro-Nicene thinkers, Apollinaris staunchly defended the
unity of Christ: there cannot be two Christs, only one. Wouldn't a Jesus
who had both a divine and a human mind be a bit divided? maybe even
two people? Apollinaris is right, of course, that such a split Jesus would
make no sense, but Apollinaris purchases the unity of Christ at the expense of his humanity.[20]

The implications of Apollinaris's position are to be found in the distinction between God and creation. We do not know *how* the one Jesus
can have both a divine and a human consciousness or principle of movement because God in God's own self is beyond human comprehension.
Next, we must recall our discussion of grace and human freedom. Apollinaris seems to take for granted that God cannot become human if human nature must include human thinking and deciding. But why should
we suppose that? Why should we doubt that God can become a human

---

20. For details of Apollinarian teaching see Lonergan, *Incarnate*, 185–95.

being—flesh as well as mind? We don't know *how* this might happen since we are talking here about the divine mystery, but if we acknowledge the transcendence of God in the sense that we have already discussed, the transcendence of God frees us of any image or concept that would limit God. Within that context we can at least recognize that it is not impossible for God to become human without ceasing to be God. In the theology of grace, for example, we have seen that a proper appreciation of God's transcendence allows for talk about human freedom and divine grace without bringing them into competition, as if they were two different versions of the same kind of thing. Instead, rather than destroying human freedom, grace is understood as perfecting and completing it.

So too in Christology, the divine nature does not annihilate the human nature of Christ. We do not understand this divine action because God's being is God's doing, and God's being is unknowable. *How* can God use human freedom to achieve God's purposes while the human being remains free? We don't know. But the logic of divine transcendence allows us—in fact requires us—to say both. If God can operate on our freedom without making us less free, there is no reason to doubt that God can set aside the distinction between God and the world and take on a complete human nature. Jesus was not less God the more human he became; instead, one must conclude that Jesus "increased in wisdom and in years [or stature], and in divine and human favor" (Luke 2:52). In other words, Jesus' human consciousness developed in conformity with his divine consciousness. [21] When we acknowledge the divine incomprehensibility, we can acknowledge that the divine Word of God was completely human. The claim is intelligible but not picturable.

Apollinaris's position is yet another case of thinking in pictures about what simply cannot be pictured. Ironically, as hostile as he was to Arius's thought, Apollinaris still shared one of his assumptions: that God's transcendence was limited. For Arius, the divine limitation translated into a reduction of the status of the Logos to a very important creature (God being incapable of becoming human because of God's status atop the Hellenistic hierarchy of being). For Apollinaris, the divinity of Jesus must exclude Jesus' full, intellectual human ability to think and make decisions as a human being. For God to take on a human nature, Apollinaris assumed that the flesh of Jesus must be informed by the divine mind, which has replaced the human mind, otherwise the work of salvation would be jeopardized and probably fail due to the weakness of human thinking and deciding.

21. Lonergan notes that Christ the human being did not have the comprehension of God that "is that knowing of God that God himself has, in accord with the identity of the act of existence itself, and the act of understanding itself" (*Incarnate*, 797).

Apollinaris used the image of a standing person who bends down to lift up one who has fallen. Our flesh has fallen through sin and the standing person (the Logos) does not have to fall down in order to do the lifting. Just the opposite: the fallen cannot lift the fallen. Jesus cannot be one in being with the Father while employing a human mind: Jesus "cannot save the world while remaining a human being and being subject to the common destruction of humans, but neither are we saved by God, except as he is mingled with us."[22] But the "mingling" is on the level of "flesh" that is apart from the human soul or mind, which is what animates the flesh in ordinary people. Jesus, in other words, cannot be like us in our mental or spiritual activity. Apollinaris has judged that God's transcendence excludes God's becoming a complete human being. His logic, based on a pre-established but unacknowledged presumption of God's limitations, has trumped the Christian claim that Jesus was a human being. Jesus was *homoousios* with our flesh but not our minds.

Opponents of his view understood Apollinaris's metaphor of the standing savior to imply that our human mind is not lifted up: Jesus saved our bodies but not our minds. The bishops at the First Council of Constantinople (381 CE) reaffirmed the *homoousios* of Nicea and they considered their disapproval of Apollinaris's doctrine to be a rejection of what he mistakenly thought were the consequences of Nicea, not Nicea itself, which focused on one specific issue. The yes-or-no question posed by Arius and answered at Nicea was whether or not the Logos is inferior to the Father. Their "no" was expressed by the word *homoousios*. Again, what Nicea's *homoousios* meant was strictly and carefully limited to the judgment that the Son is not subordinate to the Father. When the bishops at the Council of Constantinople in 381 judged Apollinaris's point of view to be false, they implicitly showed that the Nicene settlement didn't settle every question. Besides the relationship of Father to Son, there was another question to be asked, and Apollinaris stumbled upon it: can the Logos/Son be one in being with the Father while also being one in being with us human beings? This question will preoccupy the church through the next seventy years and two Councils.

The Christians had already, long before the time of Apollinaris, dismissed the notion that Jesus was not human. The earliest and perhaps the most powerful alternative to the young Christian faith was an outlook on life and the world that was constituted by beliefs and practices within which was a disdain, even loathing, for the physical, material quality of this world, a world created as the result of evil forces fighting against the good. Some

22. Quoted in Norris, *Christological Controversy*, 110.

believed in Jesus as the Savior but interpreted his presence on earth as a mere appearance of the divine, and not a real enfleshment, since the material flesh was not part of the Good God's designs or intentions. This "docetism" (from a Greek word for "appearance"), claimed that Jesus was not human. He merely appeared to have a material body, as all humans do, but was in fact purely spiritual. He did not move and breathe and eat and sleep. And he certainly didn't die. Some forms of docetism separated the Creator of this material world, which includes in it the human body, from the Redeemer of souls. The material could be despised because it did not have its source and destiny in the God who saves.

The incarnation of the divine—Jesus as God in the flesh—confirms the goodness of this creation, even though it has been distorted and defaced by human sin. The church steadfastly insisted, just as its religious parent Judaism did, that the material world is indeed good. The Creator of matter and flesh, the One who made the appetites, who designed living things to develop, grow old, and die, is also the Redeemer of the human person whole and entire, body and soul, matter and spirit. Many in the ancient world thought that divinity has this one limit: in order to act within the world it must have an intermediary. Divinity was surrounded, as it were, by a hedge that separated God from the world. A hedge over which God has no power or authority. An authentic interpretation of God's transcendence overcomes this conceptual mistake.

If Apollinaris, following the Alexandrian stress on the unity of Christ, defended the Nicene *homoousios* in a way that compromised the full humanity of Jesus, the school at Antioch was committed to defending that humanity. The theologians at Antioch were in the habit of thinking about Jesus as both *Logos* and *Anthropos*, both Word of God and human being. They distrusted the Alexandrian tendency, since Nicea, to stress the divinity of Christ because it seemed to them to compromise Christ's full humanity. They saw the condemnation of Apollinaris by the bishops at Constantinople in 381 as sufficient warning that an overzealous emphasis on the identity of Christ as God's Word could easily take the church down Apollinaris's path once more.

Ephesus (331 CE) and Chalcedon (451 CE)

Nestorius, the patriarch of Constantinople in the early fifth century, was one such Antiochene theologian who also had a nose for any doctrine that slighted Christ's humanity. Nestorius weighed in during a dispute in his diocese over the proper title for Mary, the mother of Jesus. Does the eternal Creator of the universe have a mother? By the fourth century Mary had been known for some time as *Theotokos*, Mother of God/God-bearer, but this suggested to some, including Nestorius, that Mary gave birth to divinity, as if the divine nature can have a starting point in time. Nestorius's compromise title for Mary, therefore, was Christ-bearer, Mother of Christ. His concern was to defend the transcendence of the Logos as well as the humanity of Christ. The problem he couldn't solve, however, was how to talk about the unity of Logos and Humanity in Christ. Apollinaris had tried to solve the problem of unity by compromising the human mind (and thus human nature) of Christ, which drew the sarcastic rebuke of Gregory of Nazianzus: "If anyone has put his trust in a man without a mind, he is really mindless and quite unworthy of salvation."[23] Nestorius knew that the one Christ—the unity of the person—must not be purchased at the expense of his divine or human nature. The union of the two natures, according to Nestorius, resulted from God entering the loving and obedient man, Jesus of Nazareth. The person of the Logos and the person of the man Jesus come together and form the person of the union, whom Nestorius calls "Christ," both God and man.[24]

Nestorius located the union of divine and human on the level of "person" rather than "nature," which allowed him to preserve the full humanity of Christ. Unfortunately, his solution appeared to some to defend the humanity by splitting up Christ into two Sons, divine and human. Cyril of Alexandria was one of those critics who, for political as well as theological reasons, acted decisively to have Nestorius's theology overturned. Cyril, with this emphasis on the unity of Christ, caught the weakness in Nestorius's position: Nestorius had suggested that God enters a man, whereas Cyril insisted that God became flesh. Nestorius was correctly trying to affirm the unchanging (impassible) nature of God, and so one may not say that God suffered. Cyril insisted that the utterly transcendent divine Logos, one in being with the Father, suffered as a human being. For this reason, Cyril can claim that whatever can be affirmed of one nature can also be affirmed of the other. So, for example, Mary is the Mother of God and God suffered on the cross. We can correctly talk about the two natures by exchanging properties between them without implying that God changes.[25]

23. Lonergan, *Incarnate*, 195.

24. Ibid., 197–253, esp. "Part Two, Thesis Three"; and Lonergan, "Origins," 255–57.

25. The technical term for the exchange of properties is *communicatio idiomata*. The idea must be understood correctly. For example, to say that God suffered on the cross does not mean that the unchanging divine nature suffered (and thus changed). It means rather that the identity of the man Jesus Christ, who really suffered and died, is the Eternal Logos. See Lonergan, *Incarnate*, 303–5.

Nestorius's approach leaves a division within Christ that Cyril found to be intolerable, and so he moved against Nestorius very quickly. As leader of a council at the city of Ephesus, on the western coast of Asia Minor, Cyril engineered Nestorius's condemnation by appealing to Nicea: there is only one "who," one subject whom Christians worship, and that "who" is the eternal Logos, God in the flesh.[26]So, the weakness in Nestorius's proposal for defending Christ's humanity was its division of Christ in two–but does Cyril's alternative do the job that Nestorius originally set out to accomplish? Do Cyril and the language of the Council of Ephesus perhaps fall back to an Apollinarian position in its defense of the oneness of Christ? Cyril's language could sound that way: he spoke of "one nature" (*mia physis*) after the union because "two natures" after the union seemed to split Jesus into two identities. Cyril also thought that "one nature" language could be traced back to the great defender of Nicea, Athanasius. As it turned out, the phrase was from Apollinaris, and so it is no surprise that Cyril's solution could seem to compromise Christ's full humanity. For Cyril, however, the "one nature" formula meant something quite different than what it did for Apollinaris.[27]

"One nature" for Cyril meant one identity, one "who." If we ask who was born in Bethlehem of Mary, the answer must be in terms of the identity of Jesus. And what, exactly, *was* his identity? The Logos, the Word of God, *homoousios* with the Father. Jesus has no other identity. That was the point made at Ephesus against Nestorius. But the Logos became human, was born of a woman, grew up, learned, changed, and eventually suffered and died. In other words, God became human and as human, experienced all that human beings experience. But the identity of God, the Word, does not change in the midst of the changing human life that God lived, just as anyone's identity remains the same even during one's growth and development. So, in that sense one is now the *same person* now that entered first grade, learned to drive a car, got a job, etc. That same person has changed a great deal. The change is in her humanity, not in her identity. So it is with Christ: his unchanging identity is the Word of God but in his humanity he grew, developed, made decisions, prayed, made friends, suffered and died.[28]

The unity of Christ at the heart of the Council of Ephesus' affirmations and condemnations (and Cyril's theology) reappears twenty years later at the Council of Chalcedon (451 CE), which returned to the concern of Nestorius to preserve the full humanity of Christ. After the Council of Ephesus

26. One should acknowledge the mistreatment of Nestorius by Cyril and others without affirming the adequacy of Nestorius's Christology. For a critique of Nestorius's treatment at the hands of Cyril, see Sloyan, "Injustice," 128–42.

27. Lonergan, *Incarnate*, 207–9.

28. Lonergan, "Origins," 255–61, and "Christology Today," 90–94.

(431 CE) a party of radical Alexandrine theologians led by the theologically confused but politically connected monk Eutyches intended to crush the Antiochene theology of "two natures" after the union. Eutyches insisted that, although there were two natures *before* the union, there was only one *after* their union, their coming together in Christ. There could only be one nature after the union because, in Eutyches's understanding, "nature" meant "person," and so two natures would split Christ, Nestorius-like, into two persons. But his confusion appears when, unlike Apollinaris, Eutyches affirmed a rational human soul in Christ, but was still unwilling to say that Jesus' human nature was one in being with ours. The bishops at Chalcedon judged that his way of talking about Christ's identity, the "who," (one nature after the union) threatened the full human nature of Christ.

A pro-Eutychean council met that was later rejected because of its unfair dealings with the bishops who opposed him.[29] Pope Leo of Rome, who declared that meeting to be a den of thieves, had earlier sent a "Tome" to the Patriarch Flavian of Constantinople in which he clearly stated his view of Christ's single identity while affirming two natures in Christ after the union. "Thus, in the whole and perfect nature of true manhood true God was born—complete in what belonged to him, complete in what belonged to us."[30]

After reaffirming the creeds produced by Nicea, Constantinople and Ephesus, the Council of Chalcedon followed Leo's lead in affirming the traditional Antiochene language of "two natures after the union" while insisting on the unity of Christ's identity. There is only one Christ. Chalcedon insisted that the natures are "without confusion, without change, without division, without separation; the distinction of the natures in no way being abolished because of the union, but rather the characteristic property of each nature being preserved, and concurring into one Person and one subsistence . . . "

And so, from the point of view of the teaching of these early councils at least, the controversy was decided in favor of the unity of the Christ which was not purchased at the expense of his full humanity. With Nicea and the Alexandrian tradition, Christ is one in being (*homoousios*) with the Father, while being *homoousios* with us in his humanity.

---

29. The robber council, or *Latrocinium*, took place in 449 CE. The Patriarch Dioscorus, in an attempt to defend Eutyches and his Monophysite doctrine, convoked a synod there, insulted Leo's representatives and the "Tome" he had written, and deposed bishop Flavian (to whom the Tome was addressed). The Council of Chalcedon reversed the decisions of the Robber Council.

30. Davis, *First Seven*, 175.

Incarnation and Divine Transcendence

We have seen that the distinction between God and creation is part of creation: God created not only the universe but the distinction between God and the universe. We do not understand how this could be, of course, but we know that the opposite claim—that there is no such distinction or that the distinction existed already, eternally, with God, is to deny that God, the "to-be" of all beings, is the source of all. So, as created, the distinction can be set aside by the inventor of the distinction.[31] And that is what the Christian doctrine of the Incarnation claims: God does not allow a created reality—the distinction between creation and Creator—to prevent God from sharing in human history, living a human life, being a human being. Thinking about the Incarnation requires that we not allow our imaginations to limit God's ability by picturing a compromise union, a coming together of divine and human that results in a *tertium quid*, a third thing that is neither divine nor human, as was Arius's conception. Chalcedon insisted that Christ is true man and true God, not "part human" and "part divine." Its claim can conjure up the image of two beings squeezed into one body. Images, however, no matter how carefully chosen, cannot do justice to the doctrine. The transcendence and incomprehensibility of God means that we are not dealing with two beings at all, but with the Creator and a creature. The difference between them is not like any difference between two creatures. No matter how different two created realities might be—say, a dog and a decision—they have at least the commonality of their having been created and sustained by the Creator. In other words, the word "difference" when used to describe the difference between God and the creature is a unique difference. Like every word used to say something about God, it is used analogically. There is no difference like it within creation. And because God was not compelled to create the difference in the first place, since God didn't need to create anything, it is a created difference.

Now we are in a position to appreciate an important connection between incarnation and God's transcendence. An authentic understanding of the transcendence of God implies that God, while remaining God, can become human. Yet neither God's essence nor God's incarnation are within the capacity of human understanding. A moment's reflection will reveal that we already know why the incomprehensibility of God is an indispensable component of any Christology. What God *is* cannot be known, and so *how God can do x* is also unknowable because God's acting *is* God's being. Christians know *that* God became human only because they receive

31. Burrell, *Freedom and Creation*, 60–62.

in faith what God revealed. Had it not been shown to us by God we could not know it. The claim is passed on to us from the apostles and it is received in faith. The notion *that* God became human is at the heart of Christian teaching, but to attempt to explain *how* God can become one of us is to misunderstand the transcendence of God. Theology's focus then lands on its soteriological implications of the fact.

Confusion at the pastoral level can often be traced back to the spontaneous tendency to limit God's transcendence. In part, it has to do with the need to employ cultural ideas or images already available to these ancient thinkers that would help them to explore the intelligibility of God's saving work in Christ. The use of preexisting ideas in the culture to construct analogies of what God has done in Christ is a natural and necessary theological impulse. Christianity through the ages has borrowed and used for its own purposes much from its surrounding cultural world and it has done so from an impulse that seeks to find God in all things. But such a strategy must always be corrected by an awareness of the ways in which the older ideas do not do justice to the new reality that they are set down to serve. Stoicism and Platonism enriched Christian understanding in many ways, but as the theologians tried to work out their understanding of God, Christ and the Spirit, these philosophies also revealed their insufficiencies. The same is true of modern and contemporary ways of thinking.

This Christological development through Chalcedon does not explain to us what it means to have two natures in one person; the holy mystery can never be captured in human words or grasped by human understanding. Notice the ways in which Chalcedon fashioned its language in negative terms: the two natures of Christ are not confused or separated.[32] But if the incarnation is beyond understanding, then what was all the fuss about? Why worry so much over what is being said or not said about the mystery of Christ? Christians must talk about God, and it is inevitable that they do so, and the talk is not futile. We have already seen that language about what God is not can improve our understanding and help us to avoid misunderstanding. For example, to say that God is eternal and unchanging is simply a way of pointing out the fact that God is not a part of creation but rather its source. It says nothing about what the words "eternal" and "unchanging" might mean if applied to God. In like fashion, to say that the eternal and unchanging Word of God became flesh and shared fully in our human nature is not to explain how that could be the case. Rather, it is simply to affirm that the opposite claims—that Christ is not the eternal, unchanging divine Word of God or that he was not fully human—are not only misleading but false.

32. Burrell, "Incarnation and Creation," 214.

Can the Word of God become a complete human being? If our answer is "No, God can't do that sort of thing," then we are falsely assuming that we understand what God is and therefore what God can do. God's action does not fall under the conditions and possibilities governing creation. It is certainly true that God acts through the universal instrumentality of creation, but creation itself is God's invention, not a set of pre-established rules within which God acts. Only an eternal and unchanging God can become incarnate because a changeable God will not be God if he becomes human; he would have to change from this to that. The motive for creating the world or for becoming incarnate is not the result of some need on God's part to do so. The motive, rather, is love, and love must be free.[33]

Chalcedon is an important milepost, drawing boundaries within which theologians in every age can wrestle with improved or more culturally communicative ways of talking about the relevance of Jesus. Chalcedon simply offers Christology a way of making the distinction between Creator and creature clear: Jesus is not a *tertium quid*, something neither fully human nor fully divine, as if a monster had been created after fusing two incompatible creatures. The idea that Jesus is the incarnate Word of God is a mystery of faith and we have attempted to offer some suggestions that can help improve our understanding of the mystery as mystery.[34]

If God is truly transcendent, God does not have to be reduced to "fit" into the humanity of Christ, as if God must work within the boundaries of an already-given context. If this is true, then the Incarnation is not an event that required God to "fit" anywhere. Just as one might be a mother and a sister at the same time without these relations changing that person into something other than what she is, so the Incarnation is a relation to the world that does not in any way reduce God to something less than God. God's relation to creation is parallel to God's becoming man in the Incarnation: both are relations that go beyond our understanding. What we believe in faith is not that we can understand the divine nature or the Incarnation of the divine nature in Jesus the Christ but rather that the absolutely transcendent God has, because of an incomprehensible love, shared human history, and in so doing, has drawn us into the mystery of it all.

33. See Lonergan, *Incarnate*, 745 on divine transcendence.
34. Burrell, *Peace*, 66, 73.

8

The Trinity

FOLLOWING LONERGAN'S PRINCIPLE THAT the meaning of a doctrine is inseparable from its history, in this chapter we will trace some of the highlights of the development of the doctrine of the Trinity. Lonergan's work on the Trinity and Incarnation was written within the requirements of the neo-scholastic textbooks of the mid-twentieth century, a highly technical structure that no longer communicates. Yet with patience and the help of Lonergan scholars, these books reveal to the reader the benefits of some of Lonergan's key insights.[1] For example, his illumination of the development of doctrine reveals the necessity of an accurate grasp of the operations of consciousness, as well as an historical retrieval of the horizons within which the early theologians raised and answered questions. The perceptionist or naïve realist horizon (imagining a bridge that the mind needs to cross to confront external reality) renders key theological problems insoluble. Understanding the operations of consciousness in turn is an important factor that determines one's intellectual horizon. The theology of the Trinity thus exemplifies the fact that "to understand a doctrine is to understand the history of the doctrine."[2] The historical approach is also necessary if the meaning of the doctrine is to be transposed, for meaning is found within a context. To explore the development of a doctrine is to understand its meaning.

Although the religious experience of Christians is the starting point for reflection on the doctrine, questions arise that require a shift in mentality, an expansion of horizon. The problem of understanding "is not a difficulty on the level of religion, of the spiritual life . . . The only difficulty

---

1. See Quesnell, "Scholasticism."
2. Lonergan, *Early Works 3*, 6.

lies in theoretical theology."[3] As with the doctrine of the Incarnation we begin by distinguishing between the originating experience of the early Christians and the subsequent theological questioning that led to the doctrinal formulations.

Starting with Jesus Leads to Questions about the Spirit

In the previous chapter, we noted that teachings about Christ originate in the disciples' experience of the risen Lord. As Christians found themselves in new contexts, further questions about the original experience and its continuing significance emerged, were debated and came to some sort of resolution. Christian faith affirms that Christ was human and that human beings are made with a desire for God. Human beings not only develop and learn and achieve; they also experience the love of God as a pure gift of grace that moves them to love in return. As human, Jesus experienced the pull of self-transcendence, and his love for the Father, exemplified in his life, death and resurrection, serve to communicate the Father's love for humanity. After his death by public crucifixion the disciples encountered this same Jesus as exalted and risen, no longer simply and finally dead. This experience was also one of salvation; they understood that this same Christ was the source of new life for them through the forgiveness of their sins.

The New Testament provides several examples of the early church's language of faith in the "Father" (or "God"), "Son" (or "Word" or "Lord" or "Christ") and Spirit (or "Paraclete" in John). The terms are found in several places throughout the New Testament. Trinity language, as found in the dramatic titles and imagery of the New Testament, provides data for a theology of the Trinity, but not a theology in the systematic or theoretical realm of meaning. Rather, the metaphors of Father, Son and Spirit in the early Christian writings express the language of the church's experience of God and the process of redemption that God is working through that community. The emphasis in the New Testament language is on how we are related to God through Christ and the Spirit. The symbolic language expresses how we are related to God in hope and encouragement, but it does not explain God's essence, how God is within the divine nature itself.

As we have seen in our discussion of the distinction between common sense symbolism and theoretical explanation, the language that we use to talk of things as they are related to us does have within it the potential to provoke a question about how those things are related among themselves. For example, the pleasure brought by the birds in your backyard might cause

---

3. Lonergan, *Papers 1958*, 126, esp. "Consciousness and the Trinity."

you, in a reflective moment, to ask about their pattern of migration or their mating habits. The intention of these sorts of questions require a different mentality than the one that was enjoying how the birds make you feel. In a similar way, the purpose of the symbolic biblical language is not to explain how the one God is three "persons." But biblical images do provide the impetus and some data for asking questions that can only be satisfied by a shift to a more theological or explanatory frame of mind.

To the Corinthians Paul wrote that "nobody speaking by the spirit of God says, 'Jesus be accursed.' And no one can say, 'Jesus is Lord,' except by the holy Spirit. There are different kinds of spiritual gifts but the same Spirit; there are different forms of service but the same Lord; there are different workings but the same God who produces all of them in everyone" (1 Cor 12:3–6). And again to the Galatian church he wrote, "As proof that you are children, God sent the spirit of his Son into our hearts, crying out, 'Abba, Father!'" (Gal 4:6). In these passages the unity of God is clearly presupposed: the action of God is one, not three. And yet Paul identifies the three: the Spirit, the Lord (the Christ, the Son), and the Father. Since Paul's are the earliest of the New Testament writings, and since these writings already employ the language of the one God as Father, Son and Spirit, we can safely assume that the church employed this language very early on, in response to the Christ event.

The Trinitarian language of the New Testament, in other words, describes how we are members of the body of believers as redeemed by Christ and enabled by the Spirit. The language *describes*, it does not *explain*. Description relates a thing to those who experience it; it does not explain how that thing is related to other things. The New Testament baptismal formulae serve as religious instruction, to initiate the catechumen into the life of the Christian community. The salvation that the early Christians found in Christ was inseparable from their incorporation as a social body. Given this experience, the descriptive language of Trinity in the New Testament reveals something about that communal dimension of redemption. Judaism, Christianity's parent faith, passed on its understanding of salvation as essentially communal: the awaited redemption was of the people Israel. The early Christians also inherited from Judaism the conviction that there is only one God.[4] With the disciples' experience of God's liberating grace coming through the risen Christ, however, a new question arose: how will this one God redeem all of humanity? One common Jewish assumption was that all the nations—the "Gentiles"—eventually would come to worship the one God and be saved

---

4. On the difference within ancient Judaism between intermediary beings and its strict monotheistic worship, see Hurtaldo, *Lord Jesus Christ*, 43.

(see, for example, Isaiah 49:6). Paul's insight was that this expectation, we now know, is going to be fulfilled through Christ. The early Christians then asked how humanity can be unified now that the Torah no longer provides for the unity of Jesus' disciples. After all, the new community has Gentiles in it! Jesus makes us one, but how? Paul's further insight that answers the question was "in the Spirit" (1 Cor 12:3–6). The inner word of the Spirit opens the person to receive the outer word of Christ.

The author of the gospel of Luke and its second volume, the *Acts of the Apostles*, presents the giving of the Spirit to the church as its foundation. There was a Jewish legend at the time that told of God's giving of the Torah on Mount Sinai in such a way that everyone heard it in his or her own language. Jews in the first century celebrated this miraculous reception of the Torah in the feast of Shavuot, whose Greek name was Pentecost. Luke's story of the Christian Pentecost, in which the Spirit descends as tongues of fire on Jesus' disciples gathered together after his resurrection, repeats the miracle of understanding (Acts 2:1–47). Jews from various nations and of different languages all heard Peter explain the meaning of Jesus' resurrection and its life-giving implications. Luke is complementing the ancient tradition that understood Judaism to be the source of divine blessing for the entire world. Luke names the Holy Spirit as the vehicle of that blessing. The point of the story is to identify God's holy Spirit as the foundation of the church, the community of disciples transformed by Christ. The Spirit enables the apostles to teach others about Christ and to receive them into the fellowship of the church (see also Acts 10:44–48).[5]

To summarize, the dramatic religious language of Father, Son and Spirit in the New Testament marks the start of the church's reflection that begins from the metaphoric and symbolic. The New Testament is filled with dramatic imagery but it does not contain a theory of the Trinity as it developed through the fourth century. Its language concerns God's salvation in Christ, enabled by the Spirit. The Word of God, become incarnate as the man Jesus of Nazareth, calls us into the life of God, but what causes us to hear that call? The invisible mission of the Spirit prepares us to receive the outer word of the gospel message. The new unity of humanity is thus established when the Spirit opens human hearts to hear the gospel. The biblical stories present the religious language, expressive of the lived liturgical life of the early church, and it continues today to function religiously as Christians continue to make the sign of the cross, baptize in the name of the Trinity and perform a myriad of other sacramental and devotional practices. Trinity language in the first century functions within the religious experience of

5. Lonergan, "Mission and the Spirit," 23–34.

the young church. Questions will arise, however, that require answers that go beyond what the New Testament explicitly states.

The First Council of Constantinople (381 CE)

The development to the Council of Nicea is the next phase in the story of the emergence of the doctrine of the Trinity. A quick look back to the previous chapter to review the Stoic materialism of Tertullian will remind us that Tertullian's assumption that all reality, including God, is in some way material (to be real it has to have a body) caused him to imagine the procession of the Son from the Father as a kind of material extrusion out of the original divine stuff. For Tertullian, God is real, but God must be a light, airy, invisible but still material body. When he wrote of the Son coming from the Father, he necessarily imagined that the Son is other than the Father in the way that bodies coming from other bodies must be other than the original body. The material images Tertullian uses reveal the inferiority of what is derived from the source of its derivation: the ray of light from the source of light, the shoot from the root, the stream from the river.[6]

An image of the Son or Word as "part of" God emerges when a materialist mentality such as Tertullian's names the Trinity, and yet it is strictly impossible to imagine the Trinitarian three in their mutual interrelations. In religious art it is possible and even necessary to picture the Father or the Son or the Spirit and the tradition is all the richer for these devotional expressions. The impossibility of picturing an explanation of the Trinitarian three in their inner relations, however, doesn't make the doctrine of the Trinity unreal. The real is not identical with bodies, and so God is beyond description. Yet we must talk about God, and if our talk is accurate, our understanding of God's relation to the world will improve.

In the third century Origen of Alexandria rejected all materialist assumptions about what we know when we are knowing. His Platonic language, which stressed the ideal as the real, was a distinct improvement for naming God. Origen's naming of God employs as analogies the intellectual processions of mind and will. The Son is God by participation in the action of God, by carrying out God's will. The Son proceeds from the Father spiritually, not spatially or by any type of material extrusion, and therefore not in time. And yet, Origen's approach, as we have seen, also culminated in a subordination of the Son to the Father. For Origen, the Father is an absolute spirit who cannot have any direct relationship with the world of created realities. There must be an intermediary between God and the world—the

---

6. On Tertullian, see Lonergan, *Triune God: Doctrines,* 95–105.

Logos, the Son of God—who does God's will. Origen calls the Father "the God" but the Son he calls simply "God" (implying that the Logos is God by participation in "the" God). The Trinity, in Origen's scheme, is structured as a hierarchy: the Father is highest, then the Son below him and finally, on the third rung down on the ladder of divinity, the Holy Spirit. Origen's improvement on Tertullian's imaginative presentation of the Son or Logos proceeding from the Father as a material substance was possible because of Origen's recognition that not all realities have bodies. The human intellect exhibits a kind of spiritual proceeding such that the context of space and time must be set aside as unnecessary and misleading when thinking about thinking itself. This turn to intellectual realities is a permanent step forward in the attempt to articulate the One God Who is Father, Son and Spirit. As we shall see, Augustine and Aquinas will advance the theology of the Trinity in their sustained thinking about the analogy provided by human thinking itself. But before that we must remain for a while in the late third century and the controversy that resulted in the Council of Nicea.[7]

Arius of Alexandria, a member of the same Alexandrian theological tradition as Origen, drew out the logical implications of Origen's subordination of the Logos to the Father. Arius was dissatisfied with the logic of the claim that the Logos is "God by participation." What could that mean? Was it not more logical to claim that the Logos was either "the God" (Origen's term for the Father) or not? What was this "in-between" status of the "God by participation"? Arius correctly understood that the Logos is either the Creator or a creature: if the Logos is less than "the God," then he must be a creature—the highest creature to be sure, but still a creature. The Son/Logos is not God; only the Father is God. God cannot change but the Logos does, by coming forth from the Father in time, like any other creature. This Logos thus cannot share the same being as God the Father, for that would mean, by strict syllogism, that the unchanging changes. The rigor of his logic, in addition to his interpretation of the biblical texts, as well as his commitment to the Platonic view of God as having no direct relationship with the world, led Arius to resolve the tension in Origen's theology between "the God" and "God by participation." That resolution was a fully explicit subordination of the Son to the Father.

Although the bishops at Nicea in 324 rejected Arius's proposal to speak of the Logos as created in time, still Arius's work was a theological benefit because it pushed the church to think more clearly about the distinction between God and creation. There is no "third thing" besides the Creator and the things God has brought into existence. If all reality is either God or

7. On Origen, see ibid., 117–37.

what is not God (creation) then Arius would place the Logos in the second category. As heir to the Platonic view of the absolutely spiritual God, Arius was committed to a picture of the hierarchy of beings, as well as to the temporal imagination's insistence on the idea that there must be "a time before creation." He could not, therefore, accept the Council of Nicea's insistence that the Son is one in being with the Father. Yet if God is transcendent in the sense that we have been using that word throughout this book, then it makes no sense to think of a "when," if you will, within God. There was no "when" when that making of the Son supposedly took place! Arius didn't grasp an important implication of God's transcendence: the unchanging God could in fact share human nature, because if God could *not* do that, then God would be constrained by something that must be greater than God. In other words, God would then not be the transcendent mystery; something else would be.

Arius, therefore, forced the church to deal explicitly with the distinction between the Creator and creation.[8] His answer was to put the Son clearly on the side of creation. Nicea accepted the challenge of Arius's "yes or no" question: is the Logos on the side of creation or not? Nicea issued its judgment: no, the Word of God is not a creature. The bishops at the Council were not claiming to understand the nature (or *ousia*) of God; that was not the point of their famous word *homoousios*, one in nature. Their judgment *that* Christ the Savior is God did not entail an explanation of what it means for a human being to be God. Like the distinction between the fact *that* God is and *what it means* to be God, the distinction between the fact *that* Christ must be God if Christ is the Savior does not entail an explanation of *what it means* for Jesus, a human being, to be God. The judgment of Nicea rejected the claim of Arius that Christ was less than the one and only God because the claim was inadequate to the Christian experience of the salvation brought by God in Christ.

In the Trinitarian thinking that develops through Nicea there is a growing clarity regarding the "two" in the one God: Father and Son/ Logos. Both Testaments of the Bible contain language about the "Spirit" of God. Thus, questions about the relationship between Christ and God inevitably raised similar questions about the Spirit. If the Spirit is doing the work of God and makes the human heart receptive to Christ's message, then isn't the Spirit also God? Isn't the Spirit also *homoousios* with the Father and the Son?[9]

8. Ibid., 137–47.

9. For Lonergan's discussion of the doctrinal development of the divinity of the Spirit, see ibid., 355–79.

The two most important figures arguing for the divinity of the Spirit in the fourth century were Athanasius and Gregory of Nazianzus.[10] Athanasius first recognized that the Spirit must be *homoousios* with the Father and the Son, even though, out of respect for traditional restrictions on the word, he did not label the Spirit as "God." Because they were painfully aware of the confusion and disagreement that Nicea's *homoousios* continued to cause, both Athanasius and Gregory's friend Basil tried to be mediators, often willing to compromise on language in order to heal divisions in the church.

In the long run, however, neither theology nor the unity of the church is well served by avoiding tough theological questions. The issue of the status of the Spirit needed to be resolved and it came down to this now familiar pattern: on which side of the line dividing Creator and creature does the Spirit fall? Those who followed Arius, of course, had no trouble answering: The Spirit is on the side of the creature. They had put the Word of God there, and so the Spirit was there also, and in a third rank below the Word. Eustathius of Sebaste, a figure who represents the confusion that the question generated for many at this time, answered that the Spirit occupies a middle category that is neither God nor creature. But what could possibly be in such a category? Gregory insisted that those who don't say *homoousios* about the Spirit are as bad as the Arians, who refuse to say it of the Son. His rhetorical strategy was to cut out middle positions and associate those claiming the middle with Arius even if they didn't want to be there. So, in Gregory's presentation of the matter, those who said that the Word and the Spirit are of "similar" natures were in fact claiming that the Father, Son and Spirit are all of utterly dissimilar natures.[11] With Arius, Gregory insisted on the distinction between Creator and creature; there is no middle position between Creator and creature. Unlike Arius, however, he placed the Spirit on the side of the Creator. For Gregory, those who subordinate either the Son or the Spirit are of a "crassly servile and materialistic mentality" because they are trying to picture an impossible in-between category.[12] The picturing causes the problem; in fact there is no category in between God and creation. God is the transcendent source of all that exists, and so everything else is simply not God; everything else is the created world.

Although the bishops at the First Council of Constantinople (381 CE) agreed that the Spirit should be glorified along with and in the same

10. Hedrick, "Basil," argues that the difference between Nazianzus and his friend Basil regarding the divinity of the Spirit lies in Gregory's surer grasp of the non-picturable nature of divinity.

11. For details, see McGuckin, *Gregory*, 144–45, and Gregory, "Third Oration."

12. McGuckin, *Gregory*, 293.

way as the Father and the Son, they did not affirm that the Spirit is "one in being" with the Father and Son, nor did they state that the Spirit is God. This weak affirmation of the Spirit was apparently aimed at snubbing Gregory of Nazianzus who, as president of the Council, pushed for an assertion of the Spirit as *homoousios*. But the vague language of the Council turned out to be a benefit to Gregory's point of view, because the subsequent tradition interpreted the Council to mean what Gregory wanted it to say in the first place.[13]

Distinctions and Missions

We have seen that the three in God take their names from the early narrative traditions of Christianity as Father, Son (or Word) and Spirit. Within the constraints of the symbolic language of those stories and exhortations of the New Testament, the Trinitarian names functioned to communicate God's love for humanity. We have seen that, if the Spirit creates, saves, and sanctifies, just as God does, then the Spirit *is* God. Scripture speaks of Father, Son and Spirit and so in some sense these three are also distinct. But how is the church to talk of the three as distinct from one another while avoiding the obvious mistake of implying that there are three gods? The Council of Nicea found a word to name what Father and Son have in common (*ousia*), and the tradition that followed the First Council of Constantinople, with the example of Gregory Nazianzus in the lead, extended that word to the Spirit. A *different* word, therefore, was needed to identify the distinctions that the tradition names Father, Son and Spirit, and two words emerged as candidates for the job: *prosopon* (Greek)/*persona* (Latin) and *hypostasis* (Greek).

What did these words signify for the early theologians who used them to name the distinctions—what there are three of—in the one God? A glimmer of understanding is possible if the distinctions are considered as "relations." One typical use of "relation" makes it equivalent to "relative," as in aunt, uncle, brother, daughter, mother, etc. A relation, then, is a form of relating: Peter relates to his father as a son; Sally relates to her aunt as a niece, and so on. The idea here has no meaning apart from its "relative" meaning; a mother can only be a mother because she has a son or daughter, and so on.[14]

On this category of relations in the Trinity, the great Christian thinkers of the fourth century, especially Athanasius, Gregory of Nazianzus, Basil

---

13. On the Council, see ibid., 350–69.

14. On relations see Lonergan, *Triune God: Systematics*, 231–305.

and his brother Gregory of Nyssa, as well as Augustine in the west, were the pioneers. We know that the word *ousia* or nature came to be used to name what there is one of in God—one divinity, one substance, one God. The words *hypostasis* and *prosopon* came to be used to name what there are three of in God. The meaning of *hypostasis* until this time was very slippery; both Origen and the Council of Nicea used it as a synonym for *ousia*. The key insight that their use of *hypostasis* articulates is that the distinctions in God cannot be located in the unity of the divine nature. God is thus one God, not three, but God's existence is in three: Father, Son (or Word) and Spirit. The three, then, are not ranked but exist as one; this one reality, however, is in its very being relational.

The numbers—one and three—are not used here as in arithmetic: they cannot, for example, be added together. God isn't four in any sense. What, after all, could be added to the one God? Another god? Obviously not: no being naturally possesses the divine essence because there is only one God. So, there is no ordinary counting in the Trinity. But then, how might we speak of the "three"? The linguistic convention of specifying the terms *"hypostasis"* and *prosopon* (*persona* in Latin) to identify what there are three of in the Trinity allowed the great theologians of the fourth century to maintain Nicea's *homoousios* while providing a way of identifying the three. Father, Son/Word and Spirit share the same nature while their distinctions—the way in which they are three relations and not one—do not compromise the unity of God. Just as the terms mother, daughter, or friend signify not the essence of the person who is a mother or daughter or friend, but rather how they are related to another, so too the terms of the three in God are (analogous) relations.

The words *hypostasis* and *persona*, like the word *ousia*, do nothing to explain what God is. But if that's the case, why did the early theologians even introduce these terms? Because the terms appear in the New Testament and (even earlier) in the creeds, the three—Father, Son/Word and Spirit—must have some meaning for the earliest Christians' experience of God's creative and gracious activity in the world. The naming of God as three persons or *hypostases* in one God (or one divine essence or *ousia*) is important because it provides some control over our language and helps us name the mystery that the Christian faith is charged to communicate. The need to talk about the holy mystery does not explain, let alone eliminate, the mystery; the incomprehensibility of God is not obviated by the grammatical rules that structure our talk about God. Trinitarian theology does not provide us a peek inside the divine nature. Still, Christians talk about God and they need to do so rationally. The theological challenge is to speak about the Triune God in ways that are not impossible or contradictory to reason. That can be accomplished only by way of analogy. Lonergan was convinced that the psychological analogy is the best way to improve one's analogical and therefore indirect understanding of what is finally an incomprehensible mystery.

The Psychological Analogy

In *The Triune God: Doctrines* Lonergan established through historical analysis what in fact the church came to develop and continues to teach. In *The Triune God: Systematics* he transposes his understanding of the psychological analogy that he finds in Aquinas.[15] Christians need to talk about the God they have come to know in Christ, but that need is in tension with our subject matter's nature as unknowable, ineffable, incomparable, transcending all else that we know.[16] We need to communicate our experience of God's self-gift, but it is a reality that outstrips our ability to talk directly about it. We do, however, have an indirect way of speaking. Analogy, as we have already learned, is a sort of in-between way of speaking, providing us with meanings that are neither univocal (having the same meaning) nor equivocal (having different meanings). No language can provide univocal names for the reality of God and theological language about the Trinity is no exception to the rule. Still, as we have noted when we contrasted Tertullian's materialistic imagery of the Trinity with Origen's strictly spiritual acts of the human mind, some analogies are better suited than others for talking about God. As with all "negative" language about God (e.g., God is not extended in space, not limited in time, not constrained by something greater, etc.), a good analogy can help in steering us clear of misunderstandings. Moreover, a carefully constructed analogy can be better than saying nothing, because to leave a linguistic vacuum would be to open the possibility than someone might say something even more misleading, or even downright false.

One might say that the psychological analogy increases our appreciation for the depth and infinity of meaning in the holy mystery of the three "persons" in One God. In the end, the analogy is simply a way of demonstrating that it is not impossible to think of the one God as an infinite act of understanding who speaks God's own word of self-understanding and who loves the infinite value that is God. The psychological analogy of the Trinity improves on less adequate ways of speaking about the God of Christian

15. For Lonergan's distinction between doctrinal and systematic see ibid., 59–77. Quentin Quenell ("Three Persons," 158–65) gives a clear and detailed presentation of Lonergan's use of the analogy.

16. See Lonergan, *Triune God: Systematics*, 273.

experience, but it also provides us with the best analogy for thinking hypothetically about what God might be like. Lonergan was not, of course, the
first to reflect on the psychological analogy, but he does seem to be the one
who best understood Aquinas's presentation of it. The key to the presentation
is an accurate grasp of the data of consciousness, which Lonergan explored
in depth and detail in *Insight*. In other words, if one understands what one
is doing when one is thinking and judging and deciding, and what one gets
when one performs these operations, then one can have some partial, obscure
and indirect understanding of the doctrine of the Trinity. Only an accurate
understanding of human consciousness and its operations will provide the
foundation for an adequate grasp of the psychological analogy.

The analogy is called "psychological" because it appeals to the psychological event of understanding, and this event is the key to understanding
Lonergan's interpretation of Aquinas on the Trinity. The act of understanding is the event that grasps what is going on in data, what one is trying to
understand when one asks questions like "why is it like that" or "how does
that work" or "what makes that thing the kind of thing it is?" The act of understanding is not a kind of looking and its result is not an image. One can
draw a picture of a circle without being able to define what geometers mean
by "a circle." The act is not spatial or temporal, neither extended in space nor
picturable. In the human act of understanding, there is no duration, no time
lapse. Our common speech indicates the non-temporal dimension: we usually ask something like "Do you understand X?" rather than something like
"Is understanding about X occurring in you now?" Of course, it often takes
lots of time for us to *get to* an understanding but once one *does* understand,
once one has the idea, there is no time involved in the act of understanding. Do you understand the difference between the accelerator (gas pedal)
and the brake on a car? Of course you do. But how long is it taking you to
understand it now? And where is that understanding? These questions are,
obviously, meaningless because understanding is a "spiritual" act, one that
is not located in time or space. You understand it, that's all. Once you have
it, your understanding takes no time because the insight is not extended in
space, but it is *real*. And when we have in some way expressed our understanding to ourselves, we have secured it.[17]

The basic facts of cognition that we have discussed earlier—understanding data, judging whether the understanding is true, judging the value that is
involved, acting on the good—all of these acts of human self-transcendence
make us who we are. In the analogy the relations of Father, Son, and Spirit
are like the human act of understanding that is expressed in a concept or a

17. See Quenell, "Three Persons," 159–60.

judgment or a decision; the concept or definition or expression of what we understand is related to the understanding itself by being the expression of the same content, that which is understood. Imagine yourself preoccupied with a book when suddenly you hear a puzzling high pitched noise. You pay attention to the sound and you think. Then the insight occurs: you understand that the whining noise you hear is the laboring motor of some heavy machinery in the distance, and you tell yourself (perhaps wordlessly) just that. The content of the judgment or word that is expressed internally—it's a big truck with a snow plow clearing the road in front of your house—is identical in content to your understanding of the data.

Now, this example of a simple human insight into some sound that you hear can be extended one step further. Let's imagine that your car is parked out there on that road where the heavy equipment is doing its thing. Beyond the insight ("Oh! I know what that noise is!") and beyond the concept formulated in your judgment ("It's a snow plow scraping the snow off the road!") there is also a decision to act ("I'd better move my car out of the way before it gets damaged"). The decision to move your car occurs only because of a prior judgment of value ("I need my car and don't want it to be damaged") yet the judgment of value makes the decision possible but does not cause it.

Jesus is God's wisdom or, analogously, God's judgment of value. For Lonergan, judgments of value are indeed judgments (answers to yes-or-no questions) but when they regard values, these judgments are not about what is, but what ought to be. A judgment of fact would be, for example, that Rover is a dog. A judgment of value would be that I care about him and so I ought to feed him tonight. It's not a fact yet (the feeding is in the future) but when I feed Rover I am realizing—making real—a value that I hold.

When we talk about God we are always using analogical language, but even with that limitation, we can improve our understanding. So, the Father is love and that love is expressed by the Father "speaking" God's Word, the Logos, which is a judgement of value. It's as if the Father is saying, "I love the world and so it should be saved from itself" (John 3:16). Lonergan writes that God's "judgment of value is sincere, and so it grounds the Proceeding Love that is identified with the Holy Spirit." The judgment is sincere in the sense that the Father truly wants to save the world, and so God is going to make that intention (the Logos and the gospel of Jesus) effective by sending the Holy Spirit.

The Son or Word is the Father's judgment of value. It means that the Holy Trinity saves us because of Love and through the revelation of the Son and the effective love of God poured into our hearts by the Holy Spirit (Rom 5:5), which opens our hearts to accept the truth embodied in the crucified and risen Jesus. When we decide to do something, sometimes we can get it done and sometimes not. But God's decision to do something means that it gets done; the judgment of value is effective.

All these words used concerning God—forgive me for repeating—are used in an analogous way. Lonergan uses the example of our changing understanding of the nature of fire as an example to illustrate the difference between a judgment and the varying degrees of understanding that we have of that judgment. The objective data about fire was at one time thought to be one of the essential elements of nature, along with earth air and water. Later it was thought to be a latent substance that could be released during combustion. Today, scientists recognize it as a chemical oxidation reaction. And yet, despite the very different explanations, they were all explanations of what on the common sense level is fire.[18]

The psychological analogy of the Trinity depends on an accurate understanding of these basic cognitional or psychological facts: when we understand anything, we grasp what is intelligible in data and express it to ourselves, we then affirm (or deny) the truth of that understanding by verifying it in the data to be understood, and we judge the value of whatever is at stake in the new knowledge we have acquired. When we apply the analogy to the Trinity, there are obvious differences: divine understanding occurs outside time and space, so there is no potential data to be understood. God is the pure act of infinite, unlimited understanding, with no potential to change or become something else. The divine intelligence and what that intelligence understands are the same, whereas in created intellects, the meaning of the data can be but isn't necessarily understood. The sound of the snow plow is potentially intelligible until I actually understand it, whereas in God there is no "until." God's understanding is immediate and infinite and eternal (nothing is not understood). Nor does God deliberate about what is real or what is good. Yet God understands God's own self—which includes everything that has come from God (creation)—and in doing so, God *is* himself. God's act of self-understanding is God.[19] All talk of God is analogous—indirect and imperfect—yet analogies such as the psychological analogy (when the operations of consciousness are accurately grasped) can enrich our understanding.

This creaturely event, the human act of understanding, is a better analogy for the divine relations than any material reality because understanding itself (once achieved) is, like God—the complete and infinite act of understanding—not subject to time and space. The analogy must be corrected to

18. Lonergan, "Christology Today," 87.
19. Lonergan, *Triune God: Systematics*, 173–81.

eliminate the time we human beings spend trying to understand as well as the limitations and imperfections of human consciousness. God's understanding is something that occurs in God, who immediately grasps not simply this or that here or there, now and then, but the totality of what is real. And God's self-expression perfectly captures God's understanding. when we speak of God, God's Word and God's Spirit as relations, they are real *as relations*, but there is no real distinction between the divine essence and each of the relations. The real, subsistent relations are only conceptually distinct, not really distinct, from God. In other words, when we say that the Father is God, the Son is God and the Holy Spirit is God, we make no distinction except in concept or expression between any of the three and "God." Just as the insight is expressed in the concept, so the divinity—God—is expressed in each of the relations: Father, Son and Spirit. The Son is God but not really distinct from God; the Spirit is God but not really distinct from God. But the Father is really distinct from the Son and the Spirit, and so on.

With the help of the psychological analogy we have been trying to understand a theoretical hypothesis regarding the Trinity. Traditional religious language, formulated in the symbols and metaphors of a particular, ancient common sense, can seem to be identifying something quite different from this psychological analogy. For example, the Nicene Creed says that the Word of God is "begotten" or "generated" from the Father. But we must not let traditional language confuse us here. The word "generated," when used of creatures, refers to sexual reproduction. Notice, however, how many qualifications that concept must undergo in a theory of the Trinity if it is not to mislead. Lonergan puts it this way:

> Indeed, the divine procession of the Word is not only real but also a natural generation. In us that does not hold. Our intellects are not our substance; our acts of understanding are not our existence; and so our definitions and affirmations are not the essence and existence of our children.[20]

Our parents don't *think* us into existence! Here we have an obvious way in which the *unlikeness* in the language of Trinitarian theology becomes obvious. If God is the pure act of existence, then what is "generated" in the divine nature is the divine nature shared by the Word. The term "generated" simply indicates the relation of Son to Father. Intellect provides a much better analogy than sexual reproduction for the procession of Son (or Word) from Father in the Trinity. Better because it blocks the

20. Lonergan, *Verbum*, 208.

misunderstandings that spatial or temporal metaphors are apt to generate (pun intended) in religious minds.

Gregory of Nazianzus, a master rhetorician, imagined an intellectual opponent whose materialist imagination misunderstands the Trinity in the following way: "The Holy Spirit must either be ingenerate or begotten. If he is ingenerate, there are two unoriginate beings. If he is begotten, we again have alternatives: either begotten from the Father or from the Son. If from the Father, there will be two sons who are brothers." Gregory then unleashes his satiric response:

> Make them twins if you like, or one older than the other, since you have a penchant for corporeal ideas. If he is begotten of the Son, then God has a grandson, and what could be odder than that? . . . But because the Son is "Son" in a more elevated sense of the word, and since we have no other term to express his consubstantial derivation from God, it does not follow that we ought to think it essential to transfer wholesale to the divine sphere the earthly names of human family ties.[21]

In human experience, knowing, deciding and acting in love go together. When we know something we can then judge its value. Knowing inclines the knower toward the real that is known and the desire we have for what is good follows from what we know. To love is not to add on something to our knowledge but rather to allow the mind its natural "inclination." The Spirit as the love of the Father and the Son completes, in a way, the psychological analogy of the Trinity. The "so what" question that we often ask at the end of some process of inquiry is a natural one. The question implies a desire not simply for knowledge but for what is good. It presupposes that the knowledge we acquire should matter in some way. When we know the good we are drawn toward it. And so, as we saw in the first chapter, it is perfectly natural to follow judgments about reality with judgments of value. As God's judgment of value, the Holy Spirit is God because God's knowing and God's loving are both intended in the pure act that is God. Just as the Word is God as God's self-expression, so is the Spirit God, as God's self-love. Although we can distinguish in our speech the knowing of God that is God's Word from the Loving of God that is God's Spirit, these distinctions do not divide God; rather, they help us to talk about the revealed God as Father, Son and Spirit without contradicting ourselves or making claims that are absurd and impossible. In other words, the analogy is helpful but it remains a very imperfect instrument.

---

21. Gregory, *On God and Christ*, 121, esp. "Oration 31."

The Unchanging God of Love

The psychological analogy allows us to say that God's self-knowledge is also God's self-love, and this divine knowledge and love is the creative source of all reality and all value. If our naming of God must always *deny* to God all creaturely limitation, one such limitation would be to imagine God as in need, as all creatures are. We human beings need so many things, including—especially—love. But in fact that very human need to give and receive love is itself a gift of God to us, and a gift that can only be a gift, freely given and unmerited and unforced, unless God does not need to love or be loved as creatures do. For as a creature, the human being needs what he or she does not yet have in its fullness; our potential is for the fullness of love, just as our desire to know is aimed at all being. God, however, is the fullness of being and love. If God were to need to love or be loved as creatures do, then God's love cannot deliver us from the imperfections and limitations of love as we experience it. In other words, without the gift of a divine, transcendent and incomprehensible love, the gift of human love would not be self-transcending. Its goal would be something finite, something in the world. Instead, the goal of human life and love is the Source of that life, the Giver of the gift of love.

In human relationships, the absence of need might imply distance, lack of concern, lack of love. While God's love is free of any univocal sense of creaturely need, this divine freedom must not be imagined as creating divine distance. If God is the source of all things creaturely, then our very ability to love and the desire that drives us to find it and return it, originates in what can only be the supreme, incomprehensible act of divine love that is God. And so, Christian language concerning the Holy Spirit as the communal bond of love between Father and Son is a way of identifying God as Love in action: eternally, permanently, in essence. God, in other words, is beyond our understanding not as an utterly alien unknown, but rather as the "known Unknown," the God whom we know to be unknowable.

Implications for Christian Living

Does any of this speculative thinking about imperfect analogies for Father, Son and Spirit have anything to do with everyday Christian living? First, recall from the chapter on "The Drama of Religion and the Theory of Theology" that what one accepts in faith often raises questions that theology then addresses. The natural sciences and scholarship in the humanities raise religious questions that only theological reflection, and not mere repetition of religious imagery and symbolism, or even definitions of doctrine, can manage. The concern of theology is primarily the search for a deeper understanding of what God has revealed that is fitting for us, that makes sense of our situation. Theology, in other words, searches for an ever deeper understanding of what God has done and is doing in the natural universe and in human history. Religion promotes the faith, hope and love required for the development of an ever more fully human existence. Theology is to the Christian religion as the sciences are to life in society. As a theological hypothesis the psychological analogy of the Trinity offers possible intellectual routes that increase our understanding of how God acts in the world. So, following Aquinas, Lonergan reminds us that the psychological analogy is not about holding on to a certitude; it simply helps us avoid wrong ideas about God as we encounter God in creation and its ongoing restoration.[22] God is love and love implies freedom. God does not need to create or to save human beings in order to be God. Instead, our existence and its recreation are God's acts of pure, unconstrained love. The saving acts of God are not debts repaid or the working out of some inner divine compulsion.

The second way in which the theology of the Trinity illuminates Christian living has to do with community. God's essence is a Trinity of relations. In other words, the Trinity is not merely the way God reveals God's self to humanity; the Trinity is identical with the one God. And because God creates all that exists, that creation reveals vestiges, traces, hints of its Creator. Aquinas points out that it was fitting for God to reveal something of the Trinity to humanity because the Trinity excludes compulsion in God: the Word is not something that "just has to come out" of the Father by some law or predetermined need. Rather, it is the freely spoken self-understanding of God. And Spirit as Love excludes any necessity in God's creating the universe.[23] Perfect community, modeled by the Trinity, requires freedom and excludes force. Human community can be perfected only when all human beings are liberated from whatever keeps them from realizing in their human development the image of God (*imago Dei*) according to which they are made.

Such a relational and communal vision of humanity is deeply personal, social, historical and thus other-directed, a vision far removed from the distant, uninvolved Watchmaker imagined by some thinkers of the European Enlightenment. Our participation in the life of the Trinity, then, is reflected in human solidarity. The mission of the Word is the call to imitate God through the formation of communities of intelligence, freedom

22. See Lonergan, *Verbum*, 218–19.

23. Burrell, "Incarnation and Creation," 214–15.

and love in which wounds are healed and more human ways of living are created. Indeed, in Luke's portrait Jesus says that we must be merciful as our heavenly Father is merciful (Luke 6:36) because we are all sinners in need of mercy. Just as the Spirit of Love issues forth from the bond between the Father and the Son, so the mutual regard that expresses itself in human community issues forth in faith and hope from our participation in the reality of the triune God. The community of Love is dynamic; love wants to share itself. Love unites those who share it, reconciling them to one another in the process.

Third, the Trinity is the doctrine that encourages us to participate in what God is doing in human history, no matter the cultural or religious context. As Lonergan scholar Tad Dunne explains,

> The "Spirit" very seldom is reported in Scripture to deliver a message; rather, it disposes men and women to receive a message. At times this "Spirit" is portrayed as seeking, groaning or wondering. . . . It seems, then that the mission of God's "Spirit" is experienced in our inner and immediately-felt wonder, be it the suffering kind that still searches or the enjoyable kind that appreciates the meanings embraced. God is present to us in the unmediated fashion that our own dynamic wonder is.[24]

The grace that prepares us to respond affirmatively to the desire within us (even if one doesn't hear that call from a representative of Christianity) is given as the "inner word" of the Spirit. When we look for what God is doing in the world, we are searching for concrete expressions of authentic human living: intelligent, reasonable, responsible and loving. The Spirit opens the human heart, liberating its receptivity to God's Word, no matter where or how it may be uttered.

At this point it should be clear what the doctrine of the Trinity adds to what is revealed in Christ, who called forth in his disciples a community of love. Beyond Christ's life, death and resurrection, the constitution of the church and its mission requires the reality of conversion. Why should one respond to the gospel message? Why is the Christian faith any better a solution than Naturalism, Marxism or Behaviorism? By now we should be able to reply with reference to the dynamism of human intentionality. The *telos* or goal of every human being is finally God, already present as the deepest desire of one's being, urging our transformation. Just as the hoop is the goal directing the basketball that is shot, so too the love that is the Holy Spirit directs our thinking, deciding and acting. As the Word made flesh in Christ is sent into the world, so too the Spirit is poured forth into human hearts

24. Dunne, "Trinity and History," 147.

(Rom 5:5). The objective, outer Word in history works together with the inner word of the Spirit within human subjectivity. The inner state of the person who hears God's Word in history constitutes his or her capacity to hear and respond. The Source of all speaks the Word and the human heart's search for that Meaning is its spiritual journey.

We can lose sight of the significance of this search if we have not clarified the fact that human subjectivity is "objective" in the sense that we can intend it in our questions for meaning and value. When we make the turn to the subject and appropriate our own interiority we have a foundation for clarifying the relationship of God to all of creation, not simply the Christian church. In other words, when we come to understand ourselves in our thinking and knowing and deciding, then the work of the Spirit comes into focus as utterly concrete within the dynamism of human growth and development whenever and wherever human beings happen to be found.

The theology of the Trinity has important implications for a Christian understanding of the world's many religions, philosophies and cultures. The Trinitarian Three are all *homoousios*, one in being. The Spirit sent into the many and diverse hearts of humanity throughout time and space, history and culture, is the love made manifest by Jesus' sacrifice of love on the cross. That love is made efficacious throughout all of history through the Spirit present as the gift of desire for meaning and goodness in every human heart. Frederick Crowe has suggested that the traditional neglect of the Spirit in Christian theology has led to a singular Christocentric focus on the socially and historically mediated gospel.

> Our religion cannot be Christocentric in quite the same way as it was in the past, but we are troubled by the various efforts to conceive a new center. May I suggest that we discard the image of a center, and think rather of an ellipsis with two foci? . . . In the image of an ellipse the two foci of Son and Spirit are distinct and complementary.[25]

Crowe's suggestion to shift the metaphor from one to two foci allows the Spirit to emerge out of the oblivion where an unbalanced Christocentrism has consigned it. In this more adequate Trinitarian theology, God's saving grace is not restricted to those who hear the explicit gospel message formulated within the history of Christianity.

God's self-communication through the Spirit in creation and in all human history means that everything in the universe reveals itself as the instrument of God's intelligent love. The doctrine of the Holy Spirit encourages us to expect that whatever truth and love there is in the world, there

25. Crowe, "Son and Spirit," 304.

is God, reversing evil and promoting the good. The world's great religions, in other words, are able to communicate the divine presence of God; an explicit identification with Christianity is not the only road to the redemptive self-sacrifice made manifest and effective in the cross of Christ.

9

The Church and Its Doctrines

IN THE EPILOGUE TO *Insight*, Lonergan suggested that the divine solution to the problem of evil needs to be complemented by a treatise on the church as the mystical Body of Christ. He also urged that such a treatise be contextualized within a theory of history. That context for understanding the church is needed because "it could not bear its fruits without effecting a transfiguration of human living and, in turn, the transfiguration contains the solution not only to man's individual but also to his social problem of evil."[1] After referring to the modern social encyclicals of the popes and Catholic action, Lonergan proposed the need of theology to integrate the insights of the human sciences to understand the role of the church in history and in that task of transfiguration today. "The church is a redemptive process" and that process is a concrete historical community of Christ's disciples in this world, not a platonic ideal floating above history and society. For that reason, it is incumbent on theologians to use all the tools available to understand this community of people, and that calls forth the human sciences. For Lonergan this is no afterthought. He had been working on a theory of history and a "fundamental sociology" since his days as a graduate student in the 1930s.[2]

In this chapter we examine a few of the key themes from Lonergan's work that have given fruitful directions to scholars who are developing theologies of the church. After presenting the role of the sciences in ecclesiology we turn to Lonergan's principle that the church makes itself through its thinking, deciding, and acting. Doctrines are an important element in

1. Lonergan, *Insight*, 764.

2. See *Papers 1958*, 54n. For a summary, see Shute, *Origins*, and Ormerod, "Dialectic." Crowe points out that the early papers on history focused on a theory of the history that happens, whereas Lonergan's later work on history intended to clarify the history that is written (*Lonergan*, 98).

that self-constitution of the church, and so we ask about their meaning and function. We then outline the distinction between the meaning of the doctrines and their formulation in diverse forms of communication. A few notes on the theology of prayer serve as our conclusion.

Science and the Redemptive Process

History is the arena of human redemption, but "[t]he challenge of history is for man progressively to restrict the realm of chance or fate or destiny and progressively to enlarge the realm of conscious grasp and deliberate choice."[3] Redemption requires both healing and creating, "for one cannot undo evil without also bringing about the good."[4] To create the good, theology must make use of the human sciences because it is not the sole science of human living. Theology "illuminates only certain aspects of human reality [and so] the church can become a fully conscious process of self-constitution only when theology unites itself with all the other relevant branches of human studies."[5] As a social body, the church is open to investigation for the purpose of clarifying the church's task in the process of redemption. Prior to the Second Vatican Council, Lonergan complained of the lack of attention to the social sciences. "There is so much emphasis on the legal aspect . . . in the treatise on the church simply because the one human science that is of considerable ancient lineage is the science of law. Insofar as we take over and assimilate and make our own the other human sciences we will be able to develop an adequate treatise on the church and its role in history."[6] In the next section we will say more about the role of the human sciences.

Yet social scientists are vulnerable to bias and so must not only be integrated into an ecclesiology but also criticized and purified. Lonergan's opposition to scientific reductionism is grounded in his notion of self-transcendence. When a scientist refuses to ask questions about evil and God's solution to it, and instead tries to reduce the problem and its solution to a lower viewpoint, or to deny that there is a problem and simply assume that the social surd is an aspect of reality, then the theologian cannot do without the sciences because redemption is of the whole human person in history and society. The intellectually converted theologian must also submit the sciences to a dialectical analysis. Science is not something "out there" but something done by scientists, and like theologians and all other inquirers,

3. Lonergan, *Insight*, 228.
4. Lonergan, *Method*, 366.
5. Ibid., 364.
6. Lonergan, *Early Works 1*, 300.

are subject to bias. Scientists, for example, can assume that the absurdities in society are intelligible and can be explained by science. The sciences are not so autonomous that they ignore the relevant questions that transcend their competence.[7]

Lonergan makes the foundational argument for theology's need of the sciences in *Insight*. In the epilogue Lonergan noted that "the development of empirical, human sciences has created a fundamentally new problem" for theology. Although the sciences are theoretically independent, the biases of polymorphic human consciousness create difficulties that call for a theological response grounded in self-transcendence. The rise of specialization and the division of labor opens the tendency to exclude other specializations.[8]

> In principle, other fields alone are competent to answer their proper questions. In fact, men in other fields do not triumph over all the various types of bias, to which polymorphic human consciousness is subject, unless they raise and answer successfully the further questions that belong to ever further fields.[9]

As this bias contributes to the longer cycle, the solution is only possible "by the attainment of a higher viewpoint."[10] Retreat from the sciences is not an option because that would simply cut theologians off from understanding themselves, the church and the society that the gospel is intended to transform.

The Church Makes Itself

The basic message of the Christian Church and the reason for its existence is the divine love of God, the Holy Trinity, as manifest in the life, death and resurrection of Jesus for the sake of human liberation. Jesus the Christ, God's own Word, proclaims and embodies the goal of making us a new creation, freeing us from whatever makes us less than fully human. The experience of God's love as manifest in the crucified and risen Christ is the basis for all the teachings that make up Christian doctrine. There is the message of the gospel

---

7. See Ormerod, "Dialectic," and Ormerod, "Voice."

8. Lonergan, *Insight*, 251.

9. Ibid., 766.

10. Ibid. Lonergan often appealed to Newman's theorem that omission of a part of knowledge involves ignorance of that part, mutilation of the whole, and distortion of the remainder. Theology is not immune from such distortion when it refuses to ask relevant questions that require the work of sciences beyond theology's competence. See Lonergan, *Method*, 351; *Second Collection*, 141–43 and 185–86; and *Early Works 3*, 24 and 71.

and then there are doctrines that radiate out from this original doctrine.[11] In various forms, sometimes using carefully crafted language, doctrines affirm meanings and values implicit or inchoate in the first disciples' original experience of the Risen Christ. The original teaching about God in Christ is the interpretation of the disciples' experience of liberation from the obstacles to becoming fully human—an experience offered to all of humanity in the grace of Christ's gospel and the transformative power of the Holy Spirit. As with the other areas of theology, Lonergan is not content to state clear doctrine, as important as that in fact is. He wants a systematic understanding of the social reality of the church. This systematic theology of the church will require engagement with the sociology of knowledge and other human sciences because "at the present time [1972] theological development is fundamentally a long delayed response to the development of modern science, modern scholarship, modern philosophy."[12]

If God is Unconditional Love, then love is the most important human reality; religious conversion names the process whereby Love turns and directs one's life. The mere notional affirmation of doctrinal propositions falls far short of authentic religion. By "notional affirmation" I mean the acknowledgement that a claim is true without it "making a claim" on the one who judges it to be true. Or as the common jocular rejoinder to a significant proposition would have it, "And that affects me how?" Still, those propositions are important within the context of a life informed and motivated by this Love that draws all humanity to itself. We have illustrated how religious conversion—being in love in an unconditional way—transforms our lives so that our thinking and deciding and acting now have a new foundation, a new source. C. P. Ellis began to think and act differently after he turned from hating black people to loving them. "My mind was closed," Ellis said, as he remembered the way he thought as a Klansman.[13] It is an exact description because conversion is an experience not simply of gaining new information or changing a decision, but rather of re-positioning the thinker and decision-maker. Doctrines articulate that new existential position by identifying the truths and values that are now evident to those for whom God's love has been mediated through the Christian tradition. How this mediation works has been explored by psychologists and sociologists.

Following Lonergan's methodological insights and drawing from Peter Berger's notion of the "social construction" of knowledge, Joseph Komonchak develops the sociologist's basic and interrelated facts concerning

11. Lonergan, *Method*, 295.

12. Ibid., 353.

13. See Chapter 2 of this book.

society's self-constitution and applies them to the church. Because society is a human product, even a religious society like the church depends for its existence on human thinking and deciding and acting. But society is a reality within which human beings begin by inheriting so much of what the need to develop, such as language. We are born into a social world that is already constituted by social relationships, and so we are social products. We are born into values, beliefs, and language that we do not (initially at least) choose. The result is that our identities are profoundly shaped by the worldview we inherit. As we develop, the social word into which we are born continues to shape us, to "socialize" not by making us slaves to the inheritance, but by creating in us the capacity for freedom.[14] Just as meaning is always meaning in context, so is the possible exercise of freedom.[15] In this way society creates individuals who, if they are to become intelligent, rational, and responsible, must believe what society teaches them in order to learn not only how to appropriate these meanings within their living but also how to sort out what is true and what is erroneous in that inherited fund.

The Church's Doctrines[16]

Christians inherit from the church the content of the Christian faith in a variety of forms. Initially, of course, the forms are highly symbolic, such as images, prayers, liturgy, sacraments and devotions. These forms remain important throughout life, just as common sense is not a way of thinking that theory replaces. But the authentic meanings carried by these diverse forms must be in some way stable enough to maintain the church's continuity through history and across cultures. These meanings must also generate a political polity that heads toward personal and social transformation. A community of shared meanings and values does not survive without the capacity to clarify and articulate what makes it a community and not simply a random aggregate of people. Doctrines are judgments; they articulate truths held and passed down by the community. Most of what constitutes our religious world is not a set of truths set in propositional form but a complex conglomerate of our experiences.[17] This conglomerate evokes questions regarding the control of the meanings of that conglomerate. Toward that end,

14. Komonchak, *Foundations*, 32–35, 97–120.

15. Ibid., 111–20.

16. In what follows, I have drawn from my article "Doctrine."

17. For a brief phenomenology of this conglomerate, see Crowe, "Self-Correcting Process," 30–31.

doctrines offer a critical evaluation of tradition. At the same time doctrines express the value of believing truths proposed by a religious tradition. The value is manifest when the belief and authentic appropriation of these truths of the tradition lead to transformation.

The church, the community of disciples who hand on the apostolic message of salvation, has affirmed certain doctrines as a way of specifying and defending its way of life. What everybody else is doing, however, is not a reliable reference source for Christian life. Although doctrines are both essential and critical (they hold the meanings and they call to account those who deny them), they are not sufficient. They depend on the individuals who have been genuinely formed by that tradition. The drifter, on the other hand, simply repeats what others say, affirms or denies, decides for or against certain values, without personal investment. So, when individuals drift or distort the common meanings and values while using the same expressions that stand for them, the community begins to disintegrate. When the same words are used but without the authentic meaning, then the tradition can be corrupted, only to call for purification.[18] The need for conversion, which we have discussed already, is clear. In the context of this chapter, however, we want to identify a lesser but still important issue that must be understood if the doctrines have a chance to function in the community as they should.

The need for the control of symbolic expressions emerges with questions about their meaning. We have seen that there are different realms of meaning and questioning promotes the shift from one stage of meaning to another, such as the movement from the symbolic to the theoretical.[19] The move to theory is a necessary one if there is a cognitive content to religious faith, even though that faith is normally communicated in symbols. Theoretical formulas do not exhaust the content of symbols. Abstraction from the richness of symbol does not have to be viewed as an impoverishment if it is acknowledged that, however necessary the move to theory may be, it does not usurp the primary and originating symbol in religious experience. A systematic soteriology, for example, does not replace the gospels' passion stories for liturgy and catechetical formation. An overestimation of doctrine tends to underestimate the central and originating importance of symbol, or to view doctrine as an adequate paraphrase of symbol. The opposite tendency, however, is in David Tracy's words "the assumption that 'doctrine' is either an abstract, spent or impoverished genre (compared to the concreteness of symbolic and poetic expression), or the assumption that a community does

18. Lonergan, *Method*, 299.

19. Ibid., 81–83. See also ibid., 93, and Lonergan, *Insight*, 558–60, where Lonergan recognizes the shift from common sense to theory to be an achievement made possible by the proper linguistic, conceptual, and critical conditions of a culture.

not need any explicitness or clarity to express its shared judgments on matters of belief."[20] The move to theory can also be a critical tool for determining the truth status of what symbols mean: when meaning is not controlled,
symbols are in danger of becoming oppressive, ideological obfuscations of
the transformative values latent in them, and so the question of the truth of
a symbol's meaning must be raised. But such a question cannot be settled on
the level of symbolic consciousness.[21]

Lonergan appeals to the sociologist Georg Simmel's notion that any
historically mediated community must eventually turn to "the idea" or
theory if it is to maintain continuity, "to reflect on itself, to define its goals,
to scrutinize the means it employs or might employ, to keep in mind its
origins, its past achievements, its failures."[22] In his analysis of the corrective genres in the New Testament Tracy has pointed out that the genre of
doctrine or "early catholicism"

> serves as the corrective of any temptation to shirk the ordinary,
> including the ordinary and necessary human need to find some
> clarity and explicitness for certain central shared beliefs as doc-
> trines to allow for the human need to find order in thought and
> some structure in community. The doctrines remind us that ev-
> ery *act* of proclamation involves a content that can be explicated
> to mediate the event, that every *fides qua* does involve a *fides
> quae*. The confessions and doctrines remind us as well that sheer
> intensity without any principles of ordering can lead eventually
> to a destructive chaos, that all immediacy must eventually find
> some mediation, that the witness of symbol does give rise to the
> clarifying thought of the doctrines.[23]

While the need for doctrine persists, an historically conscious concern for the development of doctrine has replaced an ahistorical "classicist"
preoccupation with certitude and universal truths. Recognizing the importance of the historicity of meaning, and the contextual understanding of
doctrines, Lonergan has often insisted that the understanding of a doctrine
requires an understanding of its development to avoid the two mistakes of
archaism ("what is not contained in the sources is a later corruption") and

---

20. Tracy, *Analogical*, 293–94. See also Lonergan, *Method*, 93–96.

21. Lonergan, *Method*, 20–21 and 83.

22. Lonergan, "Future," 159.

23. Tracy, *Analogical*, 268. As a New Testament genre, doctrines are less relatively
adequate to the communication of the meaning of Jesus; doctrine is not one of the central genres. But any adequate understanding of the other genres must include a place
for doctrines.

anachronism ("if something is taught today . . . it always was taught").[24] At the same time Lonergan rejects any tendency to leap from historical consciousness to historicism or relativism. Because there exists the possibility of knowing the context in which a doctrine is cast, it is also possible to know the doctrine's meaning, and thus to ask whether that meaning has been authentically preserved in its transposition.

Lonergan distinguishes between permanent meaning and contextual expression, but he grounds his understanding of the role of belief on an analysis of the historicity and socialization of human selfhood. As we have seen, knowledge borne of belief constitutes the vast majority of what is known. The fact of historicity warrants the judgment that believing is a value, in spite of a healthy dose of suspicion, which is always necessary.[25] Religious doctrines are believed upon the foundation of a prior judgment of value born of religious love, i.e. "the value of believing the truths taught by the religious tradition . . . ."[26] A doctrine is not immanently generated knowledge, but rather knowledge as proposed for belief by a tradition. Because of the social and historical nature of human living, it is impossible to start with absolute doubt about what tradition has proposed as true. One who judges that believing is a value "is fully aware of the fallibility of believing"[27] but realizes that there is more harm done, and in the long run less knowledge to be shared or generated, by an acceptance of the Cartesian starting point.[28]

Belief, however, does not entail a blind, naive, or uncritical stance. Human authenticity requires the raising of questions about what one has inherited. Regarding scientific method and scholarship, Lonergan cautions that, although prior knowledge gained by belief is a necessity,

> believing can be too helpful. It can help one to see what is not there. . . . The investigator needs a well-stocked mind, else he

---

24. Lonergan, *Early Works* 3, 24, 71.

25. For Lonergan's arguments concerning the factors that enter into an evaluation of the value of belief, such as the judgment that belief is a social good, that it has been accurately communicated, and that the source of the belief is reliable, see Lonergan, *Method*, 41–47, and Lonergan, *Insight*, 725–40.

26. Lonergan, *Method*, 243.

27. Ibid., 45; see also p. 223 on the difference between Descartes and Newman regarding the value of belief as a starting point for philosophy. Newman's text is in *Essay in Aid*, 242–43. The same point is employed by Crowe, "Self-Correcting Process," 22–40.

28. Lonergan appeals to Gadamer's critique of the Enlightenment: "The task for him is not the elimination of all assumptions but the elimination of mistaken assumptions" (Lonergan, *Foundations of Theology*, 228, esp. "Bernard Lonergan Responds").

will see but not perceive; but the mind needs to be well-stocked more with questions than with answers, else it will be closed and unable to learn.[29]

Our understanding does develop, along with our critical powers, and so inevitably some of what we had previously judged to be true we no longer hold.[30] Understanding and judgment are distinct operations; one can improve one's understanding of a truth. We may discover, for example, that what has been held to be part of the permanent meaning of a doctrine is now recognized as relative to an earlier context. Hence the continual need to sift the authentic from the inauthentic. In the words of Frederick Crowe, "we cannot, through any blind commitment to the past, shirk the work of research, interpretation, and history, in determining what our community has authentically held or now holds."[31] Indeed, some beliefs can be found out to be untrue after being believed by an individual or a community for a certain time.

The specialized task of systematic theology "is concerned with promoting an understanding of the realities affirmed" by the doctrines. Against any conceptualist error that holds the priority of concept over insight, systematic theology done from the turn to the subject acknowledges that its objectivity will be the result of the authentic subjectivity of the theologian.[32] In the case of ecclesiology, this will entail efforts to bring the human sciences to bear on the problems of the church's self-constitution.

Today there are new questions, many still too new to be settled, such as the question of how Christianity is related to each of the other great religions of the world. To what degree do they reveal God's truth? In what ways are they salvific? What role do their savior figures, like the Buddha, play in God's plan of redemption? Or, what about the role of women in the church? Now that the church's thinking has explicitly condemned sexism and formally separated its message from those aspects of patriarchal culture that have marred human and Christian history for so long, how will women be treated concretely within the structures of the church?

We have seen throughout this book that individuals must make themselves through their thinking and deciding; we become what we think and decide and act. This self-making, however, happens within the

29. Lonergan, "Trend," 17.

30. See Lonergan's discussion of the permanence and historicity of dogmas, based on an interpretation of Vatican I's constitution *Dei Filius*, in *Method*, 320–26. See also Lonergan, *Doctrinal Pluralism*.

31. Crowe, "Doctrines and Historicity," 121.

32. Lonergan, *Method*, 338.

community's common meanings and values. There is a difference between the authentic individual and the drifter, but the difference is not that the authentic person is isolated, individualistic, a lone ranger; rather, the individual has taken his stand on the meanings and values of the community. The meanings that inform his living are available to him because of the community, but he himself has affirmed or denied them, and this affirmation or denial is his own.

The theologian who has done the most, following Lonergan's suggestions, to recover the human dimension of the church is Joseph Komonchak. He has explored insights from the sociology of knowledge to bring a theoretical explanation to Lonergan's claim that the church is "a process of self-constitution occurring within worldwide human society. The substance of that process is the Christian message conjoined with the inner gift of God's love and resulting in Christian witness, Christian fellowship, and Christian service to mankind."[33] Komonchak has argued that ecclesiology should explore the human and social dimension of the church on the analogy of Christology's explication of the incarnation. Just as there must be no reduction in the full humanity of Christ when affirming his divinity, so the human and social reality of the church must not be slighted in favor of any affirmation of its divine origins. Neither theological nor sociological reductionism will do if the reality of the church is to be authentically presented.[34]

Doctrine and Communication

Doctrines are formulations of truth claims. But on the level of expression, "the rule is diversity." "If one is to communicate with persons of another culture, one must use the resources of their culture."[35] For this use of differing cultural resources one must acknowledge an empirical notion of culture, one which does not assume that truth and expression are coterminous. The recognition of cultural diversity through an appropriation of historical consciousness allows for the distinction between relativism vs relativity. As judgments of truth, doctrines are a critical stay against relativism, but the meanings affirmed by doctrines are open to diverse expression. Their development is a matter not of relativism but of the differentiation of consciousness and the

33. Ibid., 363.

34. Komonchak, *Foundations*, 57–75. For a good introduction to Komonchak's use of the social sciences, see Ormerod, "Voice."

35. Lonergan, *Method*, 300.

self-correcting process of learning.[36] And so there is a need to study history so that the tradition can come into the present without common sense bias that assumes the necessity of fixed and unchanging forms. Part of what the church does to constitute itself is to communicate its message, so that the hearers of the word will enter the social body that is the church or join the work of redemption in some other way. But this will not happen if the message is not communicated in a way that makes the permanent meaning of dogmas clear rather than obscure. We must expect tension and conflict, of course, because those who have not made the historical turn and have not come to a differentiation of common sense from theory will see adaptation as relativism and a loss of a dogma's permanent meaning.

Faith, as the "eye of religious love," sees the world from its vantage point made possible by a prior love.[37] The second order language of doctrines are not the original form of love's expression but they do have a function within the Christian life: they allow the church to name, communicate and encourage that love. Doctrines affirm the reality of divine love and advocate the way of life that reality entails. To be told about a loving and forgiving God is to be prepared to some degree to recognize and respond to the gift of that love, and thereby communicate it to others.

Doctrines of the Church's Basic Message

As truth claims held by the community of disciples, doctrines affirm a reality that points beyond those who hold them. The holding of these claims, however, is the glue that binds the community together. Just as the Incarnation of God embodies the wisdom and mercy of God in Jesus of Nazareth, so the community of his followers extends that incarnate presence of God in the world. The church's redemptive task is nothing short of making real in the world the healing and liberating message of Jesus. The restoration of order in a world distorted by sin will occur only when humanity is redirected by the Spirit of the Risen Christ away from egoism, group hatreds and stupidity and toward an ever fuller participation in the divine love that is the source and goal of the cosmos. Doctrines, in other words, are not arbitrary divine claims or decrees issued by church authorities; they are signposts that keep that pilgrim church headed in the right direction.

The corporate and historical character of redemption places a great responsibility on the followers of Jesus. The church is called to extend the redemptive process in the world by its witness to the gospel of forgiveness

36. Ibid., 302–5.
37. Ibid., 115–18.

and compassion. But how will the church be able to maintain its commitment to that gospel? First of all, it must remember. An obvious precondi-
tion, to be sure, but one that is too easily overlooked. Stories of cruelty,
oppression and hatred are not absent from the history of Christianity. In
one sense, that is to be expected: the church is a community of sinners. But
in another sense, if the representatives of Christ's message of self-sacrificial
love are living as if the church is simply another institution brokering
power and feathering its own nest, then the ongoing process of redemption
is going to appear as an unlikely bet.

As carriers of meaning, doctrines do certain things for the community that holds them.[38] As statements of meaning they deliver the cognitive
content of what has been communicated within the church. The language
of doctrine takes us beyond the immediate experience of the pre-linguistic
world into the world mediated by Christian meaning. When accepted in
faith, doctrines are also effective; their meanings function as a motive for
commitment and perseverance in faith.[39] There is a distinction between the
mysteries of fact and the mysteries of value which the mysteries of fact illustrate. The fact can motivate one to accept the value.[40] Without doctrines the
church as a community in history could not be constituted. Doctrines carry
the community's meanings and values, and without them the community
doesn't last very long. If the gospel is to survive, to be communicated to
future generations, then it must be formulated, not in permanent expression, but as permanent meaning rooted in God's love.[41] Doctrines also allow for the communication of the originating experience of God's love. On
the social and historical level, doctrines are linguistic formulations of the
meanings and values that hold together and direct a religious community.
To believe in the doctrines of the church is to have a sense of direction instilled in us from a living conviction of the reality of the God revealed in the
Bible and especially in the gospels, a God who has a particular concern for
each of us, who knows us and seeks in all things our happiness. To believe
that is to be strengthened to live accordingly. If "a community is one not
only by God's grace but also by a consequent union of minds and of hearts,"
as Lonergan noted, "it remains that the consequent union can be troubled,
disturbed, undergo an identity crisis; and then the solution to that crisis will

---

38. Ibid., 76–81.

39. The truth of beliefs involves the witnesses and their authenticity as well as the
claim itself. See Lonergan, "Belief," 96–97.

40. Quenell, "Beliefs," 182, and Lonergan, *Method*, 311.

41. Ibid., 323.

be a common confession of faith. It is such confessions of faith that have been given the name, dogmas."[42]

These meanings and values are most often communicated among the members of a community through feelings conveyed by images, symbols, ritual, and art; the logic of the heart precedes any formal doctrinal statement of the belief. Nevertheless, questions about the meaning of these more basic expressions calls forth the clarity that doctrine intends.

The Role of Prayer

We conclude with a brief reflection on the role of prayer in human self-transcendence. The redemptive process that is the church lives according to the three theological virtues of love, hope and faith. It is possible that faith can exist in a Christian (temporarily, at least) without love. For the long haul, however, if enough people in the church lack love, the message of faith itself is bound to suffer from incredulity and decline will accelerate. But so long as there is some faith it is possible that the message of love carried by that faith will be taken seriously again. When the gospel is no longer believed to be God's solution to the problem of evil, it is difficult to raise faith out of the ashes. We have presented examples of the value of belief in general; here we note that believing has a very significant part to play in the redemptive process. The good of world order depends on the cooperation of many people though time, and that cooperation cannot occur without widespread commitment to believing in God's solution. So, although love is the root, without belief the cooperation necessary to stem decline and promote progress is impossible.

For these reasons, an essential element in the life of Christian communities is the reality of prayer. We are creatures on the move and we make ourselves through our own thinking and deciding. Yet human life cannot be conceived in terms of self-sufficiency; to be human is to be on the way to a life that is more than what it is at any stage on the journey. As we have seen, any act of knowing takes us beyond what we were prior to acquiring that knowledge. Acts of self-transcendence on the intellectual level are surpassed when we make decisions or act on what we love. The goal of human life is God, the name for our beginning and end, our Creator and Redeemer, the Source and Goal of all creation. To be human, then, is to be oriented toward God in love, knowledge and action. To be human, in other words, is to desire God, and prayer, in the broadest sense, is the expression of that human longing. Prayer

42. Lonergan, "Theology and Praxis," 197.

is the praise of God for the goodness of creation and thanksgiving for the divine love that lifts us out of our sin and stupidity.

Prayer has a role within the larger question of divine providence and Christ's redemptive work in the transformation of human life. If nothing escapes the divine governance of the universe, then prayer must be in some way included in that governance. And if God employs instruments or secondary causes to bring about the good that God intends for God's creatures, then prayer will be one of those instruments. The question, therefore, is *how* prayer, both liturgical and devotional, functions in God's providential designs and saving grace.

Lonergan's understanding of prayer is set within Aquinas's notion of providence. God is the pure act of *to be*. God, in other words, is "good" not morally (because of his achievements) but because of God's being the cause of all being. Unlike human beings, God does not deliberate and make judgments about what is true or good or what should be done. God's relationship to the creature, then, is like someone being a help to another purely by being oneself. The helper's action is not altered for the sake of the person being helped even though the person really is being helped. This analogy does not imply that there is no bond or relationship between the two; it simply means that the help comes through being who one is rather than making a specific moral choice or performing a particular action.[43]

As the pure act of existence, God perpetually communicates being to each creature, to all reality, and so causes their being, which is what it means to say that all existing things participate, because they exist, in God who is Existence itself. God is present and active in the world not as a mere external mechanism or force like gravity or electricity. God is personal, and we relate to God personally in prayer. But personal relationships between friends often involve one friend asking for help from the other. Prayer, in other words, sometimes takes the form of "petition," requesting help from God. Yet this does not imply an anthropomorphic image of God, who operates as the cause within every creature's action.[44]

God's compassionate response to human need, a central element in the teachings of Jesus, is an unchanging love that does not fail us. God's love and care will take a multitude of forms because humanity's needs are diverse. And yet, it is "unchanging" in the sense that it is always God's love, always the divine intention for our good, and good is always concrete, which means that it is always particular and diverse.

43. Burrell, *God and Action*, 111.

44. On the elimination of anthropomorphism in thinking about God, see Lonergan, *Grace*, 323–24 and 446.

We turn to the human side of the question of prayer as petition and ask how God's love works concretely in the context of our asking God for help in prayer. God governs the sub-human natural world, for example, through the laws immanent in the evolving world. In the case of human beings, God's causing good in us is often *through* our authentically free thinking and deciding; God's "causing" is an analogous causing, and so is not humanly knowable. In faith, however, we know (1) that God is the cause of all our good works, and (2) these good works are indeed ours and not those of God's robots. The secondary causes through which God acts to bring about his intention for the universe are, in this case, human intelligence and freedom. And so, within the context of a theology of grace and freedom, we can make sense of prayers of petition.

Among other things, prayer promotes in us an awareness of our dependence on God and our need for transformation. And so, for example, we pray that God will give us more faith, hope and love. The paradoxical quality of such prayer lies in the fact that we are asking for something that we do not have and cannot generate without God's grace, and yet faith, hope and love, when they are real, are utterly *human* realities. That they are also divine gifts does not change the fact that they exist only in the form of a transformed human life. Lonergan wrote of the "barriers to enlightenment" and the means to overcome those barriers by prayer and an affective and engaged affirmation of the values implicit in the lives of the saints, in great art, in the liturgy, etc. Conversion is God's gift; what prayer does is real, but it does what it does through the praying person's transformation.[45]

God, however, is not the big being who is like us in all things except size and power. Instead, we must recall that as unlimited power, wisdom and love, God knows the world only by creating it, a knowledge analogous to the way the artist knows the work of art as it is being created. Prayer is effective not by changing God's mind but by changing us, thereby obtaining for us what God intended us to have and be by way of prayer. Prayer, in other words, is a secondary cause through which God brings about certain good things. And so, our not knowing *how* God might be at work should not discourage the faith that God in fact *is* at work in the world. Still, prayer must never be used to salve one's conscience and thereby avoid acting as God's instrument for healing and justice and peace in a suffering world. Prayer focuses our attention on the need for continual transformation, encourages in us the realization that we are dependent on God for everything, and promotes in us the trust that what goes beyond our power to understand or to do is still not impossible with God.

45. Lonergan, "Pope," 224–38.

Bibliography

Aquinas, Thomas. *Summa Theologica*. Translated by Fathers of the English Dominican Province. 5 volumes. Westminster, MD: Christian Classics, 1948.

Augustine. *Confessions*. Translated by Henry Chadwick. Oxford: Oxford University Press, 1991.

Berger, Peter L., and Thomas Luckmann. *The Social Construction of Reality: A Treatise in the Sociology of Knowledge*. New York: Doubleday, 1967.

Burrell, David. "Aquinas and Scotus: Contrary Patters for Philosophical Theology." In *Theology and Dialogue*, edited by Bruce Marshall, 105–29. Notre Dame: University of Notre Dame Press, 1990.

————. *Aquinas: God and Action*. Notre Dame: University of Notre Dame Press, 1979.

————. *Exercises in Religious Understanding*. Notre Dame: University of Notre Dame Press, 1974.

————. *Freedom and Creation in Three Traditions*. Notre Dame: University of Notre Dame Press, 1984.

————. *Friendship and Ways to Truth*. Notre Dame: University of Notre Dame Press, 2000.

————. "From Analogy of 'Being' to the Analogy of Being." *Lonergan Workshop* 17 (2002) 53–66.

————. "Incarnation and Creation: The Hidden Dimension." *Modern Theology* 12 (1996) 211–21.

Burrell, David, and Elena Malits. *Original Peace*. Mahwah, NJ: Paulist, 1997.

Chenu, M. D. *Nature, Man and Society in the Twelfth Century: Essays on New Theological Perspectives in the Latin West*. Selected, edited, and translated by Jerome Taylor and Lester K. Little. Chicago: University of Chicago Press, 1968.

Ciardi, John. *How Does a Poem Mean?* Boston: Haughton Mifflin, 1959.

Crowe, Frederick. *Christ and History: The Christology of Bernard Lonergan from 1935 to 1982*. Toronto: University of Toronto Press, 2015.

————. "Doctrines and Historicity in the Context of Lonergan's *Method*." *Theological Studies* 38 (1977) 121.

————. "Dogma versus the Self-Correcting Process of Learning." In *Foundations of Theology*, edited by Philip McShane, 30–31. Notre Dame: University of Notre Dame Press, 1972.

————. *Lonergan*. Collegeville, MN: Liturgical, 1992.

———. "Son and Spirit: Tension in the Divine Missions?" In Frederick Crowe, *Appropriating the Lonergan Idea*, edited by Michael Vertin, 297–314. Washington, DC: Catholic University of America Press, 1989.

Davis, Leo Donald. *The First Seven Ecumenical Councils*. Collegeville, MN: Liturgical, 1987.

Davis, Nuel Pharr. *Lawrence and Oppenheimer*. New York: Fawcett, 1968.

Doran, Robert M. "Introduction: Lonergan, An Appreciation." In *The Desires of the Human Heart: An Introduction to the Theology of Bernard Lonergan*. Edited by Vernon Gregson. New York: Paulist, 1988.

———. *Theology and the Dialectics of History*. Toronto: University of Toronto Press, 1990.

Doyle, Dennis. "Vatican II and Intellectual Conversion: Engaging the Struggle Within." In *A Realist's Church: Essays in Honor of Joseph Komonchak*, edited by Christopher Denny, Patrick Hayes, and Nicholas Rademacher, 99–116. Maryknoll, NY: Orbis, 2015.

Duffy, Stephen. *The Graced Horizon: Nature and Grace in Modern Catholic Thought*. Liturgical, 1992.

Dunne, Tad. "Trinity and History." *Theological Studies* 45 (1984) 139–52.

Febvre, Lucien. *Combats pour l'histoire*. Paris: Armand Colin, 1992.

Gregory of Nazianzus. *On God and Christ*. Edited and translated by Frederick Williams. Crestwood, NY: Saint Vladimir's Seminary Press, 1972.

———. "The Fifth Theological Oration (Oration 31)." In *On God and Christ: The Five Theological Orations and Two Letters to Cledonius.*, translated by Lionel Wickham, 117–48. Crestwood, NY: St. Vladimir's Seminary Press, 2002.

———. "The Third Theological Oration (Oration 29)." In *On God and Christ: The Five Theological Orations and Two Letters to Cledonius.*, translated by Lionel Wickham, 37–68. Crestwood, NY: St. Vladimir's Seminary Press, 2002.

Gregson, Vernon, ed. *The Desires of the Human Heart: An Introduction to the Theology of Bernard Lonergan*. New York: Paulist, 1988.

———. *Lonergan, Spirituality, and the Meeting of Religions*. Lanham, MD: University Press of America, 1985.

Hammond, David. "Doctrine, Praxis, and Critical Theology: An Interpretation and a Critique of Charles Davis's Option." *Method: A Journal of Lonergan Studies* 6 (1988) 71–94.

———. "The Influence of Newman's Doctrine of Assent on the Thought of Bernard Lonergan." *Method: Journal of Lonergan Studies* 7 (1989) 95–115.

Hedrick, Pamela. "Basil the Great, Gregory the Theologian, and Dialectic." *The Lonergan Review* 4 (2013) 11–36.

Hurtado, Larry. *Lord Jesus Christ: Devotion to Jesus in Earliest Christianity*. Grand Rapids, MI: Eerdmans, 2005.

Johnson, Luke Timothy. *Sacra Pagina: The Gospel of Luke*. Edited by Daniel J. Harrington. Collegeville, MN: Liturgical, 1991.

Kant, Immanuel. *The Critique of Pure Reason*, translated by Norman Kemp Smith. New York: Saint Martin's University Press, 1965.

Kinlaw, Pamela E. *The Christ is Jesus*. Leiden, Netherlands: E. J. Brill, 2005.

Knox, John. *The Early Church and the Coming of the Great Church*. Nashville, TN: Abingdon, 1955.

Komonchak, Joseph A. *Foundations in Ecclesiology*. Vol. 11 of *Lonergan Workshop Journal*, edited by Fred Lawrence. Boston: Boston College, 1995.

———. "Vatican II as an 'Event.'" *Theology Digest* 46 (1999) 337–52.

Lawrence, Frederick. "The Fragility of Consciousness: Lonergan and the Postmodern Concern for the Other." *Theological Studies* 54 (1993) 55–94.

Levenson, Jon. *Creation and the Persistence of Evil: The Jewish Drama of Divine Omnipotence.* Princeton, NJ: Princeton University Press, 1988.

Levi, Primo. *Survival in Auschwitz.* New York: Simon and Schuster, 1996.

Liddy, Richard. *Transforming Light: Intellectual Conversion in the Early Lonergan.* Collegeville, MN: Liturgical, 1993.

Loewe, William P. "From the Humanity of Christ to the Historical Jesus." *Theological Studies* 61 (2000) 314–41.

———. *Lex Crucis: Soteriology and the Stages of Meaning.* Minneapolis: Fortress, 2016.

———. "Lonergan and the Law of the Cross: A Universalist View of Salvation." *Anglican Theological Review* 59 (1977) 162–74.

Lonergan, Bernard. "Belief: Today's Issue." In *Second Collection,* edited by William F. J. Ryan and Bernard J. Tyrrell, 87–100. Philadelphia: Westminster, 1974.

———. *Caring About Meaning: Patters in the Life of Bernard Lonergan.* Edited by Pierre Lambert, Cathleen Going, and Charlotte Tansey. Montreal, QC: Thomas More Institute Papers, 1982.

———. "Christology Today." In *Third Collection: Papers by Bernard J.F. Lonergan, S.J.,* edited by Frederick Crowe, 74-99. New York: Paulist, 1985.

———. "Dimensions of Meaning." In *Collection,* edited by Frederick E. Crowe and Robert M. Doran, 232–46. Vol. 4 of *Collected Works of Bernard Lonergan.* Toronto: University of Toronto Press, 1988.

———. *Doctrinal Pluralism.* Milwaukee, WI: Marquette University Press, 1971.

———. *Early Works on Theological Method 1.* Vol. 22 of *Collected Works of Bernard Lonergan,* edited by Robert C. Croken and Robert M. Doran. Toronto: University of Toronto Press, 2010.

———. *Early Works on Theological Method 2.* Vol. 23 of *Collected Works of Bernard Lonergan,* edited by Robert C. Croken, Robert M. Doran. Toronto: University of Toronto Press, 2013.

———. *Early Works on Theological Method 3.* Vol. 24 of *Collected Works of Bernard Lonergan,* edited by Robert C. Croken, Robert M. Doran. Toronto: University of Toronto Press, 2013.

———. "The Example of Gibson Winter." In *Second Collection,* edited by William F. J. Ryan and Bernard J. Tyrrell, 189–92. Philadelphia: Westminster, 1974.

———. "*Existenz* and Aggiornamento." In *Collection,* edited by Frederick E. Crowe and Robert M. Doran, 222–31. Vol. 4 of *Collected Works of Bernard Lonergan.* Toronto: University of Toronto Press, 1988.

———. "The Future of Christianity." In *Second Collection,* edited by William F. J. Ryan and Bernard J. Tyrrell, 149–64. Philadelphia: Westminster, 1974.

———. *Grace and Freedom: Operative Grace in the Thought of St. Thomas Aquinas.* Edited by Robert M. Doran, Frederick E. Crowe, Toronto: University of Toronto Press, 2000.

———. "Healing and Creating in History." In *Third Collection: Papers by Bernard J.F. Lonergan, S.J.,* edited by Frederick Crowe, 100–109. New York: Paulist, 1985.

———. *The Incarnate Word.* Vol. 8 of *Collected Works of Bernard Lonergan,* edited by Robert Doran, SJ, and Jeremy Wilkins. Toronto: University of Toronto Press, 2016.

———. *Insight: A Study of Human Understanding.* Vol. 3 of *Collected Works of Bernard Lonergan,* edited by Frederick E. Crowe and Robert M. Doran. Toronto: University of Toronto Press, 1992.

————. "Metaphysics as Horizon." In *Collection*, edited by Frederick E. Crowe and Robert M. Doran, 188–204. Vol. 4 of *Collected Works of Bernard Lonergan*. Toronto: University of Toronto Press, 1988.

————. *Method in Theology*. New York: Seabury, 1972.

————. "Method: Trend and Variations." In *Third Collection: Papers by Bernard J.F. Lonergan, S.J.*, edited by Frederick Crowe, 13–22. New York: Paulist, 1985.

————. "Mission and the Spirit." In *Third Collection: Papers by Bernard J.F. Lonergan, S.J.*, edited by Frederick Crowe, 23–34. New York: Paulist, 1985.

————. "The Natural Desire to See God." In *Collection*, edited by Frederick E. Crowe and Robert M. Doran, 81–91. Vol. 4 of *Collected Works of Bernard Lonergan*. Toronto: University of Toronto Press, 1988.

————. "Natural Right and Historical Mindedness." In *Third Collection: Papers by Bernard J.F. Lonergan, S.J.*, edited by Frederick Crowe, 169–83. New York: Paulist, 1985.

————. "The Notion of Fittingness." In *Early Latin Theology*, edited by Daniel Monsour, Michael Shields, and Robert Doran, 483–533. Volume 19 of *Collected Works of Bernard Lonergan*. Toronto: University of Toronto Press, 2011.

————. "The Ongoing Genesis of Methods." In *Third Collection: Papers by Bernard J.F. Lonergan, S.J.*, edited by Frederick Crowe, 146–65. New York: Paulist, 1985.

————. *The Ontological and Psychological Constitution of Christ*. Vol. 7 of *Collected Works of Bernard Lonergan*, edited by Michael G. Shields, Robert M. Doran, Frederick E. Crowe. Toronto: University of Toronto Press, 2002.

————. "The Origins of Christian Realism." In *Second Collection*, edited by William F. J. Ryan and Bernard J. Tyrrell, 239–62. Philadelphia: Westminster, 1974.

————. *Phenomenology and Logic: The Boston College Lectures on Mathematical Logic and Existentialism*. Vol. 18 of *Collected Works of Bernard Lonergan*, edited by Philip McShane. Toronto: University of Toronto Press, 2001.

————. *Philosophical and Theological Papers, 1958–1964*. Vol. 6 of *Collected Works of Bernard Lonergan*, edited by Frederick Crowe, Robert M. Doran, and Robert C. Croken. Toronto: University of Toronto Press, 1996.

————. *Philosophical and Theological Papers, 1965–1980*. Vol. 17 of *Collected Works of Bernard Lonergan*, edited by Robert M. Doran and Robert C. Croken. Toronto: University of Toronto Press, 2004.

————. "Philosophy and Theology." In *Second Collection*, edited by William F. J. Ryan and Bernard J. Tyrrell, 193–208. Philadelphia: Westminster, 1974.

————. "Pope John's Intention." In *Third Collection: Papers by Bernard J.F. Lonergan, S.J.*, edited by Frederick Crowe, 224–38. New York: Paulist, 1985.

————. "A Post-Hegelian Philosophy of Religion." In *Third Collection: Papers by Bernard J.F. Lonergan, S.J.*, edited by Frederick Crowe, 206–7. New York: Paulist, 1985.

————. "Religious Knowledge." *In Third Collection: Papers by Bernard J.F. Lonergan, S.J.*, edited by Frederick Crowe, 129–145. New York: Paulist, 1985.

————. "Respect." In *Shorter Papers*, edited by Robert Doran, Robert Croken, and Daniel Monsour, 121–27. Vol. 20 of *Collected Works of Bernard Lonergan*. Toronto: University of Toronto Press, 2007.

————. *Second Collection*. Edited by William F. J. Ryan and Bernard J. Tyrrell. Philadelphia: Westminster, 1974.

————. *Shorter Papers*. Vol. 20 of *Collected Works of Bernard Lonergan*, edited by Robert Doran, Robert Croken, and Daniel Monsour. Toronto: University of Toronto Press, 2007.

————. "The Structure of the Ante-Nicene Movement." In *The Triune God: Doctrines*, edited by Robert M. Doran, Daniel Monsour, and Michael Shields, 199–255. Vol. 11 of *Collected Works of Bernard Lonergan*. Toronto: University of Toronto Press, 2009.

————. "The Subject." In *Second Collection*, edited by William F. J. Ryan and Bernard J. Tyrrell, 69–86. Philadelphia: Westminster, 1974.

————. "The Supernatural Order." In *Early Latin Theology*, edited by Robert Doran, Daniel Monsour, and Michael Shields, 53–255. Vol. 19 of *Collected Works of Bernard Lonergan*. Toronto: University of Toronto Press, 2011.

————. "Theology and Man's Future." In *Second Collection*, edited by William F. J. Ryan and Bernard J. Tyrrell, 135–48. Philadelphia: Westminster, 1974.

————. "Theology and Praxis." In *Third Collection: Papers by Bernard J.F. Lonergan, S.J.*, edited by Frederick Crowe, 177–92. New York: Paulist, 1985.

————. *Topics in Education: The Cincinnati Lectures of 1959.* Vol. 10 of *Collected Works of Bernard Lonergan*, edited by Robert M. Doran and Frederick E. Crowe. Toronto: University of Toronto Press, 1988.

————. *The Triune God: Doctrines.* Vol. 11 of *Collected Works of Bernard Lonergan*, edited by Robert M. Doran, Daniel Monsour, and Michael Shields. Toronto: University of Toronto Press, 2009.

————. *The Triune God: Systematics.* Vol. 12 of *Collected Works of Bernard Lonergan*, edited by Robert M. Doran, Daniel Monsour, and Michael Shields. Toronto: University of Toronto Press, 2007.

————. *Understanding and Being: The Halifax Lectures on Insight.* Vol. 5 of *Collected Works of Bernard Lonergan*, edited by Frederick E. Crowe, Elizabeth A. Morelli, and Mark D. Morelli. Toronto: University of Toronto Press, 1990.

————. *Verbum: Word and Idea in Aquinas.* Collected Works of Bernard Lonergan 2. Edited by Frederick E. Crowe and Robert Doran. Toronto: University of Toronto Press, 1997.

Markus, Robert. "From Rome to the Barbarian Kingdoms (370–700)." In *The Oxford Illustrated History of Christianity*, edited by John McManners. Oxford: Oxford University Press, 1992.

Mathews, William. "Kant's Anomalous Insights: A Note on Kant and Lonergan." *Method: A Journal of Lonergan Studies* 14 (1996) 85–98.

McGuckin, John. *Saint Gregory of Nazianzus: An Intellectual Biography.* Crestwood, NY: Saint Vladimir's Seminary Press, 2001.

Meyer, Ben. *Critical Realism and the New Testament.* Allison Park, PA: Pickwick, 1989.

Miller, George, dir. *Lorenzo's Oil.* 1990; Hollywood, CA: Universal Pictures, 1993.

Newman, John Henry. *An Essay in Aid of a Grammar of Assent.* Oxford: Clarendon, 1985.

————. *An Essay on the Development of Christian Doctrine.* New York: Doubleday Image, 1960.

————. *The Idea of a University.* New York: Doubleday, 1959.

————. *The Letters and Diaries of John Henry Newman.* Vol. 20, edited by Charles Dessain. London: Nelson, 1970.

————. *The Via Media of the Anglican Church.* Edited by H. D. Weidner. Oxford: Clarendon, 1990.

Norris, Richard. *The Christological Controversy.* Philadelphia: Fortress, 1980.

Ormerod, Neil. "A Dialectic Engagement with the Social Sciences." *Theological Studies* 66 (2005) 815–40.

———. "A Voice Cries in the Wilderness: The Place of the Social Sciences in Ecclesiology." In *A Realist's Church: Essays in Honor of Joseph Komonchak*, edited by Christopher Denny, Patrick Hayes, and Nicholas Rademacher, 203–20. Maryknoll, NY: Orbis, 2015.

Percy, Walker. "The Loss of the Creature." In *The Message in the Bottle*. New York: Farrar, Straus and Giroux, 1975.

———. *Lost in the Cosmos: The Last Self-Help Book*. New York: Farrar, Straus and Giroux, 1983.

Polkinghorne, John. "The Quantum World." In *Physics, Philosophy and Theology: A Common Quest for Understanding*, edited by Robert J. Russell, William R. Stoeger, SJ, and George V. Coyne, SJ. Vatican City: Vatican Observatory, 1988.

———. *The Quantum World*. Princeton: Princeton University Press, 1984.

Quenell, Quentin. "Beliefs and Authenticity." In *Creativity and Method: Essays in Honor of Bernard Lonergan, S.J.*, edited by Matthew Lamb, 173–84. Milwaukee, WI: Marquette University Press, 1981.

———. "Grace." In *The Desires of the Human Heart: An Introduction to the Theology of Bernard Lonergan*, edited by Vernon Gregson, 171. New York: Paulist, 1988.

———. "A Note on Scholasticism." In *The Desires of the Human Heart: An Introduction to the Theology of Bernard Lonergan*, edited by Vernon Gregson, 144–49. New York: Paulist, 1988.

———. "Three Persons—One God." In *The Desires of the Human Heart: An Introduction to the Theology of Bernard Lonergan*, edited by Vernon Gregson, 150–67. New York: Paulist, 1988.

Sala, Giovanni. *Lonergan and Kant: Five Essays*. Toronto: University of Toronto Press, 1994.

Shute, Michael. *Lonergan's Early Economic Research: Texts and Commentary*. Toronto: University of Toronto Press, 2010.

———. *The Origins of Lonergan's Notion of the Dialectic of History: A Study of Lonergan's Early Writings on History*. Lanham, MD: University Press of America, 1993.

Sloyan, Gerard. "Injustice at Ephesus." In *Finding Salvation in Christ: Essays on Christology and Soteriology in Honor of William P. Loewe*, edited by Christopher D. Denny and Christopher McMahon, 128–42. Eugene, Oregon: Pickwick, 2011.

Spearing, A. C., trans. *The Cloud of Unknowing and Other Works*. Baltimore: Penguin Classics, 1977.

Stebbins, Michael. *The Divine Initiative: Grace, World-Order and Human Freedom in the Early Writings of Bernard Lonergan*. Toronto: University of Toronto Press, 1995.

Tekippe, Terry. *What Is Lonergan Up To in Insight?* Collegeville, MN: Liturgical, 1996.

Terkel, Studs. *American Dreams: Lost and Found*. New York: Pantheon, 1980.

Tracy, David. *The Analogical Imagination: Christian Theology and the Culture of Pluralism*. New York: Crossroad, 1981.

———. *Blessed Rage for Order: The New Pluralism in Theology*. New York: Seabury, 1976.

Ward, Wilfrid. *The Life of John Henry Cardinal Newman: Based on His Private Journals and Correspondence*. London: Longmans, Green and Co., 1921.

Williams, Rowan. *Arius: Heresy and Tradition*. Rev. ed. Grand Rapids, MI: Eerdmans, 2001.

Made in the USA
Las Vegas, NV
26 November 2021

35306804R00105